T0259651

Patterns in the Machine

A Software Engineering Guide to Embedded Development

John T. Taylor
Wayne T. Taylor

Apress®

Patterns in the Machine: A Software Engineering Guide to Embedded Development

John T. Taylor
Covington, GA, USA

Wayne T. Taylor
Golden, CO, USA

ISBN-13 (pbk): 978-1-4842-6439-3
https://doi.org/10.1007/978-1-4842-6440-9

ISBN-13 (electronic): 978-1-4842-6440-9

Managing Director, Apress Media LLC: Welmoed Spahr
Acquisitions Editor: Steve Anglin
Development Editor: Matthew Moodie
Coordinating Editor: Mark Powers

Cover designed by eStudioCalamar

Cover image by Callum Wale on Unsplash (www.unsplash.com)

Distributed to the book trade worldwide by Apress Media, LLC, 1 New York Plaza, New York, NY 10004, U.S.A. Phone 1-800-SPRINGER, fax (201) 348-4505, e-mail orders-ny@springer-sbm.com, or visit www.springeronline.com. Apress Media, LLC is a California LLC and the sole member (owner) is Springer Science + Business Media Finance Inc (SSBM Finance Inc). SSBM Finance Inc is a **Delaware** corporation.

For information on translations, please e-mail booktranslations@springernature.com; for reprint, paperback, or audio rights, please e-mail bookpermissions@springernature.com.

Apress titles may be purchased in bulk for academic, corporate, or promotional use. eBook versions and licenses are also available for most titles. For more information, reference our Print and eBook Bulk Sales web page at http://www.apress.com/bulk-sales.

Any source code or other supplementary material referenced by the author in this book is available to readers on GitHub via the book's product page, located at www.apress.com/9781484264393. For more detailed information, please visit http://www.apress.com/source-code.

Printed on acid-free paper

To Sally, Bailey, Kelly, and Todd.
—J.T.

Table of Contents

About the Authors

John Taylor has been an embedded developer for over 29 years. He has worked as a firmware engineer, technical lead, system engineer, software architect, and software development manager for companies such as Ingersoll Rand, Carrier, Allen-Bradley, Hitachi Telecom, Emerson, and several start-up companies. He has developed firmware for products that include HVAC control systems, telecom SONET nodes, IoT devices, microcode for communication chips, and medical devices. He is the coauthor of five US patents and holds a bachelor degree in mathematics and computer science.

Wayne Taylor has been a technical writer for 25 years. He has worked with companies such as IBM, Novell, Compaq, HP, EMC, SanDisk, and Western Digital. He has documented compilers, LAN driver development, storage system deployment and maintenance, and dozens of system management APIs. He also has ten years of experience as a software development manager. He is the coauthor of two US patents and holds master's degrees in English and human factors.

About the Technical Reviewer

Jacob Beningo is an embedded software consultant with over 15 years of experience in microcontroller-based real-time embedded systems. After spending over ten years designing embedded systems for the automotive, defense, and space industries, Jacob founded the Beningo Embedded Group in 2009. Jacob has worked with clients in more than a dozen countries to dramatically transform their businesses by improving product quality, cost, and time to market. He has published more than 200 articles on embedded software development techniques and is a sought-after speaker and technical advisor. Jacob is an avid writer, trainer, consultant, and entrepreneur who transforms the complex into simple and understandable concepts that accelerate technological innovation.

Jacob has demonstrated his leadership in the embedded systems industry by consulting and working as a trusted advisor at companies such as General Motors, Intel, Infineon, and Renesas. He also speaks at and is involved in the embedded track selection committees at ARM Techcon, Embedded System Conferences, and Sensor Expo. Jacob holds bachelor's degrees in electrical engineering, physics, and mathematics from Central Michigan University and a master's degree in space systems engineering from the University of Michigan.

In his spare time, Jacob enjoys spending time with his family, reading, writing, and playing hockey and golf. When there are clear skies, he can often be found outside with his telescope, sipping a fine scotch while imaging the sky.

Acknowledgments

We'd like to thank Mike Moran for taking the time to read through early drafts of this book and for providing his usual insightful comments.

Preface

The mastermind behind this book is John. John is the one who has been working and developing code in the embedded systems space for 30 years, and this is his approach to developing software. *Patterns in the Machine*, or PIM, is his development process. If you worked with John, you'd see that his processes and his production code follow exactly what is prescribed in this book. While not all of his colleagues have been converted to his PIM approach, they can't argue with his success. John not only develops a prodigious amount of code, but he also keeps an amazing number of modules and unit tests and simulator bits current on his projects. And he does so by practicing what he preaches.

Consequently, in this book, when you see a phrase like "In my experience …" or "I worked on a project once …," it is usually John speaking. Occasionally, it's me editorializing or providing my own anecdote, but mostly it's John. We wrestled for a while about how to best alert readers to who was who, and, in the end, we decided we'd go with first-person narration. We never really were comfortable using "we." To us it sounded a little pretentious, pontificatory, and too much like the "royal we." So, when you read this book, know that "I" is John … mostly.

John and I have been involved with software development for a very long time. I wrote my first computer program in the basement of the Kiewit computer center at Dartmouth College when I was 10 years old. John was 7. Over the years, John and I have programmed in machine language, assembler, C, C++, Java, C#, Python, Perl, and so on. We've been involved in projects that range from firmware for very small hardware platforms to enterprise software for insanely large storage platforms. And while the specifics of our experience vary, we discovered over the course of writing this book that our ideas and conclusions about what constitutes smart development, what demonstrates elegance in design, and what is "the right way to do things" are surprisingly similar. When it comes to software development and programming languages, John and I are native speakers. And we speak with one voice.

—Wayne Taylor, Golden, Colorado, October 2020

CHAPTER 1

Introduction

This book is about how to be a genius—or, at least, how to design and implement software in a way that is pretty damn smart. This book is about how to build things like automated unit tests and functional simulators, which professionals in the embedded systems space hardly ever do because they feel there isn't enough time or there aren't enough resources in their programming environment or because there's never been hardware like theirs on the planet before. A lot of developers think it's unwise to write extensive code before the hardware is working, or they assume that their code can't be repurposed for a completely different hardware platform without massive rework. But that is simply not the case.

In this book, I'll show you how to apply some software engineering principles and best practices—or what I call patterns—to develop software in an efficient, sustainable manner. By applying these patterns in a deliberate way, you can develop software and firmware for embedded systems faster and with higher quality than ever before. To be clear, these patterns are not silver bullets. If, for example, your hardware platform requires you to "bit pack eight Boolean flags into a single byte," then these practices might be of limited use. Nevertheless, by implementing patterns, I think you'll find that the sum of the parts is greater than the whole. That is, the right effort applied in the right place can produce benefits far beyond what you might think.

In my experience, traditional embedded software projects tend to be monolithic applications that are optimized for their target hardware platforms. And this is understandable. Embedded projects have unique hardware characteristics, constrained resources (limited RAM, tiny amounts of Flash, no operating system support, etc.) and oftentimes require demanding real-time performance. On top of this, there are nearly always aggressive schedules and high expectations for the quality of the software. Consequently, the pressure to just get started, and to just meet the stated requirements at hand, is immense and only intensifies when, mid-project, software requirements change, hardware components become unavailable or go obsolete, and the time-to-market window gets shortened.

© John T. Taylor, Wayne T. Taylor 2021
J. T. Taylor and W. T. Taylor, *Patterns in the Machine*,
https://doi.org/10.1007/978-1-4842-6440-9_1

But referring to "traditional" embedded software projects may be the wrong word to use. Embedded software isn't developed the way it is because of tradition; rather, it is often developed this way out of a sense of desperation. As one manager I worked with put it: the process is like "building a railroad bridge over a gorge in front of a moving train while the bridge is burning down behind it." This rush to get things done, then, leads to software that is fragile and that tends to collapse if there are requirement changes or feature extensions. It also leads to software that is challenging to test, especially before fully functioning hardware and fully integrated software are available. But by following the patterns in this book, these patterns in the machine (PIM), if you will, you can create software or firmware that actually embraces change and maximizes testability. PIM does not lament the fact that change is a constant; rather, it embraces it and focuses on highly decoupled designs that can accommodate changes without sacrificing quality.

A NOTE ABOUT TEACHING PIM

If I were to teach a class on *Patterns in the Machine*, the syllabus would look something like this:

- Week 1—Hand out a board and supply the class with requirements for an application to be built on it. Tell them that a working application will be required at the end of week 5.

- Weeks 2–5—Lecture and demonstrate how to design and develop with a PIM methodology.

- Week 6—Hand out a different board and add some new requirements and change some existing requirements. A modified version of the application they just completed will be required at the end of week 8.

- Weeks 7–8—Lecture and demonstrate how to adapt the first application to the new hardware and requirements.

- Week 9—Hand out a new board, add some new requirements, and change the requirements one last time. A working application will be required to be submitted at the end of week 10 as the final exam.

It should be obvious to most of the students that unless they design their software with an eye toward accommodating the changes that will come later in the semester, they will not be successful in week 10. Unfortunately, in the "real world," project managers and development managers don't tell the team "Six weeks from now the hardware will change, and we'll add some new requirements." More often than not, they say the very opposite: "The hardware and requirements are frozen. We promise." But almost without fail, the changes come. More than anything else, it was this fact of life that led me to develop and implement the principles of PIM. It was the only way I could survive.

As an exercise, then, ask yourself this about your current project: "If in a few weeks I were to get new hardware and new software requirements, but my original deadline does not change, could my current design and implementation allow me to proceed in a reasonable, sustainable manner? Or would I be frantically working overtime to refactor my code?"

Patterns in the Machine

PIM is an amalgamation of design methodologies, best practices, software architectures, and continuous integration principles which, when applied to the embedded development space, deliver projects faster and with higher quality. As an example of faster, consider that

- PIM allows developers to start writing and testing actual, meaningful production code without hardware.

- PIM allows you to start testing early and often. Finding bugs at the beginning of the development cycle—especially bugs related to design flaws—greatly reduces the overall development time.

- PIM yields reusable code, which means there is less code to write on subsequent projects.

As an example of higher quality, consider that

- PIM emphasizes unit tests that inherently make modules more testable. One of the outcomes of this testing focus is that PIM achieves many of the quality benefits of Test-driven development (TDD). And while PIM does not embrace all TDD practices, PIM is fully compatible with it.

- PIM facilitates the ability to create a functional simulator that allows for all phases of testing to start early (i.e., before the hardware is available). Obviously, this yields greater test time, but it also enables downstream tasks like developing user documentation and training materials to start much earlier.

- PIM provides for true reuse. That is, PIM allows you to reuse source code files without modification or cloning, so there is no loss of quality or functionality in reused modules.

Other benefits to consider are

- PIM has an extendable code base. That is, accommodating new features and requirements is easier because of the inherent decoupling of the code from hardware.

- PIM allows many developers to work efficiently on the same application because the decoupled code base translates into developers not competing for access to the same files in the software configuration management (SCM) system.

- PIM is portable; when properly architected, over 90% of the source code is compiler and hardware independent.

- PIM is an agnostic development process. That is, it can be used in Agile, TDD, waterfall, and so on.

What Is Software Engineering?

Whereas there are no readily agreed-upon canonical definitions of what software engineering is, here are some interesting definitions:

> *[Software engineering is] the application of a systematic, disciplined, quantifiable approach to the development, operation, and maintenance of software.*
>
> —IEEE Standard Glossary of Software Engineering Terminology, IEEE std 610.12-1990, 1990.

[Software engineering is] the establishment and use of sound engineering principles in order to economically obtain software that is reliable and works efficiently on real machines.

—Fritz Bauer. "Software Engineering." Information Processing. 71: 530–538.

Software engineering should be known as "The Doomed Discipline," doomed because it cannot even approach its goal since its goal is self-contradictory. Software engineering, of course, presents itself as another worthy cause, but that is eyewash: if you carefully read its literature and analyse what its devotees actually do, you will discover that software engineering has accepted as its charter "How to program if you cannot."

—Edsger W. Dijkstra.
`www.cs.utexas.edu/~EWD/transcriptions/EWD10xx/EWD1036.html`

To put it simply: PIM requires you to do software engineering. And for the purposes of this book, the IEEE definition of software engineering will suffice. Unfortunately, in my experience, software engineering best practices require a level of discipline from developers (and principal stakeholders) that is, more often than not, sacrificed for the sake of tactical concerns.

Software Engineering Best Practices

Software engineering best practices can be broken down into two categories:

- Tactical—Designing and constructing individual components or modules

- Strategic—Specifying how individual components work together, how they can be tested, and how they can be architected in a way that accommodates changes in requirements or the addition of new features

In my experience, tactical best practices are routinely incorporated into projects. Strategic best practices, however, are typically a function of the tribal knowledge of an organization. As a result, they vary widely between groups and departments. Additionally, the strategic best practices that do exist are usually narrowly focused to meet past needs or present concerns. This differentiation between tactical and strategic is important because without a disciplined approach and commitment to strategic best practices, these are the first things dropped when "crunch time" arrives. While this may seem logical or even expedient, it is a net negative to the project's overall timeline and quality because it's the strategic best practices that maintain the "big picture" and integrity of the software. While tactical missteps typically have immediate consequences, strategic missteps typically aren't manifested until late in the project life cycle when they are expensive (in terms of time and effort) to fix. And, in many cases, the problems are never fixed as development teams often elect to take on "technical debt" by patching things together harum-scarum just to get the software out the door.

Here are some examples of tactical software engineering best practices:

- Design patterns
- Encapsulation
- Structured programming
- Object-oriented programming
- File organization
- Naming conventions
- Dependency management

Here are some examples of strategic software engineering best practices:

- Design patterns
- File organization
- Naming conventions
- Dependency management
- Automated unit testing
- Software architecture

Note that the two lists overlap. The reason is because most aspects of software development have both tactical and strategic characteristics. For example, let's examine naming conventions. These conventions are usually defined in the project's coding standards document. Typically, these conventions address things like case, underscores, nouns, verbs, Hungarian notation, scope of variables, and so on—all of which can be considered tactical. However, an example of a strategic naming convention would be specifying a requirement that the use of C++ namespaces (or name prefixing in C) be incorporated to prevent future naming collisions.

Another example would be requiring the use of specific design patterns. For example, applying the "observer pattern" to a module in isolation that implements a callback would be considered tactical. However, it would be considered strategic to require that the same observer pattern be applied consistently across the entire data model so that change notifications are always generated for any changes anywhere.

Chapter 2 expands on these core concepts for PIM and explains the tactical and strategic considerations for each concept.

What PIM Is Not

Patterns in the Machine is not an introduction to, nor a beginner's guide for, embedded software development. In fact, it covers very few details about tactical topics for embedded development. This book is about how to use some basic planning, architecture, and design to build highly decoupled embedded applications and then how to exploit that design and implementation to get your project done faster and with higher quality.

While the following list is not comprehensive, here are some topics that will *not* be covered in this book:

- Multi-threading programming

- Real-time scheduling

- Differences between an MCU and a CPU

- How to work with hardware peripherals (ADC, SPI, I2C, UART, timers, input capture, etc.)

- Hardware design

- Reading schematics

- Interrupt handling

- Math (floating point vs. integer vs. hexpoint, etc.)

- Low-power designs

- Cross compilers

- Optimizing for space and real-time performance

- Safety-critical applications

- IoT applications

- Watchdogs

- Networking

What You'll Need to Know

The target audience for PIM are developers who have worked on at least one embedded project and have experience with either C or C++. For example, this may be

- Software developers or firmware developers that have mid-level or higher experience.

- Technical leads

- Software architects

- Development managers

Additionally, it will be helpful if you can read and follow code written in C and C++. While this is not a strict requirement, all the sample code that is provided with this book is written in C and C++. While in many instances I do provide detailed explanations of the algorithms, sometimes it is just more effective to provide a snippet of code.

CHAPTER 2

Core Concepts

This chapter introduces the core concepts of PIM and explains why they matter. For each concept discussed here, there is a corresponding chapter in the book that provides a more detailed discussion of the material.

Software Architecture

Just like the term software engineering, the terms "software architecture" and "software detailed design" do not have concise definitions. On many embedded project teams, there is no distinction—or at least not one that the developers can articulate—between the two. The tendency, then, is to define architecture and detailed design together. This works up to a point, but teams tend to focus on the detailed design, and the architecture essentially becomes the output of that detailed design. This leads to an architecture that is rigid in terms of dependencies and oftentimes inconsistent with itself.

The problem with code designed without an architecture document arises when you try to add new features that don't quite match up with the original detailed design or when you encounter a scenario where you're trying to shoehorn a "missed feature" into the design. For example, I worked on one project where the team designed the HTTP request engine to use synchronous and asynchronous inter-thread communication (ITC) to send requests to the external cell modem driver. Later in the project, we added a watchdog sub-system that would monitor the system for locked up threads, but we found that the watchdog would intermittently trip on the thread running the HTTP engine. The root cause turned out to be that, given a specific set of preconditions related to cellular network failures, the synchronous ITC calls from the HTTP request engine would block for minutes at a time. Nothing in the original design proscribed when synchronous ITC could (or could not) be used. Because we did not have a written software architecture, there was nothing to guide or constrain the design of this feature. The developer of the HTTP engine just threw something together that reflected his minimal understanding of cell modem behavior. Ultimately, we had to leave the watchdog sub-system out of the final product.

9

© John T. Taylor, Wayne T. Taylor 2021
J. T. Taylor and W. T. Taylor, *Patterns in the Machine*,
https://doi.org/10.1007/978-1-4842-6440-9_2

You always want to have a detail-agnostic software architecture that the detailed design must conform to. It's the difference between driving a car on a paved road with guard rails and driving through an open field. Yes, the paved road has constraints on what and when and how vehicles and people can travel on it, whereas the open field has none; but getting from point A to point B is a lot faster and safer on the paved road as opposed to crossing an unbounded open field where nothing prevents you from colliding with other vehicles or local wildlife.

Software architecture best practices are strategic in nature. Define your project's software architecture first. Keep it separate from the software detailed design. There is an implied waterfall process here, but it's a good thing. Organically derived software architecture is the path to the dark side; or, without the moral overtones, it is often a quick path to "bit rot." Up-front architecture—separated from design—allows for just-in-time design, which is what you want in a development process like Agile. For example, if your software architecture defines the interface between the core business logic and the user interface as model points, then any work you do on the UI stories is completely decoupled from the business logic stories and vice versa. Only the model point instances need to be defined up front. (A more detailed discussion of model points is provided in Chapter 9.)

Automated Unit Testing

Unit tests are your friends; automated unit tests are your BFFs. Why? Because unit tests are an effective and repeatable way for developers to demonstrate that their code actually works. Manual testing may seem quicker in the moment because there is no test code to write, but it is rarely repeatable. This may not seem like a big deal until you have to make a change or have to fix a bug that requires regression testing. Additionally, without unit tests, it can be difficult to quantify actual test coverage.

In my experience, the time spent writing unit tests has always been net positive over the entire development cycle. Automated unit tests are even better because the execution of the tests can be incorporated into the project's continuous integration effort, yielding continual regression testing with code coverage metrics.

Unfortunately, writing unit tests—and especially automated unit tests—is not ingrained in the culture of embedded system development. I have no definitive explanation as to why this is, only empirical evidence that unit testing is not mainstream in the embedded world. My hypothesis is that because embedded development is tightly coupled to hardware and, consequently, bleeding-edge development, test frameworks are not readily available on many target hardware platforms. As a result, it is easy to rationalize that writing unit tests is not practical. Nevertheless, in my experience, there are no technical constraints that prevent automated unit testing from becoming the norm for embedded development. PIM's approach to unit testing is a subset of Test-driven development (TDD) in that it only requires three things:

- That you build a unit test for each module

- That you test sooner rather than later

- That you build your tests incrementally

There are two principal ways to perform automated unit tests for embedded systems. The first is to have an automated platform that can simulate the system's environment and interact with the software while it is running on its target hardware. There are many advantages to this approach, but it is costly in terms of resources, money, and time. In many ways, developing this test platform is an entire software project of its own. The second approach is to have the automated unit tests run as terminal (or console) applications on a computer. These tests return pass/fail. The obvious advantage here is that there is no simulation infrastructure to build, and there are many tools available to assist and augment the automated unit tests. The disadvantage to this approach is that it requires that the software be developed in a way that allows it to be executed both with the test computer's operating system and with the target hardware.

The PIM approach to automated unit testing is to decouple the software under development from the platform (i.e., the hardware, the OS, the compiler, etc.) so that computer-based automated testing is practical. While not all software can be abstracted away from the platform, in my experience, over 90% of an embedded application can be decoupled from the target platform with minimal extra effort. Whether it is a project on an 8-bit microcontroller or a CPU running a process-based operating system, after the source code is decoupled from the target platform and compiler, there is no downside to having computer-based automated unit testing. Of course, decoupling the software from the target platform can be tricky. But in most cases, with some up-front planning—and the discipline to follow the plan—it is a straightforward process. Furthermore, decoupling the software from the target platform also creates other benefits like being able to create a functional simulator.

To summarize, then, requiring unit tests and automated unit tests is a strategic best practice. The construction of the unit tests and test frameworks are the tactical best practices.

Functional Simulator

Just like changing requirements are a fact of life when developing software applications, "hardware is always late" is a truism for embedded projects. I have worked on numerous projects where software development begins before any hardware engineers or resources were assigned to the project, so, by definition, the hardware was already late. This creates the challenge of trying to write and test production-quality code without target hardware and without incurring a large amount of technical debt. This is where the advantages of having a functional simulator come in.

The goal of a functional simulator is to execute the production source code on a platform that is not the target platform. The simulator should provide the majority of the functionality (but not necessarily the real-time performance) of the application. In most cases, this hardware platform is a personal computer running Windows or Linux.

I first started incorporating a functional simulator in an embedded project 20 years ago as a direct result of target hardware not being available. And even after the hardware became available, the functional simulator was still used as the principal development platform. In fact, the only developer testing done on the actual target hardware were hardware-specific tests of real-time features. This was due to the fact that developing, and then executing, code on a PC was simply easier and Faster than on the target hardware where you had to cross-compile, program the Flash in the target microcontroller, and then debug the result on the target hardware. While the tools available for many target hardware platforms have improved greatly over the last two decades, developing code on a functional simulator is still easier and faster than using actual hardware.

While including a functional simulator in the project development cycle does require additional effort and planning, the complexity of that effort will vary by the nature of the project and target platforms. By starting with a minimal simulator and only then extending its capabilities on a case-by-case basis, the extra effort is minimized. The point to be emphasized here is that the effort to create a minimal functional simulator is close to free because the design work and planning that go into creating automated unit tests are 80% of the effort that is required to build the simulator.

When I first started building functional simulators, I had to convince management that constructing a functional simulator would be a net positive effort for the project. Today, I just pitch the concept of automated unit testing to management which is an easy sell. And lately I don't even have to pitch anything because management has already bought into automated unit testing. But after automated unit testing is part of the development process, constructing a minimal functional simulator becomes an uncontested line item in the schedule because the effort is small enough to be "lost in the noise."

The decision to include a functional simulator on a project is a strategic best practice. The use of the functional simulator as a substitute for the target hardware platform is a tactical best practice.

Continuous Integration

In PIM, the decision to include continuous integration (CI) on a project is a strategic best practice. As the concept of CI has been around since the 1990s, many of you have already accomplished the tactical objective of creating an automated build system for your embedded projects. Nevertheless, it is still important to articulate and define the strategic rules that govern the creation and ongoing maintenance of the CI for your project.

Martin Fowler provides this succinct definition of CI:

> *Continuous Integration is a software development practice where members of a team integrate their work frequently, usually each person integrates at least daily—leading to multiple integrations per day. Each integration is verified by an automated build (including test) to detect integration errors as quickly as possible.*

> —Martin Fowler (1 May 2006). "Continuous Integration."
> martinfowler.com. Retrieved 9 January 2014.

In the context of PIM, that yields the following strategic objectives:

- Build all work that is checked into the software configuration management (SCM) system. This should be done *before*—that is, separate and apart from—the work of merging all of the checked-in work to a mainline or otherwise stable branch of the code.

- Use the same build server for compiling daily check-ins as well as for creating formal builds from stable branches in the SCM repository.

- Execute the automated unit testing from the build server, and have the build fail if one or more automated unit tests fail.

- Build everything all the time

Setting up a CI process is nontrivial. Make sure that you include stories or tasks in your schedule to get the build server and CI process up and running. Also, periodic maintenance and support for the CI process should be included in your schedule as well.

So, how costly is it to add CI to a project? The short answer is: it depends. Here are some considerations that can complicate the CI process:

- Your experience with automation tools—There are numerous commercial and open source tools for automating builds and executing unit tests. These tools require a certain level of expertise to properly configure and use them.

- Your SCM tools—There are two primary issues here:

    1) Defining a branching or workflow strategy that explicitly incorporates CI. There needs to be steps in the workflow that prevent merging source code changes to stable branches until the CI server has successfully built and verified the changes.

    2) Defining the source code and repository organization such that it integrates with the automation tools (e.g., job construction in Jenkins is simpler when there is only one SCM repository involved as opposed to many).

- Your host build tools and environments—All of the tools used to build an embedded project must be installed on the build server (or a slave server). This also includes having compiler and tool licenses for the build server or build servers. Having build tools that execute on different operating systems further complicates the build server configuration and job construction.

- Your build engine or make files—The project's build process needs to support building the released application as well as building the automated unit tests. Depending on a project's constraints and requirements, the time and effort to define and implement this can vary greatly.

- The maintenance of the build server—Whether your build server is a physical machine or a virtual machine, you need to follow IT best practices in maintaining and backing up the platforms. The automation tools themselves will need a certain amount of maintenance as you add or update existing automated jobs.

- The build times—The amount of code that is built, and the number of unit tests that are executed, increases over time. In a perfect world, the build and test cycle for CI would be seconds. In my experience, however, for embedded projects, the reality is that the build times are minutes to hours. A general rule of thumb for build server hardware is that you can never have too much disk space, too much RAM, or too many cores because, inevitably, reducing CI build times becomes an issue.

As you can see, CI is not a simple or free addition to a project. So why do it? Going back to Martin Fowler's definition of CI, the reason to do it is to detect integration errors as quickly as possible. On the surface, this may not sound like a huge win, but CI is a significant net positive when it comes to maintaining stable branches in your SCM. For me, the best argument for detecting integration errors as quickly as possible is to avoid the pain I experienced living through broken builds that were required to be stable at all times and getting bogged down in "merge hell." I have worked with really big companies that dreaded pulling formal releases together because the build process was anything but integrated, and it had to account for a myriad of dependencies on other projects. In these environments, it could often take a week to release the project, and, in the end, I had the nagging sense that what we finally pulled together was very fragile.

This brings us to a final strategic objective for CI: build everything all the time. It is not uncommon for a project to be defined something like this: (1) release the project on ABC hardware; (2) a month later, release the software on XYZ hardware; (3) a month later, release localized versions of the software on both hardware platforms. In cases like this, it is important not to postpone the building of the XYZ project because "it hasn't really started" or to put off building the localized versions because "we haven't even sent the text off for translation." Rather, from the beginning, you should establish jobs in your CI process where all the artifacts for all the platforms and languages get built. Even if originally the jobs for the anticipated hardware start out as a lot of "stubbed" code and the localized versions only have one or two words translated, it is a net win to have these jobs building artifacts with every automated build.

Data Model

Your goal as an embedded system developer should be to design a loosely coupled system. One way to accomplish this is by never having two modules communicate directly with each other. Rather, you should place data (i.e., model points) between the modules, and the modules talk to the model points. For example, don't design like Figure 2-1.

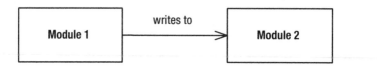

Figure 2-1. *Example of a tightly coupled design*

Instead, design like Figure 2-2.

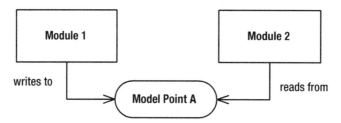

Figure 2-2. *Example of a loosely coupled design*

In the loosely coupled design in Figure 2-2, both modules are passed a reference to Model Point A in their constructors or during initialization. While this may seem like you're introducing an unnecessary layer of abstraction, in reality, you're giving your design the following advantages:

- It makes it easier to extend existing functionality without modifying existing source code. For example, you could extend Figure 2-2 by introducing a third module that takes the output of Module 1 and modifies it for input to Module 2. In this case, we would only need to create a new model point. In Figure 2-3, then, Module 3 is passed a reference to Model Point A and Model Point AA in its constructor or during initialization. The point here is that even though there has been a feature change, the original Module 1 and Module 2 do not need to be rewritten. The only change would be to the code that constructs or initializes Module 2 so that it is passed a reference to Model Point AA (instead of Model Point A).

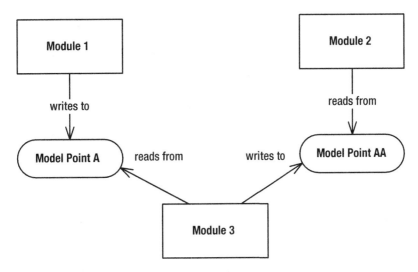

Figure 2-3. *Example of extending a loosely coupled design*

- It breaks up what might normally be a sequential bottom-up, or top-down, development process and facilitates parallel development, which is what allows you to add additional programmers to a project and have them actually contribute effectively toward shortening your development schedule.

- It simplifies the construction of unit tests.

- It simplifies writing platform-independent and compiler-independent source code.

- It simplifies the construction of a functional simulator.

- It creates a large number of reusable modules.

In the data model architecture, the modules or components interact with each other with no direct dependencies on each other. A well-defined model point will have the following features:

- Model points support any primitive data type or any data structure as their value. A model point's value should be strictly data and should not contain business rules or enforce policies (except for discrete, self-contained operations like value range checking).

- Individual model points are type specific with respect to their value. That is, all read/write operations are type safe.

- Model points have atomic operations that read or write their values. This means that accessing model point values is a thread-safe operation.

- Model points have valid or invalid states that are independent of their value.

- Model points provide a subscription mechanism for client entities to receive change notifications when the value of a model point changes or transitions to a valid or invalid state.

Figure 2-4 is an example design using the data model pattern for a hypothetical thermostat. The use case for this hypothetical thermostat is defined here:

- Use a proportional-integral-derivative (PID) controller to control a temperature loop. The output of the PID controller is a process variable that is used to drive the amount of active capacity from the system's HVAC equipment.

- The temperature input (i.e., process variable) for the PID loop can come from different temperature sensors based on configuration settings.

- If there is no valid or operational temperature sensor available for input to the PID controller, an alarm is raised.

The modules in this model are

- Temperature Driver

- Sensor Selection

- Alarm Manager

- Controller, or more specifically, a proportional-integral-derivative (PID) controller

As none of the modules have dependencies on each other, they can be developed independently. And with the possible exception of the Temperature Driver, all of the modules are hardware independent and can have automated unit tests created to verify their operation.

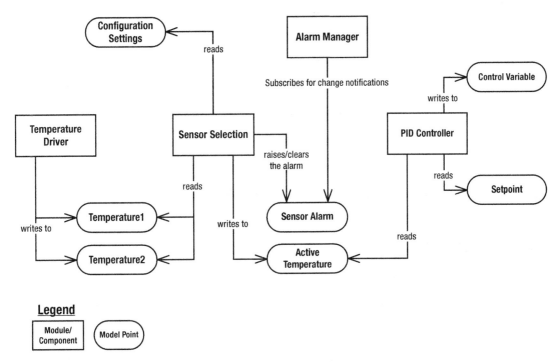

Figure 2-4. *Example design of thermostat using model points*

When your embedded project is designed with this approach, the data model becomes the canonical authority for what determines the application behavior. The data model pattern, then, is a strategic best practice because it is an architectural pattern. How the individual model points are used—whether they are polled, event driven, or used for inter-thread communications—are tactical best practices.

The data model architecture has similarities to other software patterns like Model-View-Controller (MVC), Publish-Subscribe, and Component-Based Development (CBD). The data model pattern can be used to realize a CBD architecture when the "provided" and "used" interfaces in CBD are implemented as model points. The CBD diagram in Figure 2-5 is functionally the same as Figure 2-4. As another example, the PIM example application in Chapter 16 adopts a CBD design philosophy (using the data model) to implement a thermostat control algorithm.

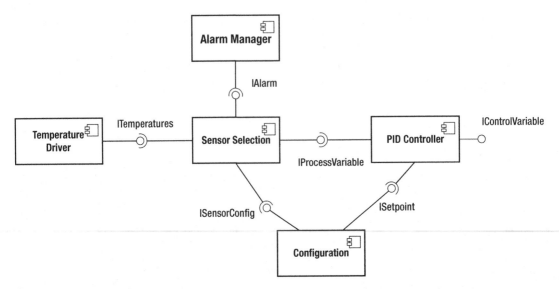

Figure 2-5. *Example of a Component-Based Design equivalent of a data model*

Finite State Machines

State machines, or specifically finite state machines (FSMs), are handy-dandy tools for embedded developers. When conducting job interviews for embedded developers, I routinely ask the question what is a finite state machine and when does it make sense to include FSM(s) in your design? Only a small minority of the job candidates are capable of articulating a cohesive answer to this question.

I place a lot of emphasis on FSMs because, when dealing with asynchronous behaviors—for example, communication protocols, time-outs, user events, external triggers, and so on—FSMs provide a robust mechanism for not only defining but also implementing asynchronous behaviors.

What is an FSM? Here is a slightly edited definition from Wikipedia along with the ubiquitous turnstile example in Figure 2-6.

> *A finite-state machine (FSM) ... is a mathematical model of computation. It is an abstract machine that can be in exactly one of a finite number of states at any given time. The FSM can change from one state to another in response to some external inputs and/or when a condition is satisfied; the change from one state to another is called a transition. An FSM is defined by a list of its states, its initial state, and the conditions for each transition.*

> —https://en.wikipedia.org/wiki/Finite-state_machine

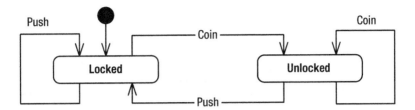

Figure 2-6. *Finite state diagram for a turnstile*

When thinking about the states for a module, it is sufficient to sketch or draw boxes and arrows freehand until you have all the states and transitions mapped out. At that point, I encourage you to draw your final or official FSM diagrams more formally. In my experience, I have found that creating FSMs using the UML syntax can help you avoid invalid FSM semantics that can become problematic during implementation. The use of FSMs in your design, then, is a strategic best practice. The use of drawing tools or code generation tools can be argued to be either strategic or tactical best practices.

Figure 2-7 is an example of an FSM diagram from the PIM example code. The diagram was drawn using Cadifra with source code generation provided by SinelaboreRT. The diagram uses the UML notation for the most part. The exceptions are that the join and choice pseudo-states are represented as () and <>, respectively. (Appendix B provides some details about state machine notation.)

The diagram describes the behavior of a single HVAC stage that provides heating or cooling capacity. Stages can be cascaded to provide additional capacity.

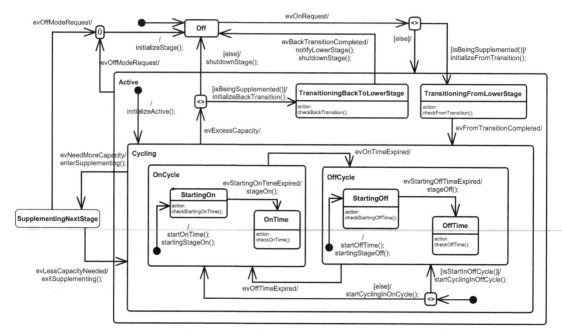

Figure 2-7. *Finite state machine diagram for the PIM example*

One principal advantage of the FSM in Figure 2-7 is that a developer (or tester or field support engineer) can determine with certainty what the behavior of a stage should be given any arbitrary set of events or preconditions. And in the embedded space, FSMs are particularly useful tools for understanding and defining an asynchronous behavior. How an FSM diagram is implemented is discussed at length in Chapter 10.

Documentation

In general, software developers don't like generating documentation. This dislike was codified in the Agile Manifesto which prefers "Working software over comprehensive documentation" (https://agilemanifesto.org/). Outside of regulated industries, the trend in the embedded software space seems to be that documentation is a waste of time. While I would agree that excessive documentation is not a net positive for a project, the other extreme, where "source code is the documentation," is a net negative. Documentation should be viewed as a tool; it is more than just a record of what was designed and implemented. Documentation adds values by

- Providing a canonical reference

- Providing a higher level of abstraction for identifying, analyzing, and specifying solutions

- Providing a concrete medium for review

- Being easier and faster to rework than source code

- Bridging the gap between individuals and disciplines

- Providing training and onboarding materials

- Providing the basis for end user and support documentation

So what is the Goldilocks amount of documentation for an embedded project? It depends. Asking the question differently, then, what should be documented? In the scope and context of PIM, the following items should be documented:

- Software development plan (SDP)—A software development plan captures the details of the development process that the software team will follow. For example, it specifies what SCM and bug tracking systems will be used, the SCM branching conventions, how code reviews will be handled, and so on. By definition, the SDP should be one of the first documents created. Said another way, the SDP documents the explicit decisions that have been made about how the software will be developed before you start the development.

- Software architecture (SA)—Chapter 5 goes into detail on what is and what is not a software architecture. By definition, the software architecture must be completed before the design and implementation begin.

- Software detailed design (SDD)—The SDD is the "how" and bridges the gaps between software requirements and software architecture and the source code. Assuming the software architecture has been defined, the detailed design can be done just-in-time or on an agile story basis.

- Best practices—If your organization has its own best practices with respect to software development, these practices need to be articulated and documented for the software team. Undocumented best practices are at best company culture and at worst individual preference.

- Source code—Everyone will agree that the source code needs to be documented. Where PIM differs a bit is that PIM encourages you to fully document all public interfaces (e.g., the syntax, semantics, thread safety requirements, example usage, etc.). In other words, the documentation for public interfaces should read like hardware data sheets for an integrated circuit or a man page in Linux or Unix. The reason is because with a highly decoupled design and implementation, the consumer of an interface does not necessarily know where to find the source files (i.e., the .c or .cpp files) that implement the interface in order to see the missing details.

Depending on the organization or industry you are in, documentation templates, formats, and document control processes can be largely dictated to the software team. If the software team has latitude in defining its documentation process, PIM encourages the practice of content over formatting. Trying to put together a formal Word document with a title page, executive summary, table of contents, headers, footers, references, glossary, actual content, change log, appendices, and so on can be exhausting. An alternative is to create a Wiki (or similar tool) page entry that just contains the actual content. You can then tag the entry or create links to it, so the entry can be found. An example of this is the `top/start_here.html` page in the PIM example GitHub repository. The `start_here.html` file is a TiddlyWiki file, which is essentially a self-contained Wiki-Server-with-content in a single HTML file.

In summary, then, the requirement that specific documentation must be completed for a project is a strategic best practice. The creation of documentation is a tactical best practice. Chapter 11 goes into more detail about documentation.

CHAPTER 3

Design Theory for Embedded Programming

One of the key concepts of this book is that embedded programming is not exempt from the rules of good software programming. Yes, there are unique challenges and difficulties when programming at a low level with very constrained resources, but, at the end of the day, it is still software. And smart, proven software design principles still apply. In particular, the design principles and theory underlying object-oriented programming are extremely useful for anyone writing embedded code.

To be clear, when I talk about object-oriented design, nothing that I am proposing requires the use of an object-oriented compiler. Object-oriented designs can be (and are) developed using ordinary C compilers.[1] If necessary, they could also be implemented in an assembly language. What's important, then, is that you use proven design principles in the creation of your software, because in a sense the design is more important than the code.

I know that may sound odd, and it isn't literally true, but consider which is easier to fix in the middle of a project: a missing semicolon in a line of code or a module with a design flaw that causes race conditions? To put it another way, consider the well-known, and sometimes dreaded, practice of code reviews or code inspections. These very detailed examinations of the software—stepping through the code line by line with the development team—would often identify problems in the syntax or implementation of the code. However, because these reviews were so focused on each line of code, they often did not uncover design defects which are vastly more problematic and more

---

[1]In my experience with embedded projects, having polymorphic functions as part of the program language is desirable, but not an absolute requirement. The C programming language can be used to implement any functionality that a C++ application has; it's just a little messier and depends on what your C compiler does and does not enforce. The first C++ compiler—Cfront—translated C++ code to C code which was then compiled by a C compiler.

25

© John T. Taylor, Wayne T. Taylor 2021
J. T. Taylor and W. T. Taylor, *Patterns in the Machine*,
https://doi.org/10.1007/978-1-4842-6440-9_3

difficult to address. In my opinion—and again overstating things a bit to make the point—design reviews would better serve a development team than code reviews. With design reviews, the reviewing team gains a common understanding of the structure of the modules, their semantics, and the design principles that were used (or valued). A design review gives everyone a better sense of how everything ties together.

So, again, while there is not anything particularly new in this chapter, I felt it was important to call out some existing software design principles and best practices that can be applied to embedded development. Specifically, this chapter provides a discussion of existing concepts and some object-oriented concepts that inform designing loosely coupled software.

SOLID

The acronym SOLID was introduced by Michael Feathers from principles developed by Robert C. Martin, and it describes five handy-dandy principles for designing loosely coupled software. The "official" abstract description of each principle is provided here and is followed by a clarifying discussion.

Single Responsibility Principle

There should never be more than one reason for a class to change.

https://web.archive.org/web/20150202200348/
http://www.objectmentor.com/resources/articles/srp.pdf

Open-Closed Principle

Software entities (classes, modules, functions, etc.) should be open for extension, but closed for modification.

https://web.archive.org/web/20150905081105/
http://www.objectmentor.com/resources/articles/ocp.pdf

Liskov Substitution Principle

Functions that use pointers or references to base classes must be able to use objects of derived classes without knowing it.

```
                              https://web.archive.org/web/20150905081111/
                     http://www.objectmentor.com/resources/articles/lsp.pdf
```

Interface Segregation Principle

Clients should not be forced to depend upon interfaces that they do not use.

```
                              https://web.archive.org/web/20150905081110/
                     http://www.objectmentor.com/resources/articles/isp.pdf
```

Dependency Inversion Principle

A. *High level modules should not depend upon low level modules. Both should depend upon abstractions.*

B. *Abstractions should not depend upon details. Details should depend upon abstractions.*

```
                              https://web.archive.org/web/20150905081103/
                     http://www.objectmentor.com/resources/articles/dip.pdf
```

Single Responsibility Principle

What the Single Responsibility Principle (SRP) is trying to say is design your software in layers, with each layer performing a specific function. Moreover, don't try to package too much work into a single module.

For example, consider the use case of storing persistent data in an EEPROM. A common implementation is to put the code that manages the EEPROM command set, the external communications, the reading and writing of data, and the data integrity checks into one module. The problem with this approach is that there is "more than one reason for [the] class to change." For example, if any of the following were to happen, it would require the entire module to be touched and retested: you need to write more data, change the data layout to a new schema, or, perhaps, even use a new EEPROM.

I once worked on one project where our team had an offboard EEPROM for storing both persistent configuration data and diagnostic data. The project started with a SPI-based EEPROM chip, which used four pins (clock, data-in, data-out, and chip-select). The code for reading and writing to the EEPROM was contained in a single module. In addition, the same module also handled the SPI communications with the EEPROM as well as checksumming the data stored in the EEPROM to detect corrupt data. Several months into the project, we discovered that we needed one additional GPIO pin to support new functionality. But there were no available pins left on the MCU.

The decision was eventually made to use an I2C-based EEPROM chip, which only required two pins (clock and data). This change freed up two GPIO pins. The new EEPROM chip had the same command set as the original SPI EEPROM chip, but the original software module had to be refactored to use I2C communications instead of SPI communications. As a result, the *entire* module had to be retested—not just the code that contained the new I2C communications. Unfortunately, a bug was introduced in the refactoring of the module, so additional extensive testing was required.

Remember that layers are your friends when it comes to unit testing, especially when implementing automated unit testing. It is also the key to decoupling code and preparing your software for future reuse. The Single Responsibility Principle is a tactical best practice, but it enables strategic best practices such as unit testing and platform-independent code.

In Chapter 4, there is an example of how we should have designed the persistent storage module. That example is written in layers and illustrates how to design with the Single Responsibility Principle in mind.

Open-Closed Principle

The Open-Closed Principle (OCP) says that you want to design your software so that if you add new features or some new functionality, you only add new code; you do not rewrite existing code. A traditional example of the OCP is to introduce an abstract interface to decouple a "client" from the "server." For example, the design presented in Figure 3-1 is straightforward but poorly designed if you're seeking to minimize rework and maximize reuse.

Figure 3-1. *Example of a design without abstract interfaces*

A more robust design that follows the Open-Closed Principle would look like Figure 3-2.

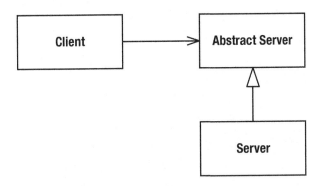

Figure 3-2. *Abstract interface designed following the Open-Closed Principle*

This design allows for new functionality and behaviors to be added to the module without modifying the original *Client* or *Server* code, as shown in Figure 3-3.

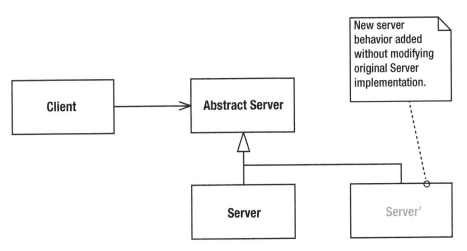

Figure 3-3. *Design extended in a way that does not require editing existing code*

PIM's interpretation of the OCP, then, is quite literally:

Adding new functionality should not be done by editing existing source code.

That is the frame of mind you need to approach designing every module with, and you achieve it by putting together a loosely coupled design.

What follows are some techniques I use in the PIM example application (discussed in detail in Chapter 16) that help realize OCP in the design:

- The use of ifndef for magic constants

- The use of model points

- The use of abstract interfaces

Using ifndef

The PIM example application is only required to support a single-stage AC unit. However, multistage AC units or heat pumps are not uncommon. So instead of hardcoding values for the type of HVAC equipment or the number of stages a compressor has, I implement a #ifndef structure to allow for the future support of heat pumps and multistage compressors. This is an example of using compile time bindings to support changes without editing existing code.

```
#include "colony_config.h"
/** The max number of compressor heating stages the system supports. */
#ifndef OPTION_STORM_MAX_COMPRESSOR_HEATING_STAGES
#define OPTION_STORM_MAX_COMPRESSOR_HEATING_STAGES      0
#endif

/** The max number of cooling stages the system supports. */
#ifndef OPTION_STORM_MAX_COMPRESSOR_COOLING_STAGES
#define OPTION_STORM_MAX_COMPRESSOR_COOLING_STAGES      1
#endif
```

Using Model Points

Additionally, the PIM example application is designed using a data model architecture. The individual modules that make up the thermostat's control algorithm use model point instances to interact with each other. Each algorithm module is passed references to the model point instances that are to be used for its inputs and outputs. The following is a code snippet from the AirFilterMonitor module that shows its constructor method taking a set of references to model point instances:

```
/** This class is responsible for monitoring how long the indoor fan has
    been running and raise an alert when it is time to change the air
    filter.
 */
class AirFilterMonitor : public Base
{
public:
    /// Input Model Points
    struct Input_T
    {
        /** The user configured number of operation hours between Indoor
            Air filter changes
         */
        Cpl::Dm::Mp::Uint32*                maxAirFilterHours;

        /// The elapsed time that the indoor blower has been on
        Cpl::Dm::Mp::ElapsedPrecisionTime*  airFilterOperationTime;

        /// The virtual system outputs
        Storm::Dm::MpVirtualOutputs*        vOutputs;

        /// The Air Filter Alert
        Storm::Dm::MpSimpleAlarm*           airFilterAlert;
    };

    /// Output Model Points
    struct Output_T
    {
        /// The Air Filter Alert
        Storm::Dm::MpSimpleAlarm*           airFilterAlert;

        /// The elapsed time that the indoor blower has been on
        Cpl::Dm::Mp::ElapsedPrecisionTime*  airFilterOperationTime;
    };

public:
    /// Constructor
    AirFilterMonitor( struct Input_T ins, struct Output_T outs );
```

This approach allows new algorithm functionality to be added by developing a new algorithm module and then wiring the new module into the existing set of algorithm modules. This allows proven algorithm modules to be static (i.e., never edited) and only the top-level start-up code needs to be changed to accommodate the new wiring. Again, this is how I achieve the goal of accommodating changes without editing existing modules.

Using Abstract Interfaces

The PIM example thermostat application also has a command-line interface (CLI) that is used to monitor and interact with the application at runtime. The CLI implementation is part of a library I created—and which I use in many production projects—called Colony.core. (This is a C++ library, and I cover it in more detail in Chapter 16.)

The design of this CLI engine depends upon abstract interfaces for reading and writing to a stream. The following code snippet shows the interface definition for the processing module of the CLI engine. The Cpl::Io::Input and Cpl::Io::Output are the abstractions of the input and output stream interfaces.

```
class ProcessorApi
{
public:
    /** This method is used to start the Command Processor, i.e. it will
        begin to process commands.  This command will not return until
        the Command Processor self terminates or a Input/Output stream
        error was encounter.  The method returns true if the Command
        Processor self terminated or was requested to stop; else false
        is returned (i.e. a Input/Output stream error was encounter).

        NOTE: This method is an 'in-thread' initialization, i.e. not
              Thread safe. The application is RESPONSIBLE for managing
              threading issues.
     */
    virtual bool start( Cpl::Io::Input& infd, Cpl::Io::Output& outfd ) = 0;
```

The Colony.core library provides an implementation of the stream interfaces for the C library's STDIO streams (i.e., stdin, stdout, stderr) as well as TCP sockets.

The selected target hardware in the PIM example is an Arduino board. In order to support the CLI engine on the Arduino board, the only change I needed to make was to provide a new implementation of the stream interfaces that delegated read and write calls to the "serial object" in the Arduino libraries. No code edits were required to the Colony.core library. This is an example of where the introduction of abstract interfaces, `Cpl::Io::Input` and `Cpl::Io::Output`, allowed the code to be extended without editing existing files.

OCP Flexibility

It is also important to recognize that a module cannot be 100% closed against all possible extensions. Furthermore, not every module needs to be OCP friendly. It is the responsibility of the designer, architect, and developer to choose what type of extensions a module is closed against. As with most things in life, good choices come with experience, and a lot of experience comes from bad choices.

OCP is very much a strategic best practice.

Liskov Substitution Principle

The Liskov Substitution Principle (LSP) addresses the subtyping of base classes so that all child classes are required to faithfully meet or implement not just the syntax but all of the semantic behavior of their base class. Because PIM does not require an object-oriented programming language, I further generalize the LSP to be

All implementations of an abstract interface are required to fully implement of the semantics of the interface definition.

The compiler knows the syntax; but semantics—all the important stuff you need to know about the interface—is not compiler enforced and is usually found in the comments of the code. For example, semantics are things like

- When is it okay to call a method?

- What needs to be done to clean up after an error?

- When do you get a callback?

- What thread does the callback run in?

- Who manages allocated memory (client, server, or both)?

Semantic equivalency, then, is the burden the developer must shoulder. Nonsemantic equivalency can be very subtle and not immediately obvious and sometimes doesn't manifest itself until the next project or until a change of functionality occurs in the current application. Loosely coupled designs are built on the assumption that they can *trust* the implementation of all the semantics of the interface definition.

I worked on one project where the data model architecture required us to create numerous application-specific model point types. The semantics for model points on this project were that all read operations returned a Boolean that indicated the valid or invalid state of the model point's data. But there was one developer who ignored the required read semantics for model points and, when creating a new model point type, defined the read operations to return the model point's data value—not its valid/invalid state.

His module that consumed the new model points (as well as the unit test for the new model point type) all passed because the unit tests always set the model points in question to valid states. However, once his code was integrated with the application, the application would randomly crash. This was because the new model point instances were not always in the valid state. (And there are legit reasons for a model point's state to be invalid.) From a compiler and unit test perspective, the new model point type was syntactically correct; however, it was semantically incorrect from an architecture or design perspective. Ultimately, the fix was relatively simple. However, finding the root cause took an inordinate amount of effort because of the intermittent nature of the failures and the assumption that since the unit tests had all passed, the problem couldn't be the new code.

The LSP is a tactical best practice that has strategic implications when not followed.

Interface Segregation Principle

The Interface Segregation Principle (ISP) says don't define an interface that does everything; instead define multiple, smaller interfaces that target specific usage models or use cases. To put it another way, you don't want to design interfaces that are Swiss army knives. Rather, you want to design and implement lots of knives with very narrowly specific uses.

A hypothetical example would be a hardware abstraction layer (HAL). The purpose of the HAL is to decouple the clients from a hardware-specific implementation. One approach to defining a HAL interface would be to have a single file or interface definition that accounts for all platform- or hardware-specific items (e.g., UART, I2C, SPI, mutexes, threads, file I/O, hardware timers, etc.). This has the advantage mapping one to one with the mental model of a HAL interface. The downside is that if you attempt to reuse the HAL interface on a different project that does not have an identical platform, then the new project has dependencies that must be satisfied at compile or link time.

For example, perhaps the first project you're assigned to uses a real-time operating system (RTOS), and, as such, the unified HAL interface includes abstractions for the RTOS. But then your next project on the same MCU is a bare-metal design that does not use an RTOS. To leverage the previous HAL interface, the methods related to RTOS abstractions would have to be reconciled and/or "mocked."

The PIM approach would be to follow the ISP. The HAL interface would be broken up into many individual HAL interface definitions, for example:

- A separate HAL interface definition for accessing UART hardware

- A separate HAL interface for accessing SPI hardware

- A separate interface for a mutex

- A separate interface for thread handling

This allows consumers of the HAL interfaces to only include what they need and nothing more.

A more concrete example would be in the PIM example application. The Colony.core C++ library's `Cpl::Io::Input` and `Cpl::Io::Output` interfaces define read/write operations that can be used to access resources such as files, serial ports, pipes, network sockets, and so on. Basically, this becomes a C++ wrapper for POSIX file descriptors. However, these interfaces only define read/write operations. For file-specific operations, additional interfaces are defined—`Cpl::Io::File::Input` and `Cpl::Io::File::Output`—by extending the `Cpl::Io` interfaces to include file operations such as `setRelativePos()`, `currentPos()`, `isEof()`, `length()`, and so on. By separating out the file-specific operations from the base read/write interface, clients that only use stream semantics (stdio, serial ports, sockets, etc.) are not forced to depend on methods or semantics that are specific to operating on files. This is especially important for embedded systems because most embedded projects have at least one stream-based interface (e.g., UART), but they do not typically have a file system. By not combining file-specific semantics into the basic read/write interface, the Colony.core C++ library can be incorporated directly without having to create any project-specific "glue code" that satisfies (at compile or link time) the unused file operations.

ISP is a tactical best practice. However, it has strategic implications because it encourages decoupled designs. Make no mistake, tactical thinking is not bad; it is a good thing when you're getting down to the nitty-gritty design and implementation of modules. What is bad is when only tactical thinking is employed in designing a module. Strategic naming conventions are a good example of this. If I were to use tactical-only thinking to design a module, I might take no thought to avoid potential name collisions that could occur when reusing the code or incorporating third-party code. I could end up causing myself unnecessary name collision problems in the future. But if I were following strategic-thinking design practices, I would use namespaces from day one.

Dependency Inversion Principle

The Dependency Inversion Principle (DIP) is something of a generalization of the previous principles in that it says introduce interfaces to break dependencies. In the following diagrams, let's start with a persistent module that is responsible for managing data stored in an offboard EEPROM chip. Figure 3-4 is a design without interfaces, which, because of dependencies, makes all of the code dependent on the Arduino platform since dependencies are transitive in nature.

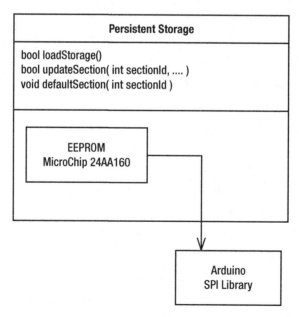

Figure 3-4. Arduino-dependent design of a persistent storage module

By adding an NV Interface and SPI Driver Interface, the original design can be broken up into layers with each layer being decoupled from each other (see Figure 3-5). Or stated another way, each layer can be reused, modified, and extended without the inclusion of the other layers or impact on the other layers. (Chapter 4 provides more implementation details for this example.)

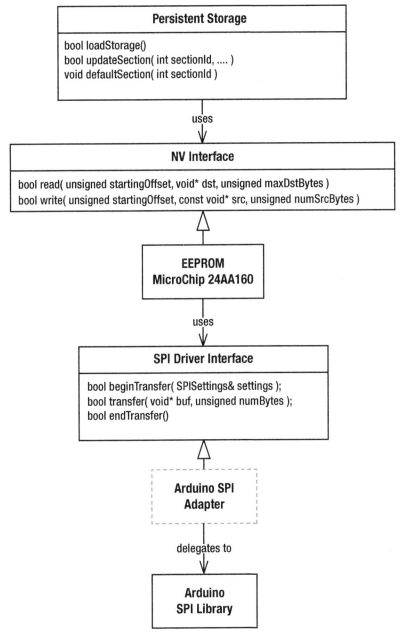

Figure 3-5. *Persistent storage module that is decoupled from Arduino*

When reading the canonical definition of the Dependency Inversion Principle, don't get too focused on the terminology of abstractions. Abstractions are just interface definitions with few if any `#include` statements. That is, they are header files that describe a set of functionality with no implementation. Abstractions just define behavior; the implementation comes later. Also, the term "details" is just a fancy way of saying implementation. So, to restate the second half of the DIP definition in terms of C/C++ coding:

> *Interface header files should not depend on implementation-specific `#include` statements.*

As an example, consider the use case of defining an interface for a mutex. The interface definition (e.g., `mutex.h`) would define the `lock()` and `unlock()` methods. However, it would not define a mutex type in terms of a specific operating system. In this way, you can avoid including the header files `Windows.h` or `pthread.h` (for a concrete mutex type) which have implementation dependencies or "details." Later in this chapter, in the "Compile Time Binding," I'll provide an example of how to define types without having implementation dependencies.

DIP is a tactical and strategic best practice.

Binding Time

The general idea behind binding time is that you want to wait as long as possible before binding data or functions to names. Or said another way, the ability to defer binding times is yet another hammer in your toolbox for designing loosely coupled software.

To be more exact in the definition, in the context of PIM, binding is the association of named identifiers with data or code. For example, the binding of the function named `main` to its implementation code for a C/C++ executable is a binding that occurs when the executable is linked.

Two major binding times are static and dynamic. Static bindings are name bindings that occur before a program is run. Dynamic bindings are name bindings that occur as the program executes. In the context of C/C++ programming, static bindings occur during the compile and link phases. Dynamic bindings are the C++ polymorphic bindings that occur at runtime when a virtual method is called. In a perfect world, everyone would be programming everything in a language that supports runtime polymorphic bindings, and every module or interface would have pure abstract interfaces that decouple them from the rest of the universe. However, polymorphic bindings are not free; they can result in poorer runtime performance and require an object-oriented programming language for a type-safe implementation. Consequently, PIM does not require polymorphic bindings. However, PIM does encourage the use of abstract interfaces when programming in C++.

Again, what I'm trying to convince you to do here is to decouple things. And the later the binding happens, the more decoupled a name is. A name that is decoupled from its implementation (e.g., a pure virtual class definition) has minimal to no dependencies. And, when it comes to unit testing, refactoring, reuse, and so on, the fewer the dependencies, the easier the task is. Consequently, PIM relies heavily on static bindings for decoupling interfaces and modules. PIM further breaks down static bindings into the following subcategories:

- Source time
- Compile time
- Link time

Source Time Binding

Source time bindings are made when you edit a source code file. This is reflected primarily in what your #include statements are and the definitions of numeric and string constants. As source code bindings are bindings that cannot be changed or undone later without editing the file, you want to minimize source time bindings. This is what you do if you embrace the OCP which allows you to add files if necessary, but to avoid editing existing files.

So what does this mean in practice? First, never include header files that are not a direct dependency. Second, design your modules and interfaces in a way where they do not directly rely on any explicit or "magic" constants. The following is an example of defining a constant value for a buffer size while still allowing an application to provide a different value at compile time. This construct defers the binding time of the buffer size from source time to compile time.

```
#ifndef OPTION_FOO_BAR_MAX_BUFFER_SIZE
#define OPTION_FOO_BAR_MAX_BUFFER_SIZE     128
#endif

    ...
uint8_t my_buffer[OPTION_FOO_BAR_MAX_BUFFER_SIZE];
```

For some additional examples of reducing source time bindings, see the sections on LHeader and LConfig in Chapter 13.

Compile Time Binding

Compile time bindings are bindings that are made during the compilation stage. The primary mechanisms involved with compile time bindings are the specification of preprocessor symbols when the compiler is invoked and setting the compiler's header file search paths. The LHeader and LConfig patterns leverage the header search path mechanism to provide concrete definitions for preprocessor symbols that were declared without any definition provided. For example, here is how you can defer the binding of the mutex data type until compile time:

File: Cpl/System/Mutex.h

```
// This is a project specific header that will resolve the _MAP symbols
#include "colony_map.h"

/** This symbol defines the structure for a Mutex. The concrete definition
    of the mutex type is deferred to the application's 'platform'
 */
#define Cpl_System_Mutex_T        Cpl_System_Mutex_T_MAP
```

The delayed binding in this example could also have been done using a forward declaration. For example, I could have used a statement like

```
typedef struct Cpl_System_Mutex Cpl_System_Mutex_T
```

and then provided the concrete definition for struct Cpl_System_Mutex in a platform-specific .c|.cpp file. The compiler allows clients (or consumers) to pass around a pointer to a mutex (e.g., Cpl_System_Mutex_T*) without a concrete type definition because all pointers have the same known storage size. The disadvantage of using the forward declaration approach is that only platform-specific code can instantiate a mutex instance. This restriction is not inherently bad, but it does bring up the issue of how memory will be allocated for the mutex instance. Will it be dynamically allocated from the heap on demand? Is there a statically allocated pool of mutexes? If so, how many instances can be created? Also, what happens when the heap/memory pool is exhausted?

The advantage of using the LHeader pattern and doing a compile time binding for the mutex type is that it allows the client (i.e., consumer) to take over the memory management for mutex instances. The client code can statically allocate as many mutexes as it needs without having to add runtime checks for possible out-of-memory conditions when creating a mutex. Remember, PIM is targeted to the embedded software space where dynamic memory allocation is strongly discouraged.

Link Time Binding

Link time binding is what most developers typically think of as static bindings.[2] These are bindings that are made during the link stage of the build process. The linker binds names to addresses or binds code with a specific function name. Link time binding allows a developer to define a function (or set of functions) and then have multiple implementations for those functions. The selection of which implementation to use is made when the build script for a project is written. Taking advantage of link time binding is a very simple mechanism for supporting multiple variants. For example, link time binding is how you can have an implementation of a function foo() for Linux and a different foo() implementation for Windows. Some of the limitations you will encounter trying to leverage link time bindings are

- The organization of the source code—PIM encourages that each implementation resides in its own file and that the preprocessor #ifdef/#else constructs are *not used* for separating the different implementations.

- It works best when used with C functions—Link binding can be used with classes (i.e., a single class definition with multiple implementations), but this provides minimal value over using the traditional object-oriented approach of inheritance.

---

[2]This section describes the process for using statically linked images. An image can also be dynamically linked at runtime when the image is loaded. Conceptually, using link time binding as a deferred binding time is the same concept as using a statically linked vs. dynamically linked image just with different implementation details.

A SOLID Conclusion

PIM is a collection of best practices with an emphasis on using strategic thinking throughout the development cycle. The SOLID principles provide time-tested guidelines for creating loosely coupled designs and implementations. While PIM does put its own spin on SOLID, it is not radically different. The following is my acronym based on a rewording of SOLID, which I unimaginatively call LSSSI:

- **L**ayers (SRP)—Break complex functionality into separate distinct modules.

- **S**trategic (OCP)—Think long term when designing and implementing modules.

- **S**emantics (LSP)—Clearly define and faithfully implement the semantics of interfaces.

- **S**kinny (ISP)—Many interfaces organized by specific functionality are better than one interface.

- **I**nterfaces (DIP)—Abstract interfaces are the golden hammers for pounding out decoupled modules.

CHAPTER 4

Persistent Storage Detailed Design Example

So enough theory already. Let's break down how to take requirements and design statements and design code in a highly decoupled way that will allow maximum reuse and hardware independence. In other words, here's how it's done with PIM.

In this chapter, I'll go through the example that was presented in Chapter 3, where we designed a persistent storage module to write to an EEPROM (more or less an implementation of Figure 3-4). Afterward, I'll show a similar persistent storage example using a PIM approach (more or less an implementation of Figure 3-5).

Persistent Storage Example

The hypothetical platform for this non-PIM exercise is a microcontroller-based board that has an external Microchip 2Kbyte SPI EEPROM that can be used for persistent data storage. The software environment supports using the Arduino libraries, specifically the SPI library.

Software Requirements

The hypothetical requirements for this exercise are

1. User settings shall be persistent.

2. Runtime data shall be persistent. Consider this to be metric data that should be updated at least once an hour.

3. The software shall revert the user settings to factory defaults if corruption is detected in the values in persistent storage.

© John T. Taylor, Wayne T. Taylor 2021
J. T. Taylor and W. T. Taylor, *Patterns in the Machine*,
https://doi.org/10.1007/978-1-4842-6440-9_4

4. The software shall change the runtime data to all zeros if corruption is detected in the values of the metric data contained in persistent storage.

5. The software shall preserve existing user setting and runtime metric data when software upgrades are performed. This includes the use case of future versions of the software which may add new user settings or new metrics' fields.

High-Level Design

Using the software requirements articulated earlier, let's write some design statements for our hypothetical software module.[1]

- Two sections of storage will be partitioned in the persistent storage to separate user settings from metric data. This will isolate potential corruption between the user settings and runtime data since the metric data are written frequently and user settings are not.

- Each section will be oversized to allow for the future growth of each section.

- Using a cyclic redundancy check (CRC), a checksum will be computed for all data stored in each section. This is how corruption will be detected.

- The size of the data for each section (not the maximum allocated section size) will be persistently stored. The data size will be included as part of a checksum.

- In each section, a schema identifier (or schema version number) is stored. This will be used to differentiate between backward-compatible changes to the data layout and changes that will break old versions of the software.

---

[1]There is a long-running debate about the difference between requirements and high-level design. At every company I've worked at, it's been different: I've seen hopelessly general requirements and nightmarishly specific requirements. There's simply not an unassailable distinction between where requirements end and where design begins. Nevertheless, in Appendix F there is a short discussion of requirements vs. design.

- On start-up, the data in each different section will be read into RAM and checksummed. If the data in EEPROM is corrupt—that is, the stored CRC checksum does not match the newly computed checksum—then that section's data (both in RAM and EEPROM) reverts to its default values. For the user setting section, this is the factory default settings. For the metrics section, the default data values are set to all zeros.

- When the application updates one or more of the user settings, the application is responsible for invoking an update to the user settings in persistent storage.

- The application is responsible for invoking an hourly update of the runtime data in persistent storage.

A Monolithic Detailed Design

Monolithic designs are the antithesis of PIM. However, as an example of how *not* to design a persistent storage module, here is a monolithic design for a persistent storage module that satisfies the requirements and high-level design. Figure 4-1 shows the module that provides an interface that an application can call on start-up to read the data from the EEPROM and to write new values to persistent storage. It has a `sectionID` argument that is used by the application to select which section to read or write. This monolithic `Persistent Storage` module contains the following business logic:

- Detecting errors and defaulting a section to factory values or zeros (in RAM and EEPROM) if corrupt data is detected

- Managing changes or additions to the data in either section during future software upgrades

- Managing the metadata associated with each section

- Encapsulating the command set for the Microchip EEPROM IC

- Issuing SPI transactions to the Arduino SPI library

You can see in Figure 4-1 how this business logic would be implemented. It consists of one class that will need to be implemented and the Arduino libraries that need to be linked in. Note also that the Arduino SPI library will be used for issuing SPI transactions to the offboard EEPROM.

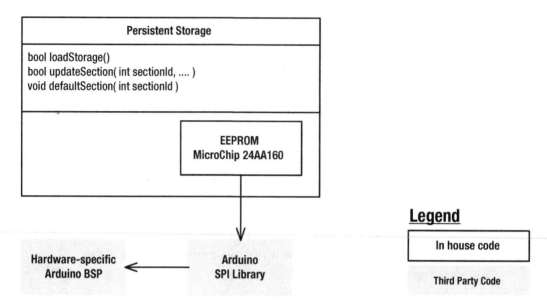

Figure 4-1. *A class diagram of a monolithic persistent storage module*

The design in Figure 4-1 is representative of numerous projects that I have worked on. It is conceptually easy to understand, relatively straightforward to implement, board specific, somewhat challenging to thoroughly test, and very tactical in its approach. Don't do it this way.

A PIM-Informed Detailed Design

The PIM approach to this design would be to apply the Single Responsibility and the Dependency Inversion Principles to break the persistent storage design into several layers. As you can see in Figure 4-2, this creates two additional interfaces which are abstract in nature—that is, they have no immediate implementation associated with them. Additionally, I created a very thin adapter layer for accessing the Arduino SPI library. This design also separates the different responsibilities that were mashed together in the monolithic design. Instead of a single module, the PIM design incorporates five modules or interfaces.

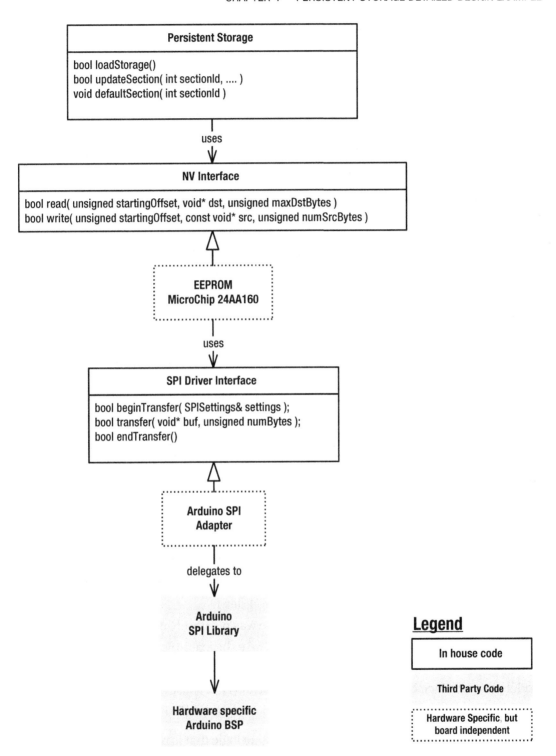

Figure 4-2. *A PIM-informed—layered—persistent storage class diagram*

With PIM, I removed the EEPROM and SPI encapsulation that was in the monolithic `Persistent Storage` module. The PIM `Persistent Storage` module only contains the following business logic:

- Detecting errors and defaulting a section to factory values or zeros if corrupt data is detected

- Managing changes or additions to the data in either section during future software upgrades

- Managing the metadata associated with each section

I added a new interface called `NV Interface` which is an abstract interface that defines the semantics for reading and writing data to persistent storage media.

I also created a new module called `EEPROM Microchip 24AA160` which implements the `NV Interface` where the persistent storage media is a Microchip 24AA160 (2KB EEPROM) chip. This module contains the following business logic:

- Encapsulating the command set for the Microchip EEPROM IC

I added a new `SPI Driver Interface` which is an abstract interface that defines the semantics for performing SPI transactions to an offboard device. Note that the SPI semantics are master/slave, with the microcontroller being a SPI master that is communicating with a SPI slave device.

And, finally, I added a new module called the `Arduino SPI Adapter` which implements the `SPI Driver Interface` with the following business logic:

- Issuing SPI transactions to the Arduino SPI library

The result is that the SPI transaction semantics of the `SPI Driver Interface` are delegated to the Arduino SPI library. Breaking out the SPI Driver interface allows the design to move to a different platform that does not use the Arduino SPI library without having to refactor or change any of the other modules.

In this example, the `SPI Driver Interface` was purposely modeled after the Arduino SPI library. This was not done just to make the example work better. It is a real-life tactic. When defining a driver or hardware-specific interface, it is a best practice to model your interface or hardware abstraction layer (HAL) based on your actual platform, software development kit (SDK), or board support package (BSP). The benefits of this are

- This minimizes the extra amount of glue logic that is needed for the initial project.

- You don't waste time trying to come up with an all-encompassing interface or HAL definition. (To be sure, your HAL definition may not be optimal as a generic library, but it is also a best practice not to optimize until you have to.)

Benefits of the PIM Design

Clearly, you can see that the PIM detailed design added more parts or layers to the design. But what, in fact, did I actually add? I added two header files for the NV and SPI Driver interfaces. I also added two concrete modules consisting of one header file and one implementation file each that encapsulate the EEPROM command set and map the SPI interface calls to the Arduino SPI library, which in this example maps almost one to one. What did I get for this extra typing? The persistent storage module can now be unit tested independent of the hardware with an automated unit test, which is a big win.

Furthermore, all the "tricky bits" of the requirements are isolated to the newly refactored and PIM-ized `Persistent Storage` module. And, as the details of the EEPROM chip are now decoupled from the rest of the design, if the requirements change and call for a different EEPROM, the only change necessary would be to replace the `EEPROM MicroChip 24AA160` module with a new module written for the new hardware. No refactoring needs to be done to the rest of the design.

Additionally, the hardware-specific Microchip EEPROM module can be used on future or other projects. I would argue that the small amount of additional work for the layered design is more than justified; it is a strong net positive for the project.

C VS. C++

The example design was done using classes and C++. However, Figure 4-2 could have been implemented just as easily using C. Remember that in the PIM world, an abstract interface is not a C++ class with virtual functions; it is simply a header file that defines a collection of functions and semantics, and its implementation is deferred. For a pure C implementation, the one item that would be different is that the Arduino SPI library would not be used because the Arduino platform is actually C++ under its IDE. An alternate SPI implementation would be needed, which is addressed in the next section.

Expanded Layering

After you have taken the plunge into a PIM-style layered design, that layered design can be extended as needed to account for changes or to be reused on different projects. Figure 4-3 is a class diagram that expands the layered design. In the diagram, the superscript numbers in parentheses are provided to help you see how the classes and modules map to the source code layout.

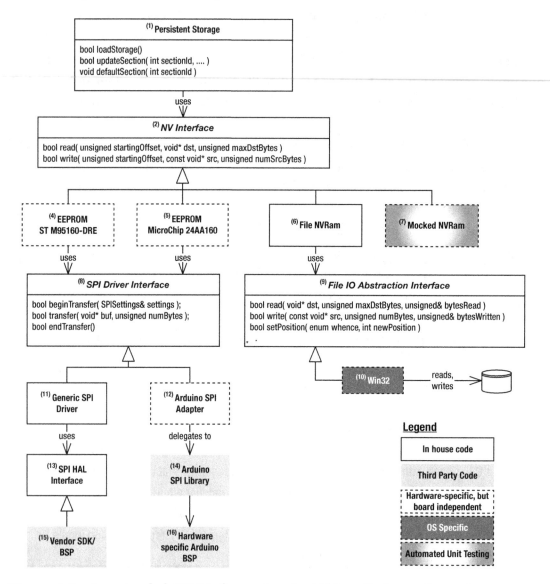

Figure 4-3. *An extended, PIM-informed and additionally layered, persistent storage class diagram*

Figure 4-4 is the source code layout of a C++ implementation of Figure 4-3. The organization is based on the PIM-recommended file or directory organization discussed in Chapter 12. A summary of the organization is as follows:

- Files are organized by C++ namespace.

- C++ namespaces map one to one with directory names.

- The hierarchical directory organization is used to represent dependencies. That is, a file depends on its containing directory. All files in a directory **cannot** have dependencies to any files in direct subdirectories of the directory they are in. For example, in the following directory tree snippet (from the Colony.core C++ library), the file `Cpl/Io/Input.h` cannot have `#include` statements that reference files from any of the subdirectories of the `Cpl/Io/` directory. Said another way, if the file `Cpl/Io/Input.h` contained the `#include "Cpl/Io/Stdio/StdIn.h"` statement, it would create a potential circular header file dependency.

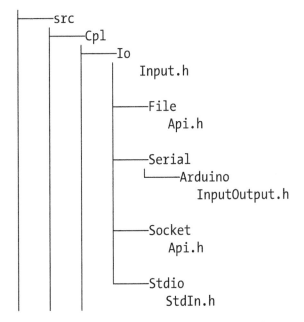

The source code including the unit tests are located under the `src/` directory. The `tests/` directory is where the unit test executables are built. For the test executables, the top-level code (i.e., the C/C++ `main()` function), compiler-specific code, and target-specific code (that is not intended to be reusable) are also located under the `tests/` directory. The bolded text indicates that the unit test is an automated unit test.

```
    ├──src                    // Root directory for the source code
    │   ├──Driver
    │   │   ├──NV
    │   │   │     Interface.h               // Class 2
    │   │   │
    │   │   │   ├──File
    │   │   │   │     Api.cpp               // Class 6
    │   │   │   │     Api.h                 // Class 6
    │   │   │   │     HalFileInterface.h    // Class 9
    │   │   │   │     // The Win32 (class 10) implementation is not shown
    │   │   │   │
    │   │   │   ├──Microchip
    │   │   │   │     Eeprom24aa160.cpp     // Class 5
    │   │   │   │     Eeprom24aa160.h       // Class 5
    │   │   │   │
    │   │   │   ├──ST
    │   │   │   │     EepromM95160DRE.cp    // Class 4
    │   │   │   │     EepromM95160DRE.h     // Class 4
    │   │   │   │
    │   │   │   └──_0tests
    │   │   │         test_nv_driver.cpp    // unit test code
    │   │   │         // Note: tests are 'common' for different NV
    │   │   │         // interface implementations
    │   │   │
    │   │   └──SPI
    │   │         Interface.h               // Class 8
    │   │
    │   │       ├──Arduino
    │   │       │     Adapter.cpp           // Class 12
    │   │       │     Adapter.h             // Class 12
    │   │       │
    │   │       ├──Generic
    │   │       │     Hal.h                 // Class 13
    │   │       │     SpiDriver.cpp         // Class 13
    │   │       │     SpiDriver.h           // Class 13
    │   │       │
    │   │       └──_0tests
    │   │             test_spi_driver.cpp   // unit test code
    │   │             // Note: tests are 'common' for different SPI Driver
    │   │             // interface implementations
    │   │
    │   └──PersistentStorage
    │       │   Api.cpp                     // Class 1
    │       │   Api.h                       // Class 1
    │       │
    │       └── _0tests
    │               test_persistent_storage.cpp // unit test code
    │
    └──tests              // Root directory for unit tests level 'build' directories
        ├──Driver
        │   ├──NV
        │   │   ├──File
        │   │   │   └──Win32                        // Testing Class 10
        │   │   │       └──Windows                  // Built host is: Windows
        │   │   │           └──vc14                 // VisualStudio 2019 Compiler
        │   │   │                   main.cpp        // Entry point for the unit
        │   │   │                                   // test. Actual tests are in:
        │   │   │                                   // src/Driver/NV/_0tests/
        │   │   │
        │   │   ├──Microchip
        │   │   │   └──Eeprom24AA160                // Testing Class 5
        │   │   │       └──grand-central-m4         // Target Hardware: Adafruit
```

Figure 4-4. *Directory structure for the PIM-informed persistent storage module*

```
                                            // Grand Central M4 board
                    └──Windows              // Built host is: Windows
                        └──gcc_arm7         // GCC Arm7 cross compiler
                            main.cpp        // Entry point for the unit
                                            // tests
        └──ST
            └──EepromM95160DRE              // Testing Class 4
                └──grand-central-m4         // Target Hardware: Adafruit
                                            // Grand Central M4 board
                    └──Windows              // Built host is: Windows
                        └──gcc_arm7         // GCC Arm7 cross compiler
                            main.cpp        // Entry point for the unit
                                            // tests
    └──SPI
        ├──Arduino                          // Testing Class 12
            └──grand-central-m4             // Target Hardware: Adafruit
                                            // Grand Central M4 board
                └──Windows                  // Built host is: Windows
                    └──gcc_arm7             // GCC Arm7 cross compiler
                        main.cpp            // Entry point for the unit
                                            // tests
        ├──Generic                          // Testing Class 11
            └──ATSAME54-XPRO                // Target Hardware: MicroChip
                                            // SAM E54 Xpro eval board
                └──Windows                  // Built host is: Windows
                    └──gcc_arm7             // GCC Arm7 cross compiler
                        main.cpp            // Entry point for the unit
                                            // tests
    └──PersistentStorage                    // Testing Class 1
        └──Windows                          // Built host is: Windows
            └──vc19                         // VisualStudio 2019 compiler
                main.cpp                    // Entry point for the unit
                                            // tests
```

Figure 4-4. (*continued*)

Example PIM Thermostat Application

This section describes the persistent storage sub-system implemented for the PIM example thermostat application. The PIM application's persistent storage requirements are very similar to the hypothetical example given earlier, but provide perhaps a more real-world layering and decoupling illustration. With respect to requirements, other than what data needs to be persistently stored, the only meaningful difference is this requirement:

- Power cycling the board shall not cause the persistent data to be corrupted. Or said another way, the scenario of power failing while writing to the physical media must be addressed such that there is no loss of data.

The thermostat persistent storage requirements are

- User settings (such as thermostat mode, setpoints, etc.) must be stored in persistent storage.

53

- The software shall default the user settings to factory defaults if corruption is detected in the values stored in persistent storage.

- Installer settings (such as equipment configuration) must be stored in persistent storage.

- The software shall revert installer settings to factory defaults if corruption is detected in the values stored in persistent storage.

- The Air Filter elapsed time and the Air Filter replacement alert state shall be stored in persistent storage.

- The software shall default the Air Filter elapsed time to zero and the Air Filter replacement alert state to not-active if corruption is detected in the values stored in persistent storage.

- The software shall preserve all persistent data when software upgrades are performed. This includes the use case of the new software adding new schema extensions to the layout of the persistent data content.

- The software shall prevent the persistent data from being reverted to its default settings if there is a power cycle during an update of the physical persistent media.

There is also a hardware difference between the two examples. The hardware platform for the thermostat application does not have EEPROM storage; instead, it has 8 MBytes of SPI data Flash available as a persistent storage media. The Arduino file system library is used for accessing the data Flash (i.e., file read/write operations to read and write Flash instead of low-level SPI transactions).

High-Level Design

The requirements stated earlier can be decomposed into the following high-level design statements:

- Each group of persistent data will be stored in separate sections in the persistent media. This is to isolate potential corruption between each data group since each data group is updated at different rates. For example, the installer data is updated rarely, while user data is updated every time there is a setpoint change.

- When determining the size of each section, additional storage space will be allocated to allow for future growth of each section.

- Using a cyclical redundancy check (CRC), a checksum will be computed for all data stored in each section in the persistent media. This is how corruption will be detected.

- The size of the data for each section (which is different than the maximum allocated section size) will be stored in the persistent media. The data size will be included as part of a checksum.

- Each section will have a schema identifier that will be used by future software versions to differentiate between backward-compatible changes and any changes that might break the layout organization of the data in each section.

- On start-up, the data in the different sections is read into RAM and a checksum is computed. If the data in the persistent media is corrupt (i.e., the stored CRC checksum does not match the newly computed checksum), then that section's data (both in RAM and on the persistent media) is reverted to its default values.

- To protect against corruption when there is a power failure while updating a section, two copies of the data will be made. The update sequence is to overwrite the oldest or corrupt copy first. On power-up, the newest, valid instance of the two copies is loaded into RAM. The worst-case power cycle scenario is that only the update that was attempted during a power cycle will be lost, but the data will not be reverted to its default setting.

- The application will update the user settings in persistent storage when one or more of the individual settings change.

- The application will update the installer settings in persistent storage when one or more of the individual settings change.

- The application will update the Air Filter elapsed time in persistent storage at least every 15 minutes. The application will also update the Air Filter alert state in persistent storage on a change of the alert state.

Detailed Design

Figure 4-5 shows the class diagram that meets the design statements earlier.

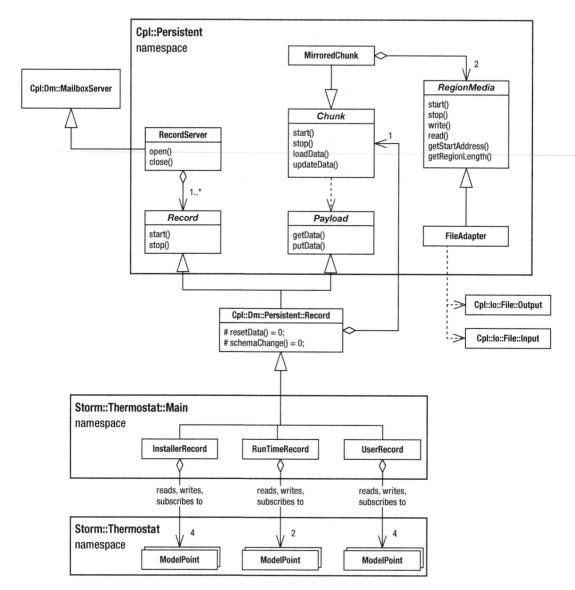

Figure 4-5. *PIM-informed, layered, thermostat class diagram*

Table 4-1 provides additional details for the preceding class diagram.

Table 4-1. *Additional details for the thermostat class diagram*

Class	Description
Cpl::Persistent namespace	
RecordServer	A concrete runnable object (essentially a thread) that supports events, inter-thread messaging, and data model change notifications. All read/write operations to persistent media will occur in this thread. The RecordServer is responsible for initiating the read-from-persistent-storage for each record on start-up of the application.
Record	An abstract class. This class decouples the RecordServer class (which has a list of records) from the concrete record types.
Payload	An abstract class. This interface defines the semantics for getting and setting the record's data from and to the application. This decouples the concrete chunk classes from specific details of how the application data that is stored in persistent storage is managed.
Chunk	An abstract class. This interface defines the top-level interface for reading and writing application data along with any metadata to the persistent storage (such as data length, CRC checksum, etc.). The semantics require this layer to provide the data integrity protection. This class decouples the application object from the details of the metadata required when persistently storing application data.
MirroredChunk	A concrete class that provides for checksumming the data and for implementing the two-copy write paradigm. A `transactionID`—which is a free running 64-bit counter—is part of the metadata (along with `datalength` and CRC) for each data copy. When comparing `transactionIDs`, the largest value represents the newest data copy.
RegionMedia	An abstract class. This interface defines the low level for reading and writing a block of data to the persistent storage media. Semantically, a "region" represents a unique set of data locations within the persistent storage media. This class decouples a concrete chunk class from the physical storage media.
FileAdapter	A concrete class that implements the RegionMedia interface. Each FileAdapter instance uses a unique file as its persistent storage media. The FileAdapter implementation relies on the file I/O interfaces from the `Cpl::Io::File` namespace.

(*continued*)

Table 4-1. (*continued*)

Class	Description
Cpl::Dm::Persistent namespace	
Record	A partially concrete class that implements the record and payload interfaces. This class adds additional logic and support for how and when application data is reset to its factory defaults and for dealing future schema changes. The class also provides the infrastructure for subscribing to model point change notifications.
Storm::Thermostat::Main namespace	
InstallerRecord	A concrete class that groups together all of the model point instances that make up the installer settings. The class configures its model points list such that they are monitored for change notifications (i.e., updates to persistent storage are performed on change). It is also responsible for providing the factory default values for the model points. It does not provide any business logic for schema change since this requirement essentially does not apply to the first release of the application.
RunTimeRecord	A concrete class that groups together all of the model point instances that make up the Air Filter elapsed time and Air Filter alert state. The class configures the Air Filter alert model point such that it is monitored for change notifications (i.e., updates to persistent storage are performed when there are changes). The class has an internal software timer that is used to update the Air Filter elapsed time model point on a periodic basis in persistent storage. It is also responsible for providing the factory default values for the model points. It does not provide any business logic for schema changes since this requirement essentially does not apply to the first release of the application.

(*continued*)

Table 4-1. (*continued*)

Class	Description
UserRecord	A concrete class that groups together all of the model point instances that make up the user settings. The class configures its model points list such that they are monitored for change notifications (i.e., updates to persistent storage are performed on change). It is also responsible for providing the factory default values for the model points. It does not provide any business logic for schema change since this requirement essentially does not apply to the first release of the application.

Storm::Thermostat namespace

ModelPoint	This class is used to represent the various application-defined model points that hold the data that is being persistently stored.

Scl::Dm namespace

MailboxServer	A concrete runnable object (essentially a thread) that supports events, inter-thread messaging, and data model change notifications.

Cpl::Io::File

Input	A concrete object that provides operations to open and read file system files. The `Cpl::Io::File` sub-system is designed to be decoupled from the underlying file system and operating system. Or, said another way, the input class is not dependent on any specific target platform.
Output	A concrete object that provides operations to open and write file system files. The `Cpl::Io::File` sub-system is designed to be decoupled from the underlying file system and operating system. Or, said another way, the output class is not dependent on any specific target platform.

The PIM-ness in the Design

The design has the following characteristics of PIM:

- Layers—The preceding design has four different abstract interfaces (which are layers), not including the interfaces and layers in the `Cpl::Io::File` sub-system.

- Highly decoupled—None of the class and interfaces in Figure 4-4 have dependencies on hardware or an operating system.

- Unit testable—All of the concrete classes except for the `Storm::Thermostat::Main` record class have automated unit tests. The `Storm::Thermostat::Main` record classes can have automated unit tests, but they were omitted from the example code because there is limited business logic in them.

- Simulator—Since the design is decoupled from any specific platform, the entire sub-system was painlessly incorporated into the functional simulator in the PIM example code.

- Strategic—Four of the concrete classes listed below adhere to the Open-Closed Principle and are essentially closed to modification, but open to extension. These classes are

  - `Cpl::Persistent::RecordServer`

  - `Cpl::Persistent::MirroredChunk`

  - `Cpl::Persistent::FileAdapter`

  - `Cpl::Dm::Persistent::Record`

When I talk about "closed to modification," I mean that new behavior can be added without modifying the source code of the file. Here are some hypothetical changes that the preceding classes are *closed* to:

- Adding more data to be persistently stored that is not model point based—In this scenario, new classes would be created that implement the `Cpl::Persistent::Record` and `Cpl::Persistent::Payload` abstract interfaces to provide the new functionality.

- Adding more data to be persistently stored that is model point based—In this scenario, either new application-specific `Storm::Thermostat::Main::Record` classes would be created or modification to the existing application-specific records or both.

- The hardware platform is updated to provide a software interrupt— An interrupt-based power-fail-pending notification along with sufficient power hold-up time to allow a single write-to-persistent-media storage to be completed would require a new module. In this scenario, a new implementation of the `Cpl::Persistent::Chunk` abstract interface would be created that only writes a single copy of the application data along with the new logic to act on the power-fail notification.

- Replace using a file system as the persistent storage medium with using direct block-level access to the data Flash. In this scenario, two new concrete classes would need to be created. One would be a new implementation of `Cpl::Persistent::Chunk` interface to manage how raw Flash sectors are used to store data (e.g., individual bytes cannot be erased, only entire sectors can be erased) and a new implementation of the `Cpl::Persistent::RegionMedia` abstract interface for handling the register/command set of the data Flash chip. Additional classes that are analogous to the `Cpl::Io::File` classes (that would handle the communications with the data Flash chip) would need to be brought into the application.

- The user settings are changing frequently—For example, if there were to be a series of single decrements to the cooling setpoint, you would not update persistent storage until it has been at least N seconds since the last change. For this scenario, a new child class of the `Cpl::Dm::Persistent::Record` would be created to implement the new requirements. Then the `Storm::Thermostat::Main::UserR ecord` would be edited to inherit from the new child class instead of directly from `Cpl::Dm::Persistent::Record`.

Note that the classes in the `Storm::Thermostat::Main` namespace are not considered closed to changes listed earlier. From a PIM perspective, this is okay because

1. These classes are just glorified lists of model points with associated factory default values. This means there is very little value in having the classes be closed to modification. However, in the future, if there were requirements for how the persistent data is upgraded or downgraded, there might be a value in closing these classes to modification.

2. Not all classes can be closed against modification. For this reason, don't spend a lot of time trying to have everything be closed. These classes are very application specific and potentially specific to future different thermostat variants and projects. This degree of potential volatility is very hard to close without overengineering or using a crystal ball to anticipate all possible changes.

The PIM Dilemma

Beyond the design and implementation details for persistent storage that were described in this chapter, you should also note herein the crux of the PIM dilemma: the cost of change-proofing your code and making it more reusable is added complexity. I would argue that added overhead is almost always worth the effort given what you gain. However, as you can see in this section, sometimes I make choices about what things will not be PIM-ized. That is, for example, I make choices about what parts of my code will not be "closed to modification."

My goal on every new software project is to design it completely in alignment with PIM. But for a range of technical, pragmatic, and political reasons, I am not always successful. Be aware, then, that embracing the principles of PIM is not an "all or nothing" commitment. That is, even if you only design a handful of modules or functions in your project using the PIM principles, you'll benefit from doing so. In my experience, anything PIM on a project is ultimately a net positive.

CHAPTER 5

Software Architecture

There is usually one member of the development team who has the title "software architect," and there may be others on the team who, while untitled, function in that capacity. You may or may not be the titled, or functioning, architect of your team, but you are certainly the architect of the code you are assigned to develop. Depending on your position on the team, some of the things discussed in this chapter may be beyond your direct control or sphere of influence. Nevertheless, even if you are only responsible for a small module in your project, you can still approach your module as something you are going to architect as opposed to something you're just going to hack together. Consequently, when I talk about software architects, I mean you.

About the Software Architect

A software architect must understand and pursue detailed design choices in order to make informed architecture decisions. Architecture decisions should not be made in vacuum, especially for those items that are new or different than what the architect or the project team is used to. That said, the architect needs to avoid mixing software architecture with detailed design. Think of defining the architecture as providing the next level of detailed requirements to the detailed design.

There is no canonical definition of software architecture. However, I am partial to Ralph Johnson's definition: "Architecture is about the important stuff. Whatever that is." I prefer not to interpret the last sentence of that quote as flippant; rather, I think of it as "Architecture is about the important stuff. [*No matter what*] that is."

In the context of PIM, software architecture is about identifying a solution at a high level and defining the rules of engagement for the design and implementation. From a top-down perspective, software architecture is the top of the software solution pyramid (even though software architecture is not a strictly top-down activity).

J. T. Taylor and W. T. Taylor, *Patterns in the Machine*,
https://doi.org/10.1007/978-1-4842-6440-9_5

Software architecture documents are working documents. Don't be afraid to make changes; but don't go wild either. Remember that after the design and implementation have begun, changes to the software architecture almost always result in rework, and one of the overriding goals of every architect should be minimizing rework. I deliberately avoided calling architecture documents "living documents" because in my experience living documents usually die before they are even finished. One notable exception was a company I worked for where the software architect for the company diligently and meticulously kept the requirements document updated. With every change of requirements, he updated the document and checked it into version control. Whenever he clarified a statement, or absence of a statement, he updated the document. It turned out that the requirements document became an extremely valuable tool for the team, and it was comforting to know that anyone on the team could consult it and get a current, authoritative answer to questions about the product. Document maintenance like this seldom happens because it requires discipline over an extended period of time. But I mention this here because the intent of this book is to convince you to treat software architecture as a discipline. It's the discipline of software architecture that distinguishes someone who simply writes code from someone who is a software engineer, someone who hacks together code from someone who engineers it. A good software architect is the difference between a team that functions well and a team where everyone has their hair on fire.

About Software Architecture Documents

As a quick summary, then, software architecture

- Should be done first.

- Should include strategic decisions and guidelines.

- Shouldn't include too many design details.

- Shouldn't be defined in isolation.

- Shouldn't be cast in stone. That is, it should allow for discovery and evolution.

So, what goes into the software architecture document? My favorite answer is "it depends." I was first introduced to the phrase "it depends" when taking internal company courses on how to be a first-line manager. It depends was the "go-to phrase" for the human resources instructor for nearly every "How do you handle this?" question. As an engineer, it was frustrating to go from the binary perspective of ones and zeros, on and off, it works or it doesn't work, to a multiplicity of possible right answers. Nevertheless, my resistance didn't change the fact that "it depends" is often the way a lot of things work.

Projects are all different with respect to requirements, scope, complexity, processes, domain, team size, and so on. Here is a list of some common items or topics that could be included in your software architecture document. This list is neither comprehensive nor required; it provides examples of things that I have included in architecture documents in the past, and they are intended to spark your thinking relative to your project.

- Major sub-systems

- Major interface semantics

- Threading/process/processor model

- Communications mechanisms

- Inter-thread communication (ITC)

- Inter-process communication (IPC)

- Processor-to-processor communication

- Memory strategies or rules

- Performance requirements or constraints

- Hardware interfaces

- Cyber security

- Functional simulator

- File organization

- Localization and internationalization

- Conventions

- Unit test strategy

- Build system

Remember that with architecture documents, a good diagram is worth a thousand words of text. Nevertheless, don't skimp on the text. Provide a context and explanation of what your diagrams illustrated so that they can be understood by someone who is new to the project. To this day, I am still tempted to simply paste a Visio diagram into my software architecture or design documents and claim that it is self-explanatory. However, my team members are quick to point out that I am not Leonardo Da Vinci, and they demand that I provide the supporting text.

Major Sub-systems

Draw a top-level logical block diagram of the system, breaking it down into logical and critical sub-systems. Show the relationships between sub-systems. In theory, all of the modules, interfaces, and components will be derived from, or be contained in, one of these top-level blocks. Figure 5-1 illustrates the major sub-systems for the PIM example thermostat application. (More about the PIM thermostat application and how to get the example code up and running is discussed in Chapter 16.)

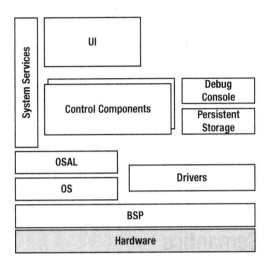

Board Support Package (BSP)

A BSP for a microcontroller is responsible for abstracting the details of MCU's data sheet. It includes the low-level code that directly accesses or configures the microcontroller unit's (MCU's) hardware registers. This also includes the use of MCU vendor–supplied drivers and SDK. For the PIM example, this includes the initialization and use of Arduino system and libraries.

Operating System (OS)

For the PIM example, FreeRTOS is used on the target hardware. For the functional simulator, it's the Windows operating system.

OS Abstraction Layer (OSAL)

The OSAL provides a services layer that decouples the application from a specific operating system. The PIM example uses the Colony.core C++ library for the OSAL.

Drivers

Modules for reading sensors, controlling relays, communicating with the HVAC bus, etc. In the PIM example, only a token relay driver that uses LEDs instead of relays is implemented.

Control Components

All of the business logic that implements the thermostat's control algorithms.

Debug Console

Command-line access to the application. For the PIM example, the debug console is the user interface.

System Services

Middleware that provides various services such as containers, checksums, string handling, software timers, inter-thread communication (ITC), data model infrastructure, etc. For the PIM example, the Colony.core C++ library provides the bulk of the system services.

User Interface (UI)

This is not implemented in the PIM example. With a full-featured application, this sub-system could be broken up into more than one sub-system depending on the complexity of the UI (e.g., if a third-party graphic package is used).

Figure 5-1. *Example of a block diagram with descriptions*

As a recommendation, don't create your initial diagrams in Visio or other computer-based drawing tool. The limitations of the tool's design and the user interface can constrain your thinking and unnecessarily distract you with the mechanics and features of the tool. Instead, draw your first and second iterations of diagrams with pencil and paper. Put down all your thoughts and ideas using whatever combination of boxes, circles, and arrows seems easiest and most natural. There is cognitive research that suggests that in the act of drawing, you are doing the "hard thinking" about the design of your code. So first think it through with a pencil, and later you can make it look pretty and legible in Visio.

Major Interface Semantics

This is where you define how various sub-systems, components, modules, and drivers will interact with each other, for example:

- Are all the interfaces synchronous?

- What interfaces need to be asynchronous?

- How do drivers interact with application modules?

- Does using the data model architecture make sense?

- Is inter-thread communication (ITC) or inter-process communication (IPC) needed?

Depending on the scope and complexity of the project, there may be one or many interface designs. Do not try to force a single paradigm here. If things are similar but different, they are still different.

This is also an area where it helps to have a good understanding of both the detailed design of the project and the specific implementation of some of the modules. Taking a "deeper dive" into the details that are available can be very beneficial at this stage. For example, I worked on an IoT device that had an external Cell/GPS modem. The interface design for the "modem stack" used a mix of synchronous and asynchronous ITC calls as the modem stack ran in its own thread. The synchronous calls were used to perform setup and configuration operations that did not require a callout to the cell network or Internet. The asynchronous calls were used when the interaction with the cell network or Internet was required (e.g., when making a RESTful call to the back-end server) because these actions could not be guaranteed to complete in timely fashion.

This worked … sort of. It was expected that the asynchronous calls could take a long time to complete or even timeout. And we wrote code to handle these scenarios. What we did not expected or initially accounted for was that if an asynchronous action was in process, a simultaneous synchronous call would be blocked by the modem until the pending asynchronous operation completed. The net result was that the main application could be blocked for minutes while waiting on the modem depending on the current cell connectivity. Since the UI ran in its own thread, nothing was visibly wrong to the end users. However, this caused the team great angst when trying to implement a watchdog for the application thread because it could legitimately be blocked for minutes at a time. (The actual worst case was over nine minutes.) In hindsight, all of the ITC calls to the modem stack should have been asynchronous. However, at the time of the interface definition, the team's knowledge on how the modem stack had been implemented was incomplete.

The PIM example application uses the data model architecture for its interfaces between all of the sub-systems. Figure 5-2 is an example of an architecture drawing that shows the interface semantics of the application.

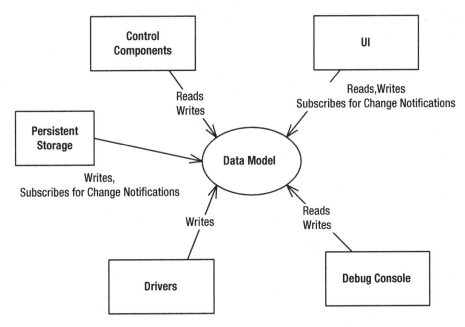

Figure 5-2. Interface semantics for the PIM example application

The PIM example also uses synchronous ITC interfaces for starting up and shutting down the application. These ITC interfaces allow sequential start-up/shutdown sequences where each sub-system is fully initialized or fully shut down while executing in their own threads.

Threading and Processor Model

The following questions need to be answered in the architecture document:

- Will the application be a bare-metal or main-loop application?

- Will the application use threads?

- Will the application have multiple processes?

- Is the system architecture a multiple processor design? (For example, is it a main board running Linux with an offboard microcontroller that performs all of the hard real-time processing?)

If the system will use threads or processes, I recommend that you document why that decision was made (i.e., what problems or requirements do threads solve or address). If the system uses multiple processors, define the roles and responsibilities of each processor.

This information doesn't necessarily need to be a separate artifact or document, but it should be noted somewhere in your set of architecture documents.

Communications Mechanisms

If your application is multi-threaded, or multi-process, or has any of the following:

- Multiple microcontroller units (MCUs).

- Multiple central processing units (CPUs).

- Intelligent offboard integrated circuits (ICs). For example, an IC might be a cell modem, Wi-Fi processor, or Bluetooth processor.

then you need to define how communications will occur between these entities. At the architecture level, you don't need to flesh out the details, but you do need to define or restrict what communications mechanisms will be used.

For multi-threaded or multi-process applications, the architecture should dictate what ITC/IPC mechanisms can be used. Ideally, there is only one ITC and one IPC mechanism. While this is a restriction, it eliminates a whole set of issues when trying to troubleshoot an application that has multiple ITC/IPC mechanisms. For example, this avoids the use case where individual developers each use different communication mechanisms because of what they are comfortable with or because it was what they used on the last project.

When dealing with communications between processors or with intelligent offboard ICs, the architecture should define the requirements for communication protocols. This includes what the physical layer is and what the protocol semantics are. For example, is the communications architecture command-response, peer-to-peer, point-to-point, master/slave, or master/slave with multiple masters? You should also note any error detection and correction processes that may be used. Many times, especially when dealing with intelligent offboard ICs, the protocol is defined by a third party, so at the architecture level, it is mostly just identifying what needs to be implemented by the project and what is provided by the vendor or third-party source code.

This information may be specified in its own document or noted in other documents.

Memory Strategy or Rules

The architecture document should define requirements, rules, and constraints for dynamic memory allocation. Because of the nature of embedded projects, the extensive use of dynamic memory allocation is discouraged. When you have a device that potentially will run for years before it is power cycled or reset, the probability of running out of heap memory due to fragmentation becomes a valid concern. A guaranteed way to eliminate memory leaks is to not use dynamic memory. In other words, "no dynamic memory allocation" means that the application does not allocate memory from the heap once its start-up process has been completed, and it never frees any memory allocated from the heap.

I worked on a telecom project that used a generic messaging framework that made extensive use of dynamic memory. Between flaws in the messaging framework, and its poorly designed memory management semantics, the project was plagued with memory leaks. The team was never able to eliminate all of the leaks. The final solution was to install an extra 128M of RAM on target hardware so that the board could run for at least a month before having to be reset. Since the board booted up rather quickly, having to reset the board once a month still met the telecom standard of "five nines" reliability over the course of a year.

The memory requirements should address when allocating memory from the heap is allowed and who is responsible for freeing heap allocated memory. These rules should address dynamic memory usage for ITC, IPC, containers, communication protocols, and third-party packages (e.g., graphic libraries).

Performance Requirements and Constraints

The architecture document should define the approach for how the application will meet its performance and real-time requirements. This is another area where a good understanding of the implementation and hardware is beneficial before committing to an architecture. The kinds of things to identify here are

- How CPU intensive are the real-time requirements?

- How much communication bandwidth is needed?

- What is the theoretical and practical performance of the hardware?

At the architecture level, these questions and others need to be broken down into the strategies for meeting them. The following questions should be answered in the context of how the software will meet the performance requirements. The following list is not a comprehensive list but is intended to stimulate the analysis process:

- What will be, or can be, interrupt driven?

- How frequent are the combined interrupts? How much time will be spent in the interrupt service routines (ISRs)?

- Which hardware drivers need to be, or can be, Direct Memory Access (DMA) driven?

- Is a main loop or cooperative scheduler sufficient?

- What is the minimum time slice for cooperative scheduling?

- What is the frequency of the system tick?

- Is a thread or process scheduler needed?

- Is preemptive scheduling needed?

- Is time slicing needed?

- What is the latency for a thread switch or process context switch?

- For a communication channel, what is the minimum bandwidth needed?

- What is the maximum latency for critical data? For noncritical data?

- What is the power budget?

- Can the processor run at full speed? Or are sleep or low-power modes necessary?

- For sleep modes, what are the wake-up latencies?

The output of the preceding analysis should be boiled down into a set of requirements or rules for the subsequent design and implementation. However, it is not the design itself. This means specifying requirements like "feature X and Y will be interrupt driven" or "a bare-metal/main-loop cooperative scheduling with a 5ms time slice will be used" or "the processor shall go into Sleep Mode 1 during idle times."

As stated earlier, it is important to have a solid understanding of the hardware capabilities and the CPU loading when making these decisions. Obviously, the more experience the architect has with respect to the project's performance requirements, the better the architectural decisions will be. Sometimes, the nature of the project allows for overspecifying the hardware as a hedge against the unknowns. Sometimes, a deeper dive into the implementation, or even prototyping, is needed to get a sufficient level of confidence to proceed. Sometimes, you just have to make a best guess with the assumption that solutions can be found later if the project does not meet all of its performance requirements. And sometimes those future solutions amount to just loosening the original performance requirements because they were unrealistic in terms of physics or the project's budget.

Hardware Interfaces

It helps to enumerate the hardware interfaces if for no other reason than to ensure that you are on the same page as the hardware team. A good place to start is by creating a block diagram representing the physical components of the system. Having brief descriptions for each component is even better. Think of a hardware interface diagram that is software focused as a high-level schematic of the system. For example, Figure 5-3 is the physical block diagram of the PIM example application.

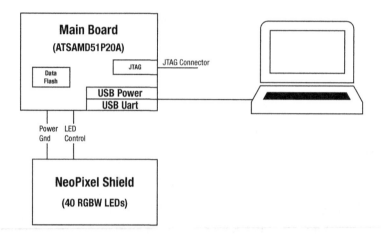

Main Board
The main board is an Adafruit Grand Central
M4 Arduino board featuring an Atmel SAMD51.
The MCU is 120MHz Cortex M4 with floating
point, 1MB of Flash, and 256KB of RAM.

LED Shield
This is an Adafruit NeoPixel Shield for Arduino
with a 40 RGBW LED Pixel Matrix. Nine of the
LEDs are used to indicate 6 Relays outputs
(G, W1, W2, W3, Y, O) and the three alarm
conditions.

JTAG
Programming and debugging interface.
A 10-pin header that supports Serial Wire Debug
(SWD) interface.

Data Flash
8MB of data flash with a FAT32 file system used
to persistently store user and installation
settings.

USB Power
The main board is powered via a USB
connection.

Figure 5-3. *Block diagram of the PIM example application*

The preceding diagram is not that interesting; the PIM example thermostat was
never intended to be a fully working prototype. A more interesting diagram is shown in
Figure 5-4: it is a hypothetical thermostat with an LCD display with touch screen that is
powered via 24VAC and has relay outputs for controlling up to a two-stage heat pump
with three stages of indoor heat.

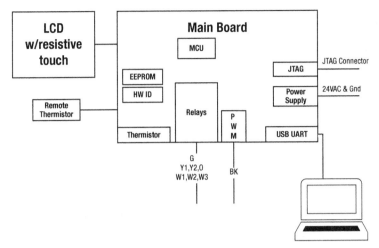

Main Board
The main board is a custom Printed Circuit Board Assembly (PCBA).

MCU
The MCU is a 120MHz Cortex M4 with floating point, 1MB of Flash, and 256KB of RAM.

LCD
With resistive touch, 2.8 TFT, 240x320 resolution, 18-bit color display with built in resistive touch panel. The LCD communicates with the MCU via a single SPI bus for both the LCD control and touch panel. A total of 6 wires (excluding power and ground signals) is required.

EEPROM
A 2Kbits, 12C EEPROM used to persistently store user and installation settings.

JTAG
Programming and debugging interface. A 10-pin header that supports a Serial Wire Debug (SWD) interface.

Power Supply
Converts the 24V AC input power to the various power rails required by the main board.

HW ID
Hardware identification circuit. This is an analog input with a resistor divider network where different resistor values are used to identify different board revisions.

USB Uart
The USB Uart is a communications device class (CDC) serial port. This UART is used for command line access to the application.

Relays
Seven relays and terminal block. Six of the relays are normally open relays capable of switching 24V AC signals. The seventh relay (the 'o' or Switch-Over-Valve) is a latching relay.

PWM
The PWM circuit is capable of generating a 24V PWM cycle with a target duty cycle of 75Hz. The MCU is responsible for generating the base band PWM signal.

Thermistor
On board NTC 10K thermistor used to measure room temperature.

Remote Thermistor
An optional NTC 10K thermistor that can be connected for an alternate room temperature measurement.

Figure 5-4. *A block diagram of a more interesting thermostat*

Operating System

Some questions to answer about the operating system are

- Will there be an OS or a real-time operating system (RTOS)?

- Will the firmware run bare metal?

- Will there be a thread scheduler?

Obviously, this is tied closely with the thread and process model and the performance requirements. When the decision is made to use an operating system, a subsequent decision is required about what the operating system abstraction layer (OSAL) will be. The OSAL is important because it enables automated unit tests and a functional simulator. (See Chapter 7 for more details about the OSAL and the functional simulator.)

Third-Party Software

Identify what external software you may be incorporating into your project. "External" in this context means source code that is not developed as part of the current project. This could be reusing in-house software, incorporating an open source project, using software provided by the board or chip manufacturers, or even purchasing a commercial software package. For example, do you use a third-party RTOS or "roll your own?" Do you create your own communication protocol or reuse a protocol from a previous project?

Note   Think twice about rolling your own middleware such as RTOSes or communication protocols. Once you start down this path, you are now in the business of developing and maintaining software that is not your primary domain expertise; it is not what your organization or company is in the business of selling.

For all third-party software you decide to use, be certain you understand the licensing model that governs it. Verify that the licensing model for the software does not restrict how you plan to sell or distribute your product. I would even go as far as to say don't even prototype with a third-party package before you fully understand the licensing. It breaks your heart when your prototype works, but you have to throw it away because the licensing is incompatible with the product plans.

Many companies require the software development manager or software architect to fill out forms detailing the licensing agreements of all third-party components of the software before release. Oftentimes, this is a gating item that can prevent or delay the release of software. If your company has these forms, or has some kind of artifact that is required, I suggest that you get a couple of blank copies and write the name of each third-party component on one of the copies and include these in your set of architecture documents.

Finally, regarding third-party software, once you start using it, it becomes a hard dependency. Or said differently, you are stuck with it for the rest of the project's life. Like all things, whether this is a good thing or bad thing, it all depends. It is good to spend some time thinking about if it makes strategic sense to create an abstract interface layer to decouple your application from a direct dependency on the third-party software in question. By having an abstract interface layer, you have the freedom later to move to something different without having to refactor your existing application code.

Functional Simulator

If you are requiring automated unit tests for your project, then creating a functional simulator is a straightforward process. The reason is because the automated unit tests impose a decoupled design that allows components and modules to be tested as platform-independent code. (See Chapter 6 for more details.) As it turns out, creating a simulator is not a lot of additional effort if it is planned for from the beginning of the project. The biggest piece of work is identifying the necessary abstraction layers (OSAL, HAL, etc.) and then determining the strategy for breaking dependencies on the board support package (BSP). The planning and implementation of this separation strategy adds minimal additional effort over not having a functional simulator.

Some decisions that need to be made for the functional simulator:

- What platform will the simulator run on (e.g., Windows, Linux, etc.)?

- What portions will be simulated? The entire application? Just the algorithms? The entire system?

- How will the hardware elements be simulated? Mocked drivers? Full hardware emulation? Functional hardware simulation?

- Are there communication channels that need to be simulated?

- Is simulated time needed or desirable? Simulating time is very useful for projects that have algorithms that are time based or where running faster than real time is desirable (e.g., simulating one month of operation in 10 minutes).

For each of the preceding items, the SW architecture should identify the requirements and strategy to meet the identified simulation needs. Chapter 7 provides details of how to create a functional simulator.

Figure 5-5 is a block diagram for the functional simulator for the hypothetical full-featured thermostat presented in Figure 5-4.

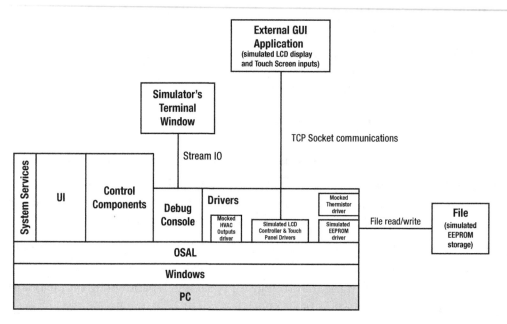

Figure 5-5. *Block diagram for functional simulator of full-featured thermostat*

File Organization

Source code file organization is very often done organically. That is, developers start writing code and organizing their files based on their immediate needs. File organization is a strategic best practice and should be thought out before any source files are created. The file organization can either hinder or facilitate in-project reuse and the construction of the build scripts. It is especially critical for in-project reuse where you build multiple images and executables from your project's code base. Unit tests and the functional simulators are examples of in-project reuse. A well-thought-out, consistent file organization will facilitate the creation and maintenance of continuous integration for your project.

Localization and Internationalization

I have been involved with a number of projects that started out with an emphatic "this project is English only," and then, halfway through development, multiple language requirements were added. This is a painful development because it is extremely difficult and time consuming to retrofit an English-only, single-byte code base.

Even though these requirements can change abruptly, it is important to state the localization and internationalization requirements regardless of how obvious they seem. Here are some examples of what to identify:

- Does your project need to display something other than numbers?

- Does your project require user input that is not menu driven or numerical? That is, does it require users to enter characters?

- What languages are you required to support? Specify these languages by country. The phrase "English only" is a very different thing than "US English only."

- If your project requires you to display characters, what encoding will you use? 7-bit ASCII has a low overhead, but 8-bit extended ASCII can give you the ability to display accent marks and other non-English characters. UTF-8 allows you to support the display of nearly every character in every language (assuming you can find a font), but it introduces the overhead that there is no longer a one-to-one mapping of the number of bytes to the number of characters in a string.

Conventions

Conventions are a collection of guidelines, best practices, and constraints that developers are expected to follow during the development of the project. One attribute of conventions is that it is the responsibility of the individual developers and the team generally to comply with and enforce the conventions. The architect and team must balance the compliance effort with the reward.

Whether these conventions are captured in the architecture document or the software development plan is a matter of preference. However, not specifying conventions is not an option; nor is specifying conventions late in the development cycle a good way to proceed. I recommend that when you encounter the need to add a new convention after work has begun, grandfather in the new convention so it only applies to new work going forward.

At a minimum, you should define the following conventions:

- Naming

  - Names for variables, functions, classes, namespaces, preprocessor symbols, and so on.

  - Naming of source files and directories. (See Chapter 12 for more details.)

- Coding conventions

  - Coding conventions define the rules, guidelines, and constraints for how the developers write their code.

Unit Test Strategy

As part of the architecture of your project, define what will be unit tested, how it will be tested (e.g., automated vs. manual), and what the expectations are for test coverage. Not every module in your project needs to have a unit test, nor is it practical to try and do so. That said, the default rule of thumb should be that every module should have at least one unit test. Another way to look at defining the unit test strategy is that it requires the software architecture to view the system from a design testability perspective, that is, what will make testing easier or harder.

The unit test strategy can be captured in either the software architecture document or the software development plan document. It's your choice.

Build System

Another thing to identify is your build system. Will it be raw makefiles, CMake, SCons, NQBP, or something else? The following items should be considered when selecting the build system:

- Where does the build engine capture platform-specific information, flags, and options? This would include which compiler toolchain has been chosen. An important rule is that the build system does not store platform-specific information in the same directories as the source code. The source code will be built for multiple platforms using several different compilers. If you break this rule, it will mean that the build files for every platform have to be aware of all of the different platform and compiler permutations that the code can be built to. Not only does this not scale well, it is a maintenance nightmare trying to keep the build files up to date.

- How does the build system integrate with the continuous integration build server?

    - Do the build tools support building from a command line (i.e., does it support automated builds?)?

    - What support tools need to be installed on the build server and what host OS is required for the tools?

- How will third-party packages, source code, libraries, and so on be included in the build process?

    - What is the file organization for these third-party packages?

    - Do they require a specific build tool? Are these build tools compatible with your source code?

On one project, we used the QT library for our graphic library. The off-the-shelf command-line support from QT was qmake or CMake. The problem was that the build paradigm put all of the generated object files into a single directory. However, our code base was organized by namespaces, and each namespace was a separate directory. The problem was that we had numerous files of the same name that were located in different directories. This meant that the object file name for these files would not be unique when omitting the directory structure. At the end of the day, though, it turned out that it was easier to fight through the nuances of building QT in our existing build system than to use QT's off-the-shelf qmake or CMake build scripts.

Creating "Real" Architecture Documents

In this chapter, I've talked about 17 different areas that will benefit from an architecture document. As you look at them, you might decide that some of these things don't apply to your project, that some are too obvious to write down, or that some have already been defined somewhere else in your organization. And in these cases, you might be tempted not to write anything down. This would be a mistake.

It is not enough just to think about software architecture. You need to create the documents. Even if all you do is handwrite a title on a piece of paper and then write "does not apply" on it, this is worth including with your software architecture documentation. For example, it would be valuable to have a piece of paper titled "Internationalization/Localization" with "US English Only" written on it. Or a piece of paper that is titled "Third-party Software" that says "No third-party software will be used." In my experience, as I write those kinds of simple sentences, I realize there is more to write down, more to clarify, and more to restrict. Sometimes, it is in the process of making the software architecture document "real"—the process of actually writing it—that I discover what it should actually say.

CHAPTER 6

Unit Testing

PIM defines a unit test as demonstrable evidence that an individual module works in isolation and that it meets all requirements and the design criteria. In this context, an "individual module" means a header file (.h) and its corresponding implementation file (.c or .cpp). If you're programming in C++, this means that essentially every class will require a corresponding unit test. In C, most of your functions will require unit tests.

I know this can sound overwhelming. If you have to write a unit test for every class, it seems like you're doubling your workload. However, it really depends on whether you look at your coding tasks from a narrow viewpoint or a broad viewpoint. I worked with one engineer who, after his code compiled and linked without errors—and it didn't immediately crash at runtime—claimed he was done with the task. Because our team's project management looked at tasks from a narrow viewpoint—that is, they didn't hold developers accountable for the rework that came out of integration testing—that engineer appeared to be a star producer. However, when you combined initial coding effort with rework effort, he was in fact one of the least productive team members.

From a broad viewpoint, a capable engineer invests X amount of effort into coding a module and Y amount of effort verifying that the code works. Even if the engineer does not view this verifying effort as unit testing, it is still part of what needs to be done before the engineer can claim that the code is finished. I argue that the X + Y effort is roughly the same regardless of whether the verifying effort is informal or embodied as a coded unit test. However, the total effort *will be substantially less* with coded unit tests if any of the following occurs:

- A module requires bug fixing.

- A module is impacted by a new requirement or by a change to an existing requirement.

Because coded unit tests are essentially "write-once, run as many times as needed" constructs, you don't have to reinvent the unit test when retesting is required.

© John T. Taylor, Wayne T. Taylor 2021
J. T. Taylor and W. T. Taylor, *Patterns in the Machine*,
https://doi.org/10.1007/978-1-4842-6440-9_6

What Is a Unit Test?

PIM requires a unit test for every completed module regardless of whether the test is manual or automated. What does this look like? For automated and manual unit tests, these are subdirectories in your source code tree. There is one test subdirectory per namespace, or component, that contains the test code. As PIM recommends organizing your source code by namespace or components, at least one test executable is created per namespace directory. These executables are test suites that run all the individual unit tests for all of the modules in the namespace directory. By placing the test code in a subdirectory of its associated component, you can facilitate reusing the test code across different target platforms.

Figure 6-1 is a UML description of the relationship between the source component and the unit tests. If some of the semantics of a UML diagram are unfamiliar, refer to Appendix C, which might help clarify things.

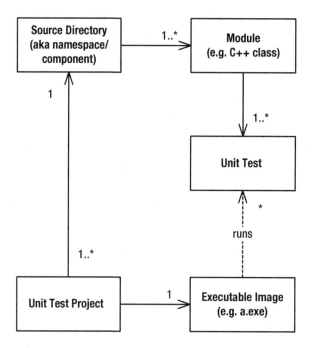

Figure 6-1. *Entity relationship diagram for component unit tests*

Using the source code tree of the PIM example program as an illustration, the file organization in Figure 6-2 shows the layout of the source code, unit tests, and test project directories for the Storm::Component namespace, which contains the control algorithm logic. The top-level tests/ directory is where the unit test executables are built. Note that the unit tests are built and run using two different compilers, Visual Studio and MinGW (which is GCC for Windows).

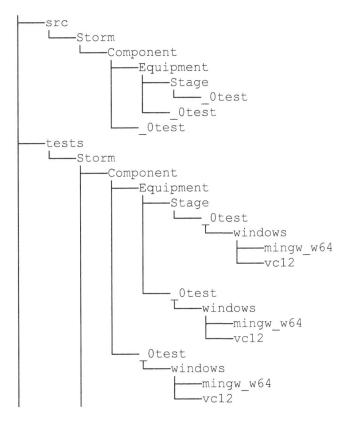

Figure 6-2. *The source and unit test directory layout for the PIM example application*

The example uses a naming and file organization convention of placing the source code for automated unit tests in a subdirectory (or a namespace directory) named _0test/. In the context of PIM, names (i.e., classes, functions, files, namespaces, etc.) are fully qualified by their namespace directory path so having multiple and nested _0test directory names does not cause name collisions. Additionally, the file organization and naming under the tests/ directory mirrors the _0test/ conventions. This is to distinguish the build directories for a component's automated unit tests from its manual unit tests. And, yes, it is perfectly acceptable to have both automated and manual unit tests for a single namespace or component.

ABOUT COMPILERS

When developing the PIM example code, I used Visual Studio because it has better tools for debugging. I also use the MinGW compiler because it generates code coverage metrics for free (whereas the code coverage metrics feature for Visual Studio is only available in the Enterprise edition).

Source Directories and Unit Tests

Referring back to the directory layout for the persistent storage example in Figure 4-4, you can see that there are only three directories that contain unit tests, but there are six different directories under src/. This seems to violate the source directory to unit test relationship shown in Figure 6-1. However, if you look at the build directories for the unit test, you can see that there are six different unit test executables that get built. This is because the same unit tests are used to validate different implementations of a single interface. For the scenario presented in Figure 4-4, the relationships in Figure 6-1 still hold, even though the relationships are not directly reflected in the file organization of the source and unit test code.

For example, these are the test directories shown in Figure 4-4:

```
src/Driver/NV/_0tests
src/Driver/SPI/_0tests
src/PersistentStorage/_0tests
```

And these are the implementation directories:

```
src/Driver/NV/File
src/Driver/NV/MicroChip
src/Driver/NV/ST
src/Driver/SPI/Arduino
src/Driver/Generic
src/PersistentStorage
```

And these are the build directories:

```
tests/Driver/NV/File/Win32/Windows/vc14
tests/Driver/NV/Microchip/Eeprom24AA160/grand-central-m4/Windows/gcc_arm7
tests/Driver/NV/ST/EepromM95160DRE/grand-central-m4/Windows/gcc_arm7
tests/Driver/SPI/Arduino/grand-central-m4/Windows/gcc_arm7
tests/Driver/SPI/Generic/ATSAME54-XPRO/Windows/gcc_arm7
tests/PersistentStorage/Windows/vc14
```

HOW MANY UNIT TESTS WILL I END UP WITH?

Each project is different in scope and complexity, and this will have a direct impact on what is the most effective way to test the code. As an example, though, here are some unit test metrics for one real-world project that I worked on:

- 110,000 lines of source code

- 8 manual unit test projects

- 74 automated unit test projects

Manual Unit Tests

A manual unit test is a test that requires interaction by the developer to execute. For embedded projects, this typically requires building the test image for the target platform, then programming and launching the test image on the target. There are different degrees of manual unit tests. They are listed as follows (in order of preference):

1. Once the test image has been launched, it runs to completion with no additional user interaction and reports pass fail. In theory, this could be an automated unit test if there is enough infrastructure to auto-deploy and execute images on the target hardware.

2. The test image runs and provides instructions or prompts to the developer on how to execute and verify individual test steps.

3. The developer launches the test image and performs ad hoc testing.

Obviously, number three, ad hoc testing, requires the least amount of planning and initial effort by a developer. However, the downside is that the actual test setup, test environment, and test coverage are completely dependent on how conscientious the developer is. Also, the reproducibility of these tests when there are changes, bugs are fixed, or code is refactored is very undependable. Nevertheless, this is sometimes the most practical method (in terms of effort and reward) for testing hardware-specific code (e.g., a SPI driver). In these cases, PIM recommends applying the Single Responsibility Principle to isolate your hardware-specific code to make the testing effort more manageable. By minimizing what the code does, it also bounds and focuses the test effort.

Referencing the persistent storage example in Chapter 4, only the `Arduino SPI Adapter` and the `EEPROM MicroChip 24AA160` classes are hardware dependent and would need manual unit tests. The manual unit test for the `Arduino SPI Adapter` class only needs to verify the functionality and semantics of the `SPI Driver Interface` (or, in other words, does the class perform valid SPI transactions?). The manual unit test for the `EEPROM MicroChip 24AA160` class only needs to verify the set of EEPROM commands that are implemented by the class. In both these unit tests, the testing is very focused and bounded.

Automated Unit Tests

Automated unit tests are your BFFs. An automated unit test is a stand-alone executable that returns the pass/fail results of the test. An automated unit test could also be a script that interacts with the test executable and reports the results. All components that do not have a direct dependency on your target hardware should have an automated unit test. There should also be unit tests for all components with hardware dependencies, but these can be manual tests. Another exception to the there-must-be-an automated-unit-test rule is when human feedback is required for the test. This might be the case, for example, if the unit test is running against the presentation layer of your user interface (UI).

PIM recommends creating automated unit tests that execute as terminal or console applications on a personal computer. With a well-defined HAL layer, it is possible to run automated tests on the actual hardware, but that requires some additional work. To run an automated unit test on actual target hardware, you need some external automation to deploy the test image (i.e., program the board or Flash), launch the test, provide stimulus or input to the test, and then capture the pass/fail results. This kind of automation becomes a return on investment (ROI) decision (i.e., a project unto itself, which is outside of the scope of PIM).

Referencing the persistent storage example in Chapter 5, the `Persistent Storage` class should have an automated unit test since it has no direct hardware dependencies.

UNIT TESTS AND PLATFORM INDEPENDENCE

Code that has automated unit tests, as they are described in this chapter, is by definition platform independent. Platform independence is also the majority of the work you need to do in order to create a functional simulator. By creating a fully automated unit test suite for your code, you are creating a foundation that you can build your functional simulator on.

Code Coverage Metrics

How good is your automated test coverage? This is where code coverage metrics come in. Once you have automated unit tests, you can then "instrument" them to generate data that can be processed into code coverage metrics. Typically, "instrumenting" means enabling specific compile time options, running the test executable (which generates "execution data"), and then postprocessing the execution data into human-readable results. For example, the GCC toolchain includes a tool called gcov that processes the execution data in various human-readable formats. Figure 6-3 provides an example of code coverage metrics from the PIM example code.

Line Coverage for the Storm::Component::Equipment module:

```
                    GCC Code Coverage Report
                 Directory: \workspaces\pim\src
-----------------------------------------------------------------------
File                                     Lines   Exec  Cover   Missing
-----------------------------------------------------------------------
Storm/Component/Equipment/Cooling.cpp      34     32    94%    41,43
Storm/Component/Equipment/Cooling.h         1      0     0%    66
Storm/Component/Equipment/IndoorHeating.cpp 101    89    88%    71,73, 159-160,
                                                                206-209,212,215,
                                                                224-225
Storm/Component/Equipment/IndoorHeating.h   1      0     0%    89
Storm/Component/Equipment/Off.cpp          15     15   100%
Storm/Component/Equipment/Off.h             1      0     0%    49
Storm/Component/Equipment/StageApi.h        1      1   100%
-----------------------------------------------------------------------
TOTAL                                     154    137    89%
-----------------------------------------------------------------------
```

Branch Coverage for the Storm::Component::Equipment module:

```
                    GCC Code Coverage Report
                 Directory: \workspaces\pim\src
-----------------------------------------------------------------------
File                                    Branches Taken  Cover   Missing
-----------------------------------------------------------------------
Storm/Component/Equipment/Cooling.cpp      24     20    83%    30,72,76,85
Storm/Component/Equipment/Cooling.h         0      0    --%
Storm/Component/Equipment/IndoorHeating.cpp 124    79    63%    32,108,112,144,
                                                                158,159,160,173,
                                                                192,203,207,208,
                                                                209,223,224,225,
                                                                239
Storm/Component/Equipment/IndoorHeating.h   0      0    --%
Storm/Component/Equipment/Off.cpp           2      2   100%
Storm/Component/Equipment/Off.h             0      0    --%
Storm/Component/Equipment/StageApi.h        0      0    --%
-----------------------------------------------------------------------
TOTAL                                     150    101    67%
-----------------------------------------------------------------------
```

Figure 6-3. *Code coverage metrics from the example program*

In the preceding example, there are both line coverage and branch coverage metrics. Line coverage represents actual lines of code executed. Branch coverage is an evaluation of all of the possible paths for conditional statements that were actually taken. It is possible to have 100% line coverage and less than 100% branch coverage. For example, in the following code snippet, if during the test the variable isReady was always TRUE, then line coverage would be 100%, but branch coverage would only be 50%:

```
bool isReady = checkSomething();
if ( isReady )
{
    doSomethingInteresting();
}
doMoreStuff();
```

One final note about code coverage metrics: you can have 100% line and branch coverage but still have low-quality test coverage. This is because an invalid stimulus (with respect to the module's requirements) can generate the desired code coverage metrics, but effectively provide little in the way of meaningful test coverage. In short, don't rely solely on code coverage metrics when evaluating the quality of a unit test.

About Testing Frameworks

When discussing automated testing, the topic of unit test frameworks inevitably comes up. Do you have to use a test framework to implement automated unit testing? The short answer is no. Unit test frameworks simplify—in theory—the process of constructing, organizing, executing, and reporting results for unit tests. But at their core, unit test frameworks are just glorified ASSERT macros. That is, the ASSERT says "fail a test if the code under test didn't generate the expected result."

PIM does recommend that you do have a unit test framework, if for no other reason than to be consistent in how you construct and execute the unit testing. But this does not mean that you have to use third-party tools or products.

TESTING FRAMEWORKS: BUY VS. BUILD

Many third-party options are available for unit test frameworks that make a strong case for the buy option. There are literally dozens of commercial and open source frameworks to choose from. When selecting a third-party unit test framework, you need to evaluate the framework's build paradigm. For example, some frameworks are packaged as header file–only implementations that are essentially build system agnostic. Other frameworks require a specific build system or require you to run preprocessing scripts that auto-generate boilerplate code, mocked code, test runners, and so on, before compiling the tests. This is important because PIM's recommendations for directory organization do not always fit cleanly with these build requirements. Also, remember that just from a logistics perspective, you will have many unit test projects (and the count only goes up over time) so the build process for the unit tests needs to scale. Currently, I use Catch2, which is a "header-only" framework. Consequently, there are no build/script issues, and it is compatible with mixing in other frameworks like Hippomocks.

Also, when researching unit test frameworks for a C project, don't restrict your search to C-specific unit test frameworks. C++ unit test frameworks are fully capable of unit testing C code, and many of these C++ frameworks have richer feature sets (e.g., self-registration of unit tests).

If you feel, however, that your requirements can be best met by building your own framework, then by all means do so. Personally, though, I would never want to build my own testing framework. But if I needed a certain feature from a third-party testing framework—but it required me to use CMake—I would definitely consider rolling my own testing framework or possibly trying to build the feature into a less constrained framework.

Continuous Integration

Automated unit tests lose much of their value if they are not set up to be automatically built and executed. Generally, automated tests should be executed upon submission of your module into your SCM repository. More details about how to set up continuous integration with your projects are provided in Chapter 8.

Tips for Unit Testing

Here are some things you can do to be more successful in your unit testing.

Minimize Dependencies

The most useful thing you can do for better unit testing is to minimize your module's dependencies. The simplicity of the unit test is a function of how decoupled a module is. A module with no dependencies (assuming it is not just a monolithic implementation) is an easy unit test to implement. However, "easy" in this context does not necessarily mean less code. For example, unit testing a doubly linked list is a nontrivial amount of test code—but if the list has no external dependencies, the unit testing will not require mocked functions, classes, or an advanced class in the unit test design.

Use Abstract Interfaces

A module that depends on interfaces where the interfaces are abstract is easier to unit test than a module that depends on a specific concrete implementation because concrete implementations inevitably bring in additional dependencies. And since dependencies are transitive in nature, you end up having to include the entire kitchen sink just to get your unit test to link and run. Using abstract interfaces to break dependencies is PIM in action.

Referencing the persistent storage example in Chapter 4, the NV Interface was introduced to break the Persistent Storage class's dependencies. So instead of the Persistent Storage class being dependent on the EEPROM Microchip 24AA160 class, the Arduino SPI Library, and the Arduino hardware, it only depends on the abstract NV Interface.

ABOUT ABSTRACT INTERFACES

An abstract interface does not have to be a pure virtual class in C++. An abstract interface is any interface that defines a behavior that has a deferred binding (i.e., not a source time binding) for its implementation. See the "Binding Time" discussion in Chapter 3 for additional details.

Use the Data Model Pattern

Using the data model pattern is a very effective way to decouple a module's dependencies. A model point is not an abstract interface (since by definition model points are concrete, type-specific entities), but it does stop transitive dependencies. When a module uses a model point, the only dependency it incurs is that the model point must exist. There are no dependencies to any upstream/downstream entities; there is no requirement that an actual application somewhere is setting or consuming the model point.

The data model also simplifies the construction of unit tests because the test code can directly read, write, or inspect the model points. For model point unit testing, the test code only needs to instantiate the model point, and there is no need to mock the implementation of an interface as part of the test code.

Test Early

When you are developing your code, PIM strongly recommends that you create and run your unit test projects sooner rather than later. Do not wait until all the modules in a namespace have been created before you start writing and executing unit test code. For example, simply creating the test project for a module that has a single test that does nothing is a very effective way to resolve compiler and linker errors in real time. This becomes even more important when you have many modules that are very similar in structure (e.g., if you are cloning and editing module A to start module B).

Develop and Test Incrementally

Don't be in a rush to fully complete a module before writing and exercising its corresponding unit test. In the spirit of Test-driven development (TDD), you can write the test function first or at any point in the process of developing your module. Obviously, this depends on the nature of any given module, but by constructing a module incrementally—for example, doing the easy parts first—and then testing the recently completed increment of the partially finished module, you can continue building your module on a proven set of increments. If you don't test your module until the very end of its development—the big bang approach to unit testing—in the end, testing the module is going to consume considerably more time than an incremental approach.

ABOUT TEST-DRIVEN DEVELOPMENT

PIM is agnostic with respect to TDD. There is a lot of overlap between TDD and what PIM recommends for unit testing. But if your organization embraces a broader use of TDD than PIM requires, by all means, go all in on TDD.

The Dark Side of Unit Testing

While I am a big fan of unit testing, there are a few potentially problematic things to be aware of:

- Unit tests are fragile. That is, even minor code refactoring has a tendency to break unit tests. This is actually a good thing, but it also means that sometimes you spend more time refactoring the unit test code than you did refactoring the production code. While this can be frustrating, it is just part and parcel of refactoring. Do not skip refactoring your unit tests to account for a new change regardless of the effort and time required. Not keeping your unit tests up to date is an anti-strategic practice that creates technical debt. It also gives you a false sense of the quality of your code, and it is the first step toward bit rot. Always keep your unit tests up to date.

- The value of a unit test is only as good as the developer writing the tests. It is possible to write unit tests that have designated code coverage, but still does not provide meaningful test coverage. This is particularly easy to do when unit testing algorithms. Software developers are typically not domain experts with respect to the embedded systems they build, so trying to determine what is or is not a valid input test vector for a unit test can be challenging. A set of invalid input test vectors can pass and generate the desired code coverage metrics, but effectively provide little in the way of meaningful test coverage.

- Over time, you will end up with many tests. Eventually, this will become a logistical issue with respect to continuous integration (i.e., at some point, it will take a long time to build everything). Possible solutions to this are listed as follows in order of most to least desirable:

1. Get a faster build machine.

2. Run the tests periodically (e.g., nightly) instead of every time there is a pull request or SCM check-in.

3. Consolidate tests into a single build to reduce building the same infrastructure and framework code over and over.

4. Run the tests weekly instead of nightly. The downside to this option is that you could have a week's worth of work to review if tests fail.

5. Have fewer tests. This is a bad option, and I hesitated to bring it up, but it can be a real issue. I worked on one project where every "system service" component had three unit test executables built—one for each compiler. But because of resource constraints on the build server, we dropped building and running the Linux version of the unit tests. As the project was at a point where the system services were very mature, skipping the step of validating the code for Linux was not considered a big risk.

Unit Testing vs. Integration Testing vs. System Testing

Unit testing does not replace integration or system testing. For example, unit testing (by definition) catches only a subset of potential errors because the modules are being tested in isolation. Errors that are present when individual modules are combined together will not be caught by unit tests, but rather will be caught by integration testing and system testing.

Consequently, from a project planning aspect, unit tests should be limited to only providing a repeatable means for a developer to demonstrate that their code works before integrating it into the system; integration testing and system testing are still required. However, in my experience, having good unit test practices drastically reduces integration testing times and the integration effort generally. In addition, with good unit testing, the bugs found during system testing are measurably fewer and less severe.

CHAPTER 7

Functional Simulator

A functional simulation is the execution of production source code on a platform—that is **not** the target platform—which provides the majority of the functionality (but not necessarily the real-time performance). Or, more simply, functional simulation is being able to develop, execute, and test production code without target hardware.

From a project management perspective, a functional simulation of the hardware eliminates the finish-to-start dependency the software has on the hardware and allows the hardware and software to be developed in parallel. It allows for meaningful software development and testing even though no hardware is available. On one project, my team worked on the software for 18 months before the hardware was ready because we were able to create a functional simulator.

A functional simulator, then, in real life, is a big win because there are any number of reasons why the hardware may be unavailable to be used for software development. It might simply be there aren't enough target boards to make the hardware available to all the software developers on the team. Or perhaps a global pandemic has prevented physical access to the lab.

So how much effort is it to create a functional simulator? In my experience, most of the effort is in the planning. And the key piece of that planning is starting with a decoupled design that can effectively isolate compiler-specific or platform-specific code. The other important ingredient is using the Main pattern for building your application. This means that the top-level creator is dependent on all of the specifics of the target platform (including the compiler) and is responsible for connecting and wiring all of the modules together. It is analogous to a top-level diagram in a hierarchical hardware schematic. By using the Main pattern, the difference between constructing the target application or constructing the function simulator is isolated to the top-level creator. This means that a functional simulator uses over 80% of the same modules as the actual application. But, again, for this wiring magic to work, there must be explicit interface boundaries for all platform-specific functionality, which is what you get when you design with PIM.

© John T. Taylor, Wayne T. Taylor 2021
J. T. Taylor and W. T. Taylor, *Patterns in the Machine*,
https://doi.org/10.1007/978-1-4842-6440-9_7

Figure 7-1 illustrates the dependencies of a hypothetical embedded application on its target platform.

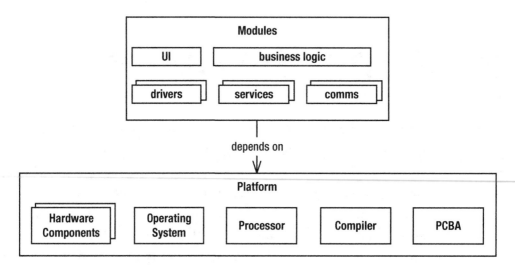

Figure 7-1. *Application platform dependencies*

By using hardware abstraction layer (HAL) interfaces and operating system abstraction layer (OSAL) interfaces, we can decouple the core application from the target platform. Note, however, that the separation of the platform-specific entities can be done with any abstract interface—not just at a HAL or OSAL interface. The concepts of HAL and OSAL interfaces are used here because they are more familiar and conceptually easier to understand. Figure 7-2 shows the same hypothetical embedded application with its hardware dependencies decoupled from the application.

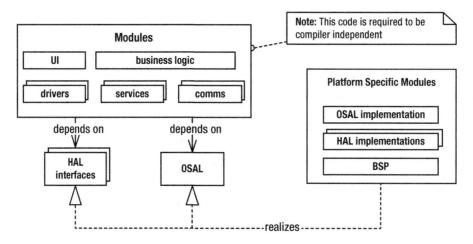

Figure 7-2. *Decoupled application platform dependencies*

Operating System Abstraction Layer

An OSAL provides interfaces for all functionality provided by the underlying operating system. For an embedded system that is using a basic thread scheduler, it would typically include interfaces such as

- Elapsed time (replacement for the standard C library `clock()` function)

- Non-busy wait delay (replacement for the standard C library `sleep()` function)

- Thread management (create, delete, suspend, etc.)

- Mutexes

- Semaphores

Chapter 16 provides details on the OSAL used in the PIM example application.

Hardware Abstraction Layer

A HAL interface is an interface with no implementation. That is, the interface is abstract; it defines behavior for a hardware-specific or platform-specific device. At some point in the build process, or at runtime, there is a binding of a device-specific implementation. A HAL interface is no different than any other abstract interface—the terminology just attempts to categorize what it is abstracting. For example, one could view an OSAL as just a collection of HAL interfaces that define an operating system behavior.

In general, HAL interfaces should be defined or created on an as-needed basis, and they should be created at the level that will provide the most return for the effort. This means that you should not try to create an all-encompassing HAL interface. It adds no value, and it breaks the Interface Segregation Principle and Single Responsibility Principle.

Main Pattern

After defining your OSAL and HAL interfaces, the next step is to add in the Main pattern. The Main pattern encapsulates all of the platform-specific knowledge and dependencies about how to interconnect the platform-independent modules with the platform-specific modules.

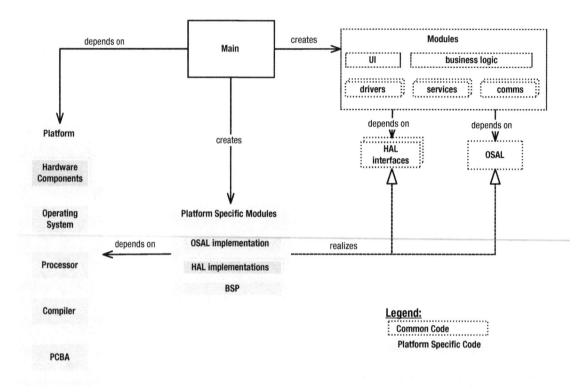

Figure 7-3. *Application with the Main pattern*

In Figure 7-3, the differences between the target application and the functional simulator are contained in Main, the platform-specific modules, and platform blocks. The core of the application, everything contained in the Modules block, can stay the same regardless of which Main instance uses it. While in the diagram shown in Figure 7-3, the platform and platform-specific entities take up most of the diagram, in practice, the common entities in Modules constitute over 80% of the code base. For the PIM example thermostat application, Table 7-1 lists the lines of common code, simulator-specific code, and target hardware code.

Table 7-1. *PIM thermostat lines of code (LOC)*

Top-Level Namespace	Total	Common	Sim Only	Target Only
src/Cpl	24420	23082	1129	1338
src/Storm	8299	7906	231	162
Totals	**32719**	**29859**	**1360**	**1500**
		(91%)	**(4%)**	**(5%)**

Simulated Time

With some additional effort and planning, you can create a functional simulator that not only simulates the target platform but also simulates time. Since a functional simulator's primary goal is to simulate a functional behavior and not real-world timing, the jump from running the functional simulator in real time to simulated time is possible. The following is a brief list of use cases for having simulated time:

- Run faster than real time. If your application has features that include time features that span hours, days, months, or years, one way to verify these features is to use the simulated time feature to speed up time.

- Run slower than real time. If your application has real-time behaviors that occur faster than a user can observe or interact with, you can use the simulated time feature to "single step" the application one system tick at a time. With slower time, you can also present simulated input signals at each system tick.

- Connect to an external model simulation. External tools such as Matlab/Simulink can model some or all of the ecosystem that your embedded device is part of. If you want to incorporate the functional simulator into a model that the external tool simulates, the tools generally control the advancement of time as the model runs.

How to Implement Simulated Time

As in most software-related efforts, there are many ways to simulate time, and there is no one definitive right answer. PIM recommends the following approaches:

- Use an OSAL that incorporates the concept of simulated time. The advantage of this approach is that it requires minimal planning and no extra design effort for your application. The disadvantage is trying to find an OSAL that simulates time and meets your application needs; this can be difficult.

- Build the ability to control or simulate time directly into the parts of the application that will use the simulated time feature. Then instead of building a full functional simulator, build a variant that only includes the features that benefit from simulated time. For this approach to work, you need to design your modules so that their time source code is isolated to a single source and that single source is behind an abstract interface. The single time source must be the root for all timers and elapsed time calculations. You can create algorithm code that is time based by

  - Reading the current time from the time source interface at the start of an execution cycle.

  - Passing the current time to all modules that make up the algorithm. All your modules need to be written to use the time that was passed to them as the current time.

Note   This approach to simulated time works for periodic timing, that is, if your modules are polled rather than event driven. For event-driven modules, PIM recommends that you use an OSAL that supports simulated time.

All of this is pretty simple to design and implement up front. However, coming back later and attempting to refactor existing algorithm code to accommodate simulated time can be challenging. Once again, up-front planning is what makes a functional simulator low effort.

Platform Boundaries

As stated earlier, given a decoupled design for your embedded application, the bulk of creating a functional simulator is to identify where platform boundaries are with respect to the functional simulator. The first question to answer is: how will a particular platform-specific entity be simulated? This is important because the answer determines which software layer is used as the platform boundary. There are three basic options:

- Mocked

- Simulated

- Emulated

Mocked Simulation

A mocked simulation is where you provide a minimal implementation of the device's HAL interface so that the application compiles, links, and does not cause aberrant behavior at runtime. A mocked device may have an optional white-box interface that allows a developer to manually alter the behavior of the mocked device at runtime.

An example of a mocked device is the HVAC output driver in the PIM example thermostat program. This driver does nothing other than to satisfy at link time the `Storm::Thermostat::Outputs` interface. This works because the semantics of the interface are to read a model point containing the current values for the HVAC output signals and then update the platform's outputs. The mocked driver does nothing because the developer already has access to the HVAC output signal model point via the debug console. The platform boundary in this case was not actually a HAL interface per se, but an application-level abstract interface.

Simulated Devices

A simulated device is where the majority of a device's behavior is implemented. Some examples of a simulated device are

- Using a PC's file system to mimic an EEPROM IC (see the `File NV` class in Chapter 4). In this case, the platform boundary is the `NV Interface` class.

- Simulating an LCD using an external C# Windows application that uses a bit image to display the LCD's pixels. (See the "Simulated LCD" use case later for additional details.) In this case, the platform boundary was the SPI interface definition. That is, a simulated SPI driver was created that transferred LCD pixel data to an external C# application.

Emulated Devices

An emulated device is where you replicate a device's behaviors at its lowest, most basic level. For example, emulating an EEPROM IC would mean writing code that interprets and executes the IC's individual registers or EEPROM commands. Typically, emulating a device is by far the largest effort and requires in-depth knowledge of the device being emulated. PIM does not recommend emulating devices unless there is a clear and significant return on the effort required.

Simulated Use Cases

This section provides several real-world examples of a functional simulator.

A Simulated LCD

The project was an IoT device that contained a small LCD display (320x300, 24-bit color) and four physical buttons for its user interface. The LCD and buttons were simulated using an external C# Windows application. The C# application used a bit image that was the same pixel dimensions as the physical LCD and provided button widgets for each physical button. In addition, the C# application was a TCP socket listener. The functional simulator would communicate with the C# application via a TCP socket connection. The connection was used to pass pixel data to the application and receive button events from the C# application. The effort to create the C# application was a couple of days of work.

The actual interface to the physical LCD controller was a SPI interface that was unidirectional to the LCD. The LCD controller had numerous commands to power up and configure the display, but only one command to transfer pixel data. This command contained starting X,Y coordinates followed by N pixels, where each pixel consisted of 24-bit color data. For the functional simulator, I created a simulated SPI driver. This driver ignored all of the LCD controller commands except for the pixel data command. It processed the pixel data by transferring the commands content (starting coordinates and pixel data) over the socket connection to the external C# application. Since the simulation boundary was at the SPI driver level, the LCD simulation was completely transparent to the application's graphic middleware.

The hardware interfaces to the physical buttons were discrete input signals connected to external interrupt pins on the MCU. For the functional simulator, the HAL interface for the button driver was simulated. The simulated HAL interface would trigger an interrupt on button press or button release events received over the socket connection. Because the simulation boundary was at the HAL interface, we were able to test and verify the complete button driver in a simulated environment.

An Algorithm with Simulated Time

The project was a medical device that separated blood. The hardware and software platforms the device had been built on had gone end-of-life, and our job was to port the system to newer hardware and software platforms. In addition to a complete functional simulator for the project, a separate simulator was implemented that just exercised the blood processing algorithm, and that simulation supported simulated time. The simulation time was advanced in 2ms ticks. For each tick, all of the sensor inputs could be specified. This allowed us to generate scripts to fully exercise the nuisances and edge cases for the algorithm.

An unexpected side effect of the algorithm simulation was that we were able to execute the algorithm code on the original legacy hardware. Aside from the fact that the simulator was running in real time, the only change to the initial simulator was to replace the simulated drivers with drivers for the legacy hardware (and of course compiling for the legacy software platform). The benefit of this was that we were able to validate the algorithm on the new architecture long before the new hardware was available.

A Model Simulator with Simulated Time

The project was an HVAC control system for commercial HVAC rooftop equipment. The functional simulator supported simulated time. That is, we could advance time on the simulator in 1ms increments. The functional simulator's debug console was used to advance the simulated time. When management saw how this worked, they gave us a new requirement to include our control system as part of an overall Matlab/Simulink model simulation of the unit. For this we used Matlab's SDK to create a custom Matlab driver that could talk with our functional simulator over TCP sockets. For the functional simulator, we only had to add support for accessing the debug console over a TCP socket. After the functional simulator was connected to the Matlab simulation, Matlab would set the functional simulator's principal inputs, advance time by 1ms, then read back the simulator's HVAC output signals.

A Communication Channel

The project was a two-processor design: a CPU running Linux and an MCU that performed all of the real-time processing. The target hardware used a point-to-point UART for communication between the two processors. The functional simulator for the project consisted of two applications: one that simulated the application running on the CPU, and one that simulated the firmware running on the MCU. We used TCP sockets to simulate the UART between the two applications. The OSAL used for both applications provided the abstraction for stream I/O (i.e., the equivalent of POSIX file descriptors).

For the functional simulators, the only change (with respect to the communication channel) between the production code and the simulators was how the stream instance (i.e., file descriptor) for the communication channel was created.

The Functional Simulator for the Thermostat Example

The PIM thermostat example includes a functional simulator. Figure 7-4 shows the relationship between the software for the target platform and the simulator.

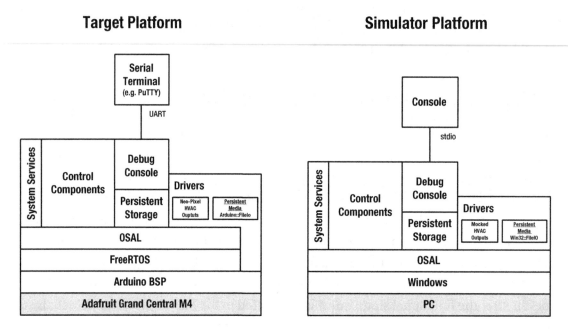

Figure 7-4. *Block diagram for the PIM thermostat example*

The "Mocked HVAC Outputs" driver is only a stub; it does nothing except to satisfy at link time the `Storm::Thermostat::Outputs` interface. This is because the semantics of the driver interface are to read a model point containing the current values for the HVAC output signals and then update the platform's outputs. The mocked driver does nothing because the developer already has access to the HVAC output signal model point via the debug console.

Also note that the functional simulator does not use simulated time. However, several of the automated unit tests for the thermostat algorithm components use simulated time to execute the tests faster than real time. Essentially, these unit tests are microfunctional simulators that only include the algorithm components.

CHAPTER 8

Continuous Integration

PIM is about designing, writing, and maintaining source code in a strategic, efficient, reusable manner. However, in addition to writing the source code, there is all the file manipulation and management activity that go along with building the code and the unit tests. Figure 8-1 gives you a rough idea of the scope of the file management activities that are involved in creating and maintaining an embedded systems project.

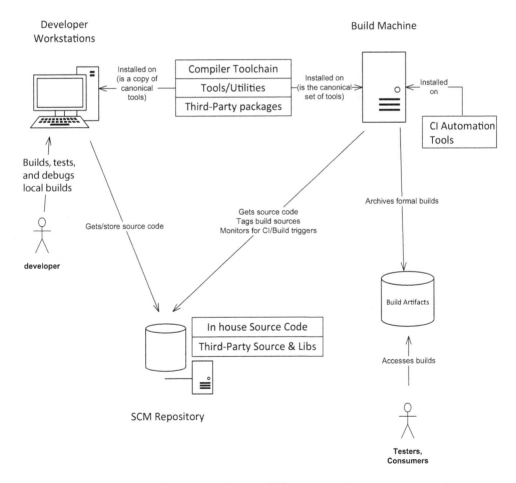

Figure 8-1. *Locations and relationships of files in continuous integration*

© John T. Taylor, Wayne T. Taylor 2021
J. T. Taylor and W. T. Taylor, *Patterns in the Machine*,
https://doi.org/10.1007/978-1-4842-6440-9_8

While, strictly speaking, PIM doesn't really have patterns addressing these activities, there are, nevertheless, strategies that you can implement to avoid bugs and rework when you design your build processes. This chapter, then, is less about how to set up a CI infrastructure and more about how to design your CI to accommodate a project designed with PIM methodology.

At this point, let me also add that I am not a build expert nor a continuous integration (CI) expert. I only take on this task when there is no one else who is willing or capable of doing it. In many ways, CI is an art unto itself, and it can be difficult and time consuming to set it up "right." It takes some trial and error and ultimately some experience to design a robust CI system and to fully master it. But it is always worth the effort. Few things are as disheartening and bewildering as watching an organization or a development team flail and scramble every time they need to pull together a formal build.

Implementing Continuous Integration

In order to implement continuous integration, you will need the following:

- A build machine—This machine should have all the required development tools installed on it.

- Ongoing IT support for the build machine and build automation tools—Specifically, you need to have IT keep the build server updated and up to date with security patches. Additionally, as the build machine quickly becomes the canonical reference for the development tools, it is critical that the server be backed up regularly and, if possible, have high availability.

- A Software Configuration Management (SCM) process—This process needs to be explicitly defined. It should delineate things like "there must be a successful CI build with new code before it can be merged to a stable branch." In the vocabulary of Git, this maps to "pull requests." Or, to phrase it in the language of Git, "a pull request should not be merged until the CI build passes."

- A build automation tool—This can be Jenkins, CruiseControl, Microsoft's Team Foundation Server (TFS), and so on.

- Build scripts—This typically means that you have the ability to build from the command line. In my experience, building projects from an IDE is antithetical to good CI practices. And while there may be occasions when it might make sense to do this, using an IDE to build a part of your project is invariably slower and more error prone.

Continuous Integration and PIM

In a perfect world, there would be a person or team in charge of designing, creating, running, and maintaining the continuous integration hardware and software. If you happen to be in this situation, consult with the CI person or team about incorporating some of the requirements listed below into your CI. They are probably doing many of these things already. But if they're not, collaborate with them on incorporating some of the features described as follows.

But, if there is no CI team, and you're it, here's what you want to make sure happens:

- Ensure that all individual developer code that gets checked into the software configuration management (SCM) system compiles and passes all automated unit tests. This ensures there will be a basic CI build.

- Ensure that a basic CI build completes successfully before the source code for that build is merged to mainline or stable branches.

- Ensure that every CI build builds all unit tests (both manual and automated) as well as all the final application executables. It is critically important that all automated unit tests are built and executed—even the ones that don't seem to be related to the changes that were made in the code. Oftentimes, what I think are just localized changes end up having system-wide impact.

- Ensure that the simulator or simulators—if you have them—build every time. I worked on one project where the developer quit building the simulator one day because it broke the build. Because the hardware had arrived, he didn't think anybody was using the simulator anymore and he didn't bother to fix the build problem; he just commented it out of the build script. Once this was discovered, the team insisted that he get the simulators building again because, even though the hardware was now available to everyone on the team, the simulators were still widely used, and, for some use cases, they were superior to using hardware. Certainly, there will be times when you take a simulator or unit test out of service, but it should be a strategic decision, not something that happens because a build breaks.

- Ensure that all the unit tests are built, even if they're not automated unit tests. It is important that all manual unit tests are built even though they are obviously not executed as part of the build process. This helps guards against accumulating technical debt with respect to the manual tests. Since the manual tests are typically not often executed, it is crucial that when you do have to run them (e.g., after refactoring or bug fixing), they have been kept up to date and are ready to run.

- Ensure that the build server that is used for the CI builds is the same build server used for creating formal builds from stable branches in the SCM repository.

- Ensure that formal builds, or releases, are done from mainline or some other stable branch. Formal builds are required to pass all automated unit tests just like CI builds.

- Ensure that the formal builds are tagged or labeled in the SCM repository.

- With both CI and formal builds, ensure that all permutations of the final application and simulators and release variants and engineering-only variants get built every time.

- Incorporate, at your discretion, any automated "smoke tests" or "sanity tests" into the build process.

About the Build Machine

The build machine is where all CI and formal builds are done. The build machine may be a single PC, a virtual machine (VM), a cloud-based service, or a collection of PCs and VMs. There are many possible configurations; it just depends on the needs of the project and the company's IT infrastructure. Nevertheless, the hard requirement is that the build machine has all of the tools (and licenses) required to transform source files into final images. Unit tests can, but are not required to, be run on the build machine.

Consequently, the build machine should never be an individual developer's PC as the build machine is the canonical reference for the development tools. For this reason, the build machine must also be backed up to protect against these kinds of occurrences:

- A build machine failure (hardware failure, natural disaster, malware attack, etc.). You should be able to recreate your build machine in a timely fashion lest it become a bottleneck for ongoing development and releases.

- One or more of the development tools (compiler, code generators, host operating system, etc.) go end-of-life.

- Your project requires an update years after a project has been completed.

Maximizing Build Machine Performance

Regardless of the build machine's physical or virtual hardware, you will want your build machine to have as much performance as your budget can afford. This is because

- You want CI build times to be short. As a successful CI build is required before code can be merged to a mainline branch, CI builds can become a critical path when trying to get changes into a release for developers or testers.

- When the automated unit tests execute on the build machine, you want the test time to be as short as possible for the same reason you want the CI build time to be short.

- The number of automated unit tests always increases. While automation tools themselves do not require a lot of horsepower and only execute sporadically, running the unit tests, running code analyzers, and running report generators are CPU intensive. Nevertheless, it is a common, and often useful, configuration to have all the build automation tools execute on the build machine.

To improve the performance of your builds, consider implementing the following strategic practices:

- Configure your build or makefile scripts to perform parallel builds.

- Configure the automated unit tests to run in parallel.

- Have additional slave build machines so that CI and formal builds are not forced to be serialized. For example, you could configure a set of machines or VMs so they can build multiple pull requests at the same time.

- Get better hardware, that is, more RAM, solid-state disk drives, more CPU cores, higher CPU clock rates, and so on. You can never have too much hardware when it comes to a build machine.

About Software Configuration Management

When you are planning your project and thinking about how to organize your SCM and store your code in repositories, you need to consider potential constraints and complications that might arise from build automation tools. For example, Jenkins' classic jobs are cumbersome when trying to incorporate multiple repositories.

The simplest organization for a project is to have a single SCM and a single repository. However, this approach is not always an option. For example, you may need to work with legacy repositories, preexisting processes, or cross-department collaboration. In these situations, I strongly recommend you prototype continuous integration and formal builds with your build automation tool (using stubbed or mocked code) before making any final decisions about your SCM organization. Trying to change your SCM organization and repository structure late in a project can be a very painful experience.

I also recommend that you check all third-party sources into your SCM repositories. This includes items such as Linux kernel source. Be sure, however, never to pull code from the Internet when building a CI or a formal build. If your Internet connection is unavailable—even temporarily—you can't build. Furthermore, without capturing the actual source and storing it in your local SCM, you may not be able to reproduce a prior build. By definition, all formal builds must be recreatable down to the byte level for every object that is built. Years ago, I saw this principle modeled to near perfection by the

AT&T Unix System Laboratories. They were fanatical and meticulous about being able to identically recreate every version they had ever released of their Unix operating system. Furthermore, they held my team to the same standard. Even if our only change was a single update to a man page, we had to show that our build system allowed us to create an exact replica of that release at any point in the future.

Implementing Branching Strategies

The requirements that PIM has for CI assume that the project will follow some kind of SCM branching strategy. It is not uncommon for embedded projects to use a trunk-based strategy because projects are often small and there are often only one or two developers working on it. But even for the single-developer scenario, I recommend using branches instead of a trunk-based paradigm.[1] If for nothing else, branches add a layer of protection that prevents a single developer from polluting the trunk with code that does not compile or does not pass all of the unit tests.

So, what branch strategy should you use? It depends. If your software team size is small, collocated, and releases are infrequent, then a very basic branch model such as Git Flow, or derivatives thereof, will suffice. But regardless of what branching strategy is selected for a project, it needs to support performing a CI build on a developer branch before the branch is merged to a mainline or stable branch. Once again, Git's pull request mechanism is a great example of this, and it has a lot of support with respect to build automation tools (e.g., Jenkins has numerous plugins for building Git pull requests).

PIM does not require that your CI strategy perform a CI build every time a developer checks something into the SCM repository. In my experience, this doesn't scale, and it discourages developers from checking their code in frequently. I recommend that you only do a CI build once a task (e.g., a user story, bug ticket, feature) has been completed by a developer.

---

[1]In its simplest form, a trunk-based paradigm allows all developers to have access to the mainline branch (aka the "trunk") and perform direct checkouts and check-ins to mainline. A branch-based paradigm requires developers to create individual branches (based on feature or work task) to perform the daily check-ins and checkouts. Then once the task associated with a branch has been completed and unit tested, it then goes through additional steps to merge it back to its parent branch. In terms of Git, the "merge a work branch back to its parent" would be done through the pull request mechanism.

About Formal Builds

A formal build is a successful build—a build that has compiled without errors and has passed all of its associated automated unit tests. Formal builds should be given a unique identifier. Furthermore, a formal build is one that can be recreated from the SCM repository if need be. In other words, formal builds are builds that can be given to a customer or to testers.

Note   Testers should only log bugs against formal builds because a regular CI build or a developer's private build has no guaranteed provenance. That is, unless the bug was found using a formal build, it might not be a bug at all. Any bugs found on a CI build should be immediately reproduced on a formal build before any development resources are spent troubleshooting it.

About the Build Automation Tool

There are many choices for build automation tools. PIM is agnostic to which build automation tool you select. In the PIM context, a build automation tool must

- Automate the triggering of CI builds and the execution of the associated automated unit tests.

- Flag a build as failed if there is failure in the compiler, linker, or one or more automated unit tests.

- Automate the triggering of formal builds (and the execution of unit tests) when new code is merged to mainline or stable branches.

- Generate and enforce a unique build identifier for each formal build. In addition, if multiple build automation jobs are required, then the tool should use a single, or common, build number when it creates the complete set of the release images.

- Ensure that the SCM repositories used for a formal build are tagged and labeled appropriately. At a minimum, the tagging must include the formal build's build identifier.

- For both CI and formal builds, ensure that defined metrics and documentation are generated, for example:

    - It should collect and report automated unit testing coverage.

    - It should run Doxygen or a similar tool over the compiled source code to auto-generate documentation mined from the raw source.

    - Generate and report lines of code (LOC) metrics.

    - Run static code analyzers and report the findings or metrics.

Note   While the generation of metrics and documentation can be optional, it is okay, and often desirable, for these steps to fail a build. For example, it often makes sense to fail a build if Doxygen reports errors, or if the static code analyzer detects errors or complexity violations. If the output of the metrics and documentation is part of the formal development process, then failing the CI and formal builds on errors prevents the accumulation of technical debt with respect to these processes.

- Archive all the release artifacts of a formal build. At a minimum, this should be all of the executables, images, documentation, and so on that make up a release package. It should also contain information about what is in the build (e.g., the SCM change log comments) and the build's unique build identifier. How these archived artifacts need to be kept (and where) will be dictated by your team or organization's processes for releasing software.

- Support the ability to manually trigger CI and formal builds. In real life, automation does not always work as expected. There are almost always instances where the technical lead needs to override the CI automation and force specific builds and behaviors.

As mentioned previously, there is a learning curve with respect to build automation tools. If the CI infrastructure is already set up, then typically adding a new project or job is fairly simple. However, be prepared to spend some time standing up the CI infrastructure for the first time. And you also always want to allocate some amount of time and resources to maintaining the build automation tools.

About Build Scripts

The reality of developing software today is that developers start with an IDE. The IDE is magical in that it is an editor, real-time syntax checker, build tool, and debugger all in one. No other tools are required, and all of the messy details are hidden or dumbed down for the developer. While this can be useful, it is also bad when it comes to continuous integration and build scripts. The exception might be if you have a fully integrated tool set that includes everything from build automation tools to the SCM to the developer's IDE to the compiler toolchain. In my experience, this rarely happens. Over the course of my career, I've only seen it once. The problem with IDEs is

1. Build automation tools work best with command line–driven build scripts. Depending on your IDE, it can be difficult to generate (and maintain) a command-line build script. That is, it is not easy to create makefiles (or build scripts) that can be used with build automation tools and at the same time be the build scripts that a developer would invoke from the IDE. And, of course, you want the developers to use the same build scripts that are used on the build machine. If they don't, then diagnosing compiler and linker failures on the build machine is going to be time consuming and painful.

2. The default behavior for IDEs is to organize all files under a single parent root directory. This is fine if you are doing a project in isolation and there is no shared source code from other projects. Most IDEs do provide alternate structures (e.g., Microsoft Visual Studio Solution File, which is a collection of individual project files). Unfortunately, a lot of embedded projects start with the silicon vendor's IDE and example code, and how the IDE integrates into the build process is seldom considered until the project is well underway. And, at that point, it's a nontrivial effort to restructure the code organization.

The first item mentioned earlier is an issue when it comes to CI and has a direct impact on your project's build scripts. The second item is an example of a strategic antipattern, and it impacts your build scripts because it involves the directory structure of the source code.

PIM recommends that you start with command line–based scripts from day one. This can be anything really: raw makefiles, CMake, SCons, NQBP, and so on. If you're using an IDE, don't build inside the IDE; rather, configure the IDE to invoke your build scripts. Or, if your IDE doesn't support this, simply have a terminal window open next to your IDE and build directly from the command line.

You will also need to have your team agree up front on how your source code will be organized in the file system. This includes both deciding how to organize the code that is native to your project and anticipating what reuse opportunities there may be for other projects. You also need to consider what code is being reused from other projects as well as third-party sources (e.g., the silicon vendor, open source projects, purchased libraries, etc.). Chapter 12 goes into detail about the PIM recommendation for file organization.

Here are some of my recommendations for your build scripts:

- Make them command line based.

- Have the build machine and the developer use the same build scripts.

- Design the scripts to support building the application as well as an unlimited number of unit tests.

- Ensure the scripts scale up to accommodate the fact that the number of unit tests and application variants increases over time.

- Design the scripts so that adding a new file to the build script is no effort or very little effort for the developer. At the turn of the century, I worked on a project that used the Symbian operating system and toolchain. The makefile structure was so complex that developers didn't create new files, but rather added new features to existing files (which were only related at a high feature level) because it was so painful and error prone to add anything to the makefiles. Remember, PIM is all about the OCP and extending code without modifying existing source files. This means that you will be adding new files and directories all the time.

- Ensure that any script file that is located in the same directory as the source code does not have any unique compiler flags, linker directives, or -D symbols. The reason is because any given directory may be built for different output images (e.g., as part of the application or as part of a unit test image).

- Has the ability to just build selected directories. That is, don't build in the assumption that building a top-level directory will recursively build all of its subdirectories. Depending on whether you are building the application or a unit test, the required directories can differ.

Be aware that if you develop on Windows, the Windows command line (cmd.exe) has a limited length of 8191 characters. This can cause problems if you have a large number of include paths (or other options) as part of compiler arguments and your root directory has a lengthy path (e.g., more than 20 characters). This is especially problematic when it comes to the build automation tools because they can have a deep path for the starting root directory for build.[2] The moral of the story here is to minimize the number of header include search path options whenever possible. I have worked on a project where the silicon vendor's SDK added an individual header path option (-I) for every directory in the SDK. And yes, we exceeded the 8191-character limit and had to get creative with our build scripts.

---

[2]Sometimes, with a "deep path" on Windows, you can shorten it with the subst command. This command lets you set a drive letter (which is a directory root) at any level of your path. For example, if my directory path were something like this: D:\SC\perforce\user_dev\product\project\sc\1.0\en_US then a command like subst m: D:\SC\perforce\user_dev\product\project\sc\1.0\en_US will set the drive letter M: to start at en_US.

CHAPTER 9

The Data Model Architecture

The data model software architecture pattern is a data-oriented pattern where modules interact with each other via data instances (a.k.a. model points) with no direct dependencies between modules. For example, Figure 9-1 illustrates the difference between a literal architecture and a data model architecture. By implementing a data model, you introduce a layer of indirection that allows one module to change without requiring other modules to change.

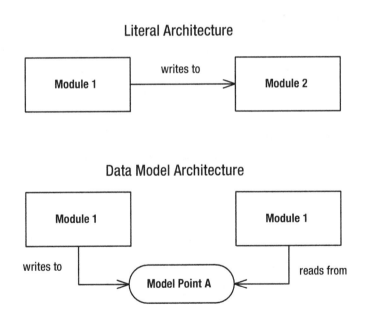

Figure 9-1. *Literal architecture vs. data model architecture*

"The data model" consists of all the model point instances in your design, and it is the canonical authority for the data, which determines the application behavior. Model points have the following features:

- The value stored in a model point can be of any type or any data structure. A model point's value should be strictly data and not an object. That is, model points do not contain business rules or enforce policies (except for things like value range checking).

- Model point instances are type safe. That is, all read and write operations are specific to the model point's value type.

- Model points have atomic operations for accessing their value or state. This means that accessing model point values is a thread-safe operation.

- Model points have a valid or invalid state independent of their value.

- Model points provide a subscription mechanism for clients to receive change notifications when a model point's value changes or if the model point's validity changes.

Using model points can be viewed as analogous to the introduction of abstract interfaces per the Dependency Inversion Principle (DIP). Even though model points are concrete, they are very stable. This means that if Module A has dependency on a model point, then the transitive dependencies that it incurs are well bounded and unlikely to change. The net effect is that a dependency on a model point means that Module A is dependent on the data model framework—not the hardware or application-specific dependencies. As long as your design can live with a dependency on the data model framework, model points are functionally equivalent to using abstract interfaces to decouple modules.

The data model pattern has similarities to the Model-View-Controller (MVC), Publish-Subscribe, and Component-Based Development (CBD) software patterns.

Figure 9-2 is an example design using the data model pattern for the following hypothetical use case. In this example, all four modules—Temperature Driver, Sensor Selection, Alarm Manager, and PID controller—have no dependencies on each, and they can be developed independently of each other. And with the possible exception of the Temperature Driver, all of the modules are hardware independent and can have automated unit tests to verify their operation.

Here are the requirements for the example design:

- Use a PID controller to control a temperature loop. The PID controller reads from the Setpoint and Active Temperature model points and writes to the Control Variable model point.

- The temperature input (or process variable) for the PID loop can come from different temperature sensors based on configuration settings.

- If there is no valid or working temperature sensor available for input to the PID controller, an alarm shall be raised.

In the design shown in Figure 9-2, the PID controller module reads the Active Temperature model point instance. However, how that model point gets its value— whether it comes from an onboard or remote temperature sensor—has no impact on the PID controller module because the PID controller is decoupled from its temperature input source. Additionally, it is decoupled from consumers of its output. All of which results in a high degree of reusability for the PID controller module.

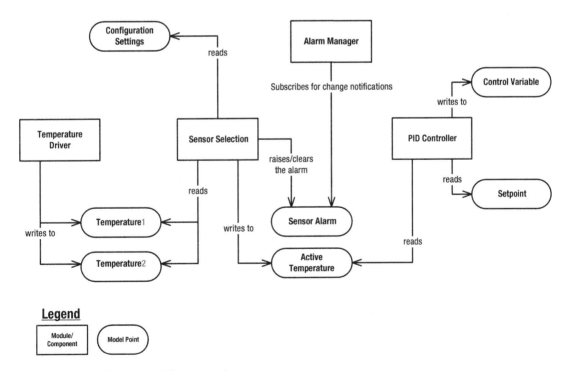

Figure 9-2. *data model example*

The Sensor Selection module reads the `Configuration Settings` model point instance. In a complete application, the `Configuration Settings` would be persistently stored. However, the Sensor Selection module has no knowledge of, nor needs to have any knowledge of, whether the `Configuration Settings` are persistently stored nor what the mechanism is for storing and retrieving the configuration values. This means the work on the Sensor Selection module can begin immediately and does not have to wait for the `Configuration Settings`' value to be actively stored and retrieved from persistent storage.

The Temperature Driver, Sensor Selection, and PID controller modules use a polling paradigm for reading and writing to model points. The Alarm Manager module on the other hand is event driven because it relies on the data model change notification mechanism. Applications can use only polling strategies, or only change notifications, or any combination of both.

To extend the design shown in Figure 9-2, new behaviors or new features would be implemented by creating new modules and new model point instances and "wiring in" these new entities to the existing design. For example, if there were a requirement to add additional filtering of the temperature values, then a new module Temperature Filter (two instances) and two new model points `Filtered Temperature1` and `Filtered Temperature2` would be created and inserted into the design between the Temperature Driver and the Sensor Selection modules. The design to accommodate this new requirement is shown in Figure 9-3.

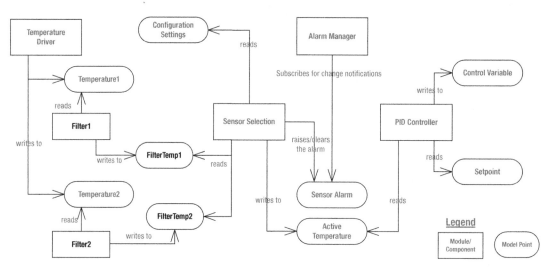

Figure 9-3. *Data model with extended requirement*

When designing with model points, here are some additional semantics to keep in mind:

- Never cache a model point value across function calls. It is okay to read a model point value in a method and then use a local value for the rest of the method. But never read a model point value and then store it in a class member variable for later use.

- Always check the valid state of a model point before operating on the read value. The application cannot assume that a model point always has a valid value, and any module interacting with the model point needs to include logic for dealing with an invalid data. And it is not uncommon to have invalid states in embedded systems. For example, here are some common contributors to invalid states:

  - A sensor may be broken or missing.

  - There can be a delay before the first value is available.

  - Communications may be down or not yet started.

  - Optional equipment may not be installed.

- The data model's change notification semantics guarantee that a client will get a notification when there is a change to a model point's value or state. However, the client is not guaranteed to get notified for every change—just a notification for the last one. For example, consider a system that is configured for the following behavior:

  - A Sensor Driver is updating model point A every millisecond with a different analog value.

  - Module B subscribes for change notification from model point A.

  - The Sensor Driver and Module B execute in different threads.

  Depending on thread priorities, CPU performance, and other activities in the system, Module B is unlikely to be able to process a change notification every millisecond. If, let's say, Module B's thread is delayed by 5ms before the change notification can be executed, Module B will receive a single change notification (not five), and the value of the model point A will be the latest value written by the Sensor Driver.

- There is no synchronization between model points. Operations on a single model point instance are atomic. The application cannot infer the state or value of model point A based on the state or value of model point B. For example, consider a thermostat application that has cooling and heating mode setpoints where the heating setpoint is always required to be less than the cooling setpoint. If the cooling and heating setpoint values are stored in different model point instances, then reading the cooling setpoint before comparing against a new proposed heating setpoint will not always work because there is no guarantee that the cooling setpoint value that is read has not changed before it is compared against the proposed new heating setpoint value.

When synchronization across model points is required, it must be provided by the application. How complex this additional synchronization logic is will depend on requirements. If the requirements are fairly simple—like the preceding thermostat example—a possible solution would be to create a new model point type that contains both the cooling and the heating setpoint, hence a single model point instance. This allows for an atomic read-modify-write operation when changing one or both of the setpoint values.

- The application must view each model point type as unique and different, not as a hierarchical base class with specialized subtypes. Model point types have distinct semantics and are not interchangeable with other model point types even if the underlying model point values are the same. For example, the Colony.core C++ library used in the PIM example thermostat application has a model point type `Cpl::Dm::Mp::Float` that contains a float value. The semantics for a change notification for this type is a simple not-equal test. Since the value is a float, any change, no matter how small or numerically insignificant, will trigger change notifications. But this is less than optimal when using an event-driven paradigm. A solution would be to create a new model point type, perhaps `Cpl::Dm::Mp::FloatDelta`, that still holds float values but has a minimum delta threshold for triggering change notifications. The semantics of what triggers change notifications are different between the two types and, therefore per the LSP, cannot be interchanged. That is, you would never provide a reference to a `Cpl::Dm::Mp::Float` instance to a module if that module needs a reference to `Cpl::Dm::Mp::FloatDelta` instance.

This is especially important from an architectural design perspective because the most efficient way to implement the `Cpl::Dm::Mp::FloatDelta` class would be to inherit from the `Cpl::Dm::Mp::Float` class. This means that the compiler, potentially, could happily accept a reference to the `Cpl::Dm::Mp::FloatDelta` class even though the syntax calls for a `Cpl::Dm::Float` class. But even though the compiler might allow this, your application should not.

- PIM recommends that the application instantiate model points in their invalid state. First, this helps reinforce developer behavior of always checking the valid/invalid state when reading model point values. Second, it provides a consistent paradigm for developers to follow since not all model points can be initialized to a valid value when instantiated. For example, a model point that holds a sensor value will not have a valid value until the driver responsible for reading the sensor has been initialized and has enough time to collect a valid value.

- PIM recommends that all model points be statically instantiated. By statically creating the model points, it avoids the whole dynamic memory issue. Additionally, this ensures that all of the model point instances are always in scope. And finally, it simplifies debugging because you can watch (in the debugger) any model point instance at any time.

- For application-specific modules, using hard-coded model point names (instead of pointers or references to model point instances) is acceptable. This can greatly simplify start-up and construction of modules and unit testing. The downside of using hard-coded model names shows up in the scenario where a new behavior requires that new model points be "inserted into the data flow." For example, see the discussion of Figure 9-2 where the `Filter Temperature1` and `Filter Temperature2` model points were added. In this scenario, the Sensor Selection module would have to be updated to use the `Filter`

125

Temperature1|2 model points instead of the original Temperature1|2 model points. If the set of application-specific model points is well defined or the "insert" use case is not common, then using hard-coded model point names is a good simplification.

- For non-application-specific modules, PIM recommends that modules use references to model points and not hard-code model point instance names.

Additional Model Point Features

The data model pattern assumes the following basic functionality for model points:

- Type safe (by the model point's value type)

- Atomic operations (e.g., read/write operations are thread safe)

- Change notifications

- Separate valid/invalid state from the model point's value

That said, nothing precludes you from including additional features into your data model framework. The only caveat is that the new functionality cannot violate any of the previously defined data model semantics. Here is a pseudocode snippet that is an example of a "minimal" model point class that holds an unsigned 32-bit integer:

```
#include "ModelPointSubscriber.h"
#include <stdint.h>

/** Model Point that holds a uint32_t value.  All methods on this class
    are thread safe.

    The Model Point's sequence number is used to track when the MP value's
    or valid state changes.  That is every time the MP value or valid state
    changes the MP's sequence number is incremented.  Note: The sequence
    number is a free running counter and it will 'roll over' once the max
    uint16_t value has been reached. However, the sequence number will
    never be zero.
 */
class PtUint32
{
```

```
public:
    // Constructor. Initialize the Model Point in its invalid state.
    PtUint32();

    // Constructor. Initialize the Model Point with an initial/valid value.
    PtUint32(uint32_t initialValue);

public:
    /** This method returns the model point's value via the 'dstData'
        argument and optionally returns the MP's sequence number (at the
        time of read operation) via the 'seqNumPtr' argument.

        The method returns the true if the model point value is a valid
        value.  When false is returned, the argument 'dstData' will not be
        updated.
    */
    bool read(uint32_t& dstData, uint16_t* seqNumPtr = 0) const;

    /** This method updates the model point's value to 'newValue'.  In
        addition this method sets the MP's valid state to true.

        The method returns the MP's sequence number after the 'newValue'
        has been applied.
     */
    uint16_t write(uint32_t newValue);

    /** This method puts the model point into the invalid state

        The method returns the MP's sequence number after being changed to
        the invalid state.
     */
    uint16_t setInvalidState();

    // This method returns true when the model point is the invalid state.
    bool isNotValid() const;

public:
    // Type specific subscriber
    typedef ModelPointSubscriber<PtUint32> Observer;
```

127

```
/** This method is used to register the 'observer' for a change
    notification when there is change in the MP's value or valid state.
    A change notification is generated when the 'observer' sequence
    number differs from the MP's sequence number.  When subscribing
    with an 'initialSeqNumber' set to 'SEQUENCE_NUMBER_UNKNOWN' the
    observer will receive an initial callback to provide it a
    starting-value for the MP.
 */
void attach(Observer& observer,
            uint16_t  initialSeqNumber = SEQUENCE_NUMBER_UNKNOWN);

/** This method is used to cancel a previous change notification
    subscription
 */
void detach(Observer& observer);
};
```

As examples of some possible extensions of a data model, the following list identifies some extended features used in the PIM example application:

- Serialization—The framework supports both binary and text-based serialization of a model point's value as well as any supporting metadata. The text serialization (which uses JSON formatting) is especially useful because it provides the infrastructure for reading and writing model point values and states from a command-line interface.

- Invalid codes—The framework supports application-defined invalid codes rather than a simple Boolean valid/invalid flag.

- Locking—This is where an entity can freeze or lock a model point's value, and all subsequent write operations to the model point's value will fail silently. This feature is especially helpful for testing scenarios such as when a tester injects (and locks) a "bad value" for a sensor output without disturbing the underlying driver to test the upper layer's error handling logic.

- Association of static data—The application can define and bind nonmutable information specific to each model point instance, such as valid data ranges, units of measure, symbolic names, and so on.

- Type information—The frameworks support each model point type having a unique (text base) type identifier. The type identifier facilitates dynamic discovery scenarios.

The following pseudocode snippet is an example of an "upsized" model point class that holds an unsigned 32-bit integer:

```
#include "ModelPointSubscriber.h"
#include <stdint.h>

/** Model Point that holds a uint32_t value.  All methods on this class
    are thread safe.

    The Model Point's sequence number is used to track when the MP value's
    or valid state changes.  That is every time the MP value or valid state
    changes the MP's sequence number is incremented.  Note: The sequence
    number is a free running counter and it will 'roll over' once the max
    uint16_t value has been reached. However, the sequence number will
    never be zero.
 */
class PtUint32
{
public:
    /// Options related to the Model Point's locked state
    enum LockRequest_T
    {
        eNO_REQUEST, /* No change in the MP's lock state is requested */
        eLOCK,       /* Request to lock the MP.  If the MP is already lock,
                        the request is ignored and the update operation
                        is completed */
        eUNLOCK,     /* Request to unlock the MP.  If the MP is already
                        unlocked - the request is ignored and the update
                        operation is completed */
    };
```

```
public:
    // Constructor. Initialize the Model Point in its invalid state.
    PtUint32( const char* modelPointName );

    // Constructor. Initialize the Model Point with an initial/valid value.
    PtUint32( const char* modelPointName, uint32_t initialValue);

    /// This method returns the model points name
    const char* getName() const;

public:
    /** This method returns the model point's value via the 'dstData'
        argument and optionally returns the MP's sequence number (at the
        time of read operation) via the 'seqNumPtr' argument.

        The method returns the true if the model point value is a valid
        value.  When false is returned, the argument 'dstData' will not be
        updated.
     */
    bool read(uint32_t& dstData, uint16_t* seqNumPtr = 0) const;

    /** This method updates the model point's value to 'newValue'.  In
        addition this method sets the MP's valid state to true.  The
        caller can optional lock, unlock, or maintain the current lock
        state when performing the write operation.  When a Model point
        is in the locked state all subsequent write operations (that have
        'lock' set to eNO_REQUEST) will silently fail.

        The method returns the MP's sequence number after the 'newValue'
        has been applied.
     */
    uint16_t write(uint32_t      newValue,
                   LockRequest_T lock= eNO_REQUEST);

    /** This method performs an atomic read-modify-write operation that
        increments the model points' value by 'count'.
```

   The method returns the MP's sequence number after the increment
   operation has occurred.
 */
uint16_t increment(uint32_t   count = 1,
                   LockRequest_T lock = eNO_REQUEST);

/** This method is similar to increment(), except that the model
   point's value is decremented.
 */
uint16_t decrement(uint32_t   count = 1,
                    LockRequest_T lock = eNO_REQUEST);

/** This method puts the model point into the invalid state

   The method returns the MP's sequence number after being changed to
   the invalid state.
 */
uint16_t setInvalidState(LockRequest_T lock = eNO_REQUEST);

// This method returns true when the model point is the invalid state.
bool isNotValid() const;

/** This method updates the lock state of the Model Point. Note: This
   method never triggers change notification(s).

   The method returns the MP's sequence number at the time of when
   then lock request was applied.
*/
uint16_t setLockState(LockRequest_T lockRequest);

/** This method does NOT alter the MP's data or state, but
   unconditionally triggers the MP change notification(s). The method
   returns the Model Point's sequence number after the method
   completes.
 */
uint16_t touch();

```
public:
    // Type specific subscriber
    typedef ModelPointSubscriber<PtUint32> Observer;

    /** This method is used to register the 'observer' for a change
        notification when there is change in the MP's value or valid state.
        A change notification is generated when the 'observer' sequence
        number differs from the MP's sequence number.  When subscribing
        with an 'initialSeqNumber' set to 'SEQUENCE_NUMBER_UNKNOWN' the
        observer will receive an initial callback to provide it a
        starting-value for the MP.
     */
    void attach(Observer& observer,
                uint16_t  initialSeqNumber = SEQUENCE_NUMBER_UNKNOWN);

    /** This method is used to cancel a previous change notification
        subscription
     */
    void detach(Observer& observer);

public:
    /** This method converts the Model Point's data to JSON string and
        copies the resultant string into 'dst'.  If the Model Point's data
        cannot be represented as a JSON object then the contents of 'dst'
        is set to an empty string and the method returns false; else the
        method returns true.

        If the converted string is larger than the memory allocated by
        'dst' then the string result in 'dst' will be truncated. The caller
        is required to check 'truncated' flag for the truncated scenario.

        Format:
        { "name":"<mpname>", "seqnum":nnnn,
          "valid":true|false, "locked":true|false, "val":<value> }
     */
    bool toJSON(char* dst, size_t dstSize, bool& truncated) const;

    /** This method attempts to convert the null terminated JSON formatted
```

'src' string to its binary format and copies the result to the Model Point's internal data. The expected JSON object/format is the same format as the toJSON() method.

If the conversion is successful true is returned; else false is returned.

The method optional returns - via 'retSequenceNumber' - the Model Point's sequence number after the conversion. If the method returns false then 'retSequenceNumber' has no meaning.

```
    */
    bool fromJSON( const char* src, uint16_t* retSequenceNumber = 0);
};
```

Model Points vs. Global Variables

Aren't model points, then, just global variables? And aren't global variables bad? Well, it depends. There are certainly good reasons to avoid global variables. Here is a partial list in no particular order of reasons why the global variable is the *bête noir* of programming:

- Non-CONST global variables are dangerous because their values can be changed at any time and there is no easy way for the developer to know when, how, or if this will happen.

- Global variables are not inherently thread safe.

- Clients have to spend time searching for all the places a global variable is referenced.

- Global variables can bring in hidden dependencies and make testing code in any predictable fashion extremely difficult.

- No module that depends upon a global variable can be closed against any other module that might write to that variable.

- Global variables pollute the standard namespace.

And, yes, from a compiler perspective, statically instantiated model points are global variables. But model point semantics are not traditional variables and therefore are not subject to the whole global-variables-are-bad argument. Here is a list of reasons why model points are good despite their similarities to global variables:

- The semantics of a model point instance is that it can be changed at any time, and there is never an assumption that its value has *not* been changed by some external entity.

- Model point types are required to be thread safe.

- While a developer may spend time searching for where a particular model point is used, this activity is done to understand how the application works. However, knowing every place a model point is used is not required to construct a module that will consume the model point instance.

- Model points only have a dependency on the data model framework, nothing more. That is, there are no hidden dependencies. In addition, using model points makes testing easier because the individual tests can control exactly when, and what, values are written to the model points.

- There are advantages to using hard-coded model points in modules; it greatly simplifies creating classes and modules because you don't have to propagate a bunch of model point references through initialization or constructor calls. Also, when using hard-coded model point names in modules that are application or project specific, there is little downside because these modules only need to be closed within the context of the application. And they are.

  For non-application-specific modules (e.g., a temperature driver), using hard-coded model point names is a bad thing. You should instead pass the necessary model point reference into the initialization or constructor call.

- The namespace issue can be resolved either by putting the model instances into their own namespace or by using a naming convention for model point names that avoids namespace collisions.

Model points, then, may be global variable-like, but they have sufficiently different semantics to exempt them from the don't-use-global-variables best practice. In some ways, it's similar to why `if-else` or `switch` constructs are okay to use even though they are technically just gussied up `goto` statements (and everyone knows `goto` statements are bad). The reason `if-else` and `switch` constructs are okay to use is that they provide syntactic cues that bound the `goto` actions. The same is true with model points: it may be "global data," but there are syntactic cues that their usage semantics are not that of traditional global variables.

CHAPTER 10

Finite State Machines

State machines, or finite state machines (FSM), are handy-dandy tools for providing a deterministic framework for your application to deal with asynchronous behaviors. These are things like

- Software timers

- Communication protocols

- Hardware interrupts

- User events

- Polled events

Here is a good, general-purpose definition of what a state machine is:

> *A finite-state machine (FSM) is a mathematical model of computation. It is an abstract machine that can be in exactly one of a finite number of states at any given time. The FSM can change from one state to another in response to some external inputs and/or when a condition is satisfied; the change from one state to another is called a transition. An FSM is defined by a list of its states, its initial state, and the conditions for each transition. (Wikipedia, citing Wang, Jiacun (2019). Formal Methods in Computer Science. CRC Press. p. 34. ISBN 978-1-4987-7532-8.)*

State machines can be drawn up as diagrams or as tables. State diagrams are very useful for understanding your application's operation, and state tables are very helpful in ensuring that every possible transition has been identified. But regardless of which format you use to describe your state machine—and you can use both—these documents should be included with your software architecture and design documents.

State machines can also be used to analyze and describe system behaviors. That is, their use is not limited to just a software design and implementation tool. For example, Figure 10-1 shows a state machine for the life cycle of a hypothetical IoT device.

© John T. Taylor, Wayne T. Taylor 2021
J. T. Taylor and W. T. Taylor, *Patterns in the Machine*,
https://doi.org/10.1007/978-1-4842-6440-9_10

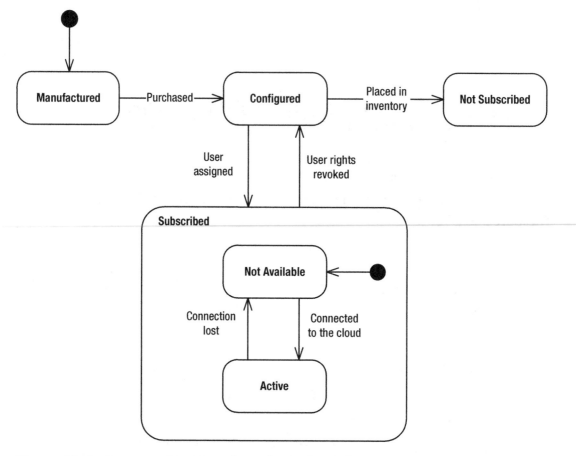

Figure 10-1. *State machine for a hypothetical IoT device*

If you are planning to implement a state machine directly in software, then you will want to take special care to ensure that your state diagrams conform to the syntax of one of the formal state machine definitions (e.g., UML, Harel, etc.). See Appendix B for a description of some UML state machine syntax.

Example of a Thermostat FSM

Figure 10-2 is an example of a simplified thermostat stage cycling state machine drawn up in UML syntax. It is a version of the example presented in Figure 2-7 that has some of the complexity removed to better illustrate the state machine mechanics.

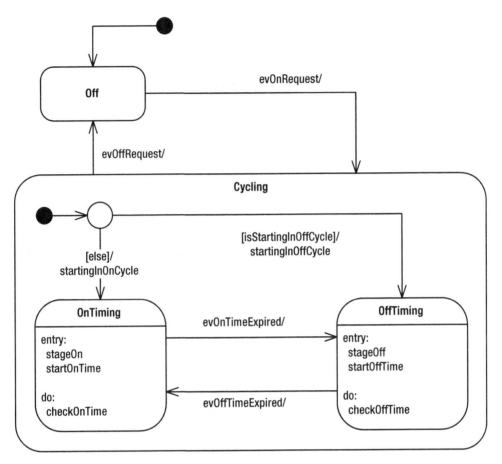

Figure 10-2. *Simplified HVAC stage cycling FSM*

The following table provides a brief description of the actions and guards in Figure 10-2.

Action/Guard	Description
stageOn	This action is responsible for turning the HVAC equipment on, i.e., actively condition the space.
stageOff	This action is responsible for turning off the HVAC equipment.
startingInOnCycle	This action provides for setup and initialization activities when cycling is started, specifically when the cycling is started in the "on cycle" state.

(*continued*)

Action/Guard	Description
startingInOffCycle	This action provides for setup and initialization activities when cycling is started, specifically when the cycling is started in the "off cycle" state.
startOnTime	This action is responsible for capturing the current or starting time for the duty cycle "on time."
startOffTime	This action is responsible for capturing the current or starting time for the duty cycle "off time."
checkOnTime	This action is responsible for calculating the duty cycle "on time." If the elapsed "on time" is greater than the newly calculated "on time," the action generates the evOnTimeExpired event.
checkOffTime	This action is responsible for calculating the duty cycle "off time." If the elapsed "off time" is greater than the newly calculated "off time," the action generates the evOffTimeExpired event.
isStartingInOffCycle	This guard is used to force the duty cycling to start either with an on cycle or an off cycle. The guard action reports the result of the policy decision of whether to start in the on or off cycle state; it is not responsible for making the policy decision.

The state machine is responsible for duty cycling a single stage of HVAC equipment where the duty cycle is a function of a PID controller output that is defined as

$$dutyCycle = \frac{onTime}{onTime + offTime}$$

This means the maximum PID output value maps to the stage always on: dutyCycle=1. A minimum PID output value maps to the stage always off: dutyCycle=0. The medium PID output value maps to the stage being on half of the time and off for the other half: dutyCycle=0.5. Because the PID output is constantly changing, the on and off times are continually re-recalculated. The state machine is executed periodically (at the same frequency as the PID controller) to process events and to run the "do" actions. The evOnRequest event is generated when the operator enables active HVAC conditioning. The evOffRequest event is generated when the operator disables active HVAC conditioning.

State Tables

Along with state diagrams, state tables can be used to describe an FSM. Table 10-1 is an example of Figure 10-3 rendered as a state table. As the behavior of your application will depend on both the event and the state of the machine when the event occurs, the columns of the table represent events, and the rows of the table represent states. The cells at the intersection of these rows and columns are where you define the application behavior. The initial/started state for the state machine is S1, and actionA is executed when the state machine is initialized.

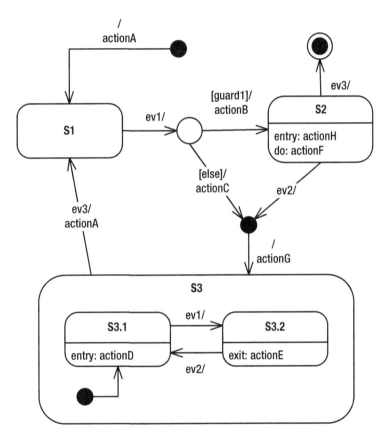

Figure 10-3. *State machine diagram*

Table 10-1. *Example state table*

Events/States	ev1	ev2	ev3	Notes
S1	guard1 is true -->S2 guard1 is false -->S3.1	ignored	ignored	When new state is S2: actionB and actionH are executed. When new state is S3.1: actionC, actionG, and actionD are executed.
S2	Ignored	S3.1	**FinalState**	When new state is S3.1: actionG and actionD are executed. While in S2, actionF is continually executed.
S3	Ignored	ignored	S1	When new state is S1: actionA is executed.
S3.1	S3.2	ignored	S1	When new state is S1: actionA is executed.
S3.2	ignored	S3.1	S1	When new state is S1: actionE and actionA are executed. When new state is S3.1: actionE and actionD are executed.

Design vs. Implementation

PIM strongly encourages the use of state machine diagrams in your design documentation. The process of drawing a valid state machine for handling asynchronous behavior is a good way to understand and visualize the problem space. In addition, the word *valid*, used earlier, means you need to evaluate—before implementation and testing—that all possible events are handled correctly in all possible states. This is a great way to make sure that all error conditions and edge cases have been accounted for. An edge case, for example, might be something like this: "what should happen when Event6 occurs in State2, which is not expected and is very unlikely, but is still physically possible?"

Even though PIM recommends that you create a valid state machine diagram, it does not mean the diagram needs to be implemented as a formally coded state machine. For example, consider the turnstile state machine discussed in Chapter 2. Figure 10-4 is a reproduction of that figure.

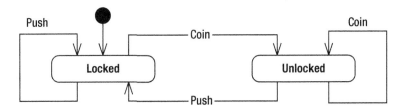

Figure 10-4. *State diagram for a turnstile*

Would it make sense to implement the preceding state machine using the canonical State pattern from the book *Design Patterns: Elements of Reusable Object-Oriented Software*? Or could the state machine be implemented as a simple collection of if/else statements? Assuming that you were using C++, to implement the Turnstile state machine using the State pattern would require at least the four classes illustrated in Figure 10-5.

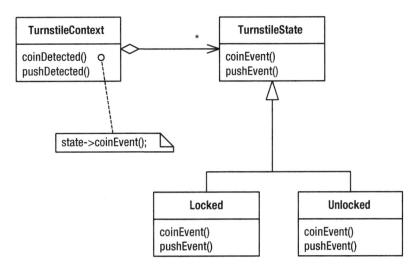

Figure 10-5. *Classes required to implement Turnstile as a formal State pattern*

However, it could also be implemented as a single class. For example, here is how a class called Turnstile might look:

```
class Turnstile
{
public:
    /// Constructor
    Turnstile() :m_locked( true ) {};

public:
    // This method is called when a Coin has been deposited into
    // the turnstile
    void coinDetected() {
        if ( m_locked ) {
            m_locked = false;
        }
    }

    // This method is called when the Turnstile has been pushed
    void pushDetected() {
        if ( !m_locked ) {
            m_locked = true;
        }
    }

protected:
    // My current state
    bool m_locked;
};
```

It is pretty clear, then, that a formal state machine implementation is overkill.

But the converse might also be true. For example, consider the PIM example thermostat application. To *not* implement the stage cycling mechanism of that application as a formal state machine is a train wreck waiting to happen.

When it comes to the actual implementation of a state machine diagram, it is a judgment call of the designer and developer on how to "best implement" a state machine diagram. If you are unsure on which way to go, err on the side of implementing a formal state machine. The reason is because as projects go on, and you learn more about the problem space or as requirements change, the tendency is to add more transitions, events, and states to your machine. And formal state machine implementations are better suited to handle these kinds of changes.

Code Generation Is a Good Thing

Let's talk some more about what a formal state machine implementation is. PIM's definition is a formal state machine implementation is one where your implementation uses a well-defined pattern such as the State pattern or perhaps function tables. You might also create the implementation with a code generator. Or you could do both. What is important here is that the pattern or code generator is not specific to a particular state machine instance, but that it is generalized for all state machine instances.

There can be a lot of boilerplate code when it comes to implementing a state machine diagram. The boilerplate is the code that manages how events, transitions, and actions are processed—that is, the mechanics of executing the state diagram. The "context" of the state diagram is where events are generated along with the contents of the action and guard methods. The ideal scenario is that you have a code generator that can consume a state machine diagram and spit out the execution portion of the diagram with interface definitions for the context. With this approach, the developer can focus on implementing the context instead of getting bogged down in writing the code for the boilerplate execution code. If such a tool is not available, the next best option is to have code templates or scripts that assist in generating the boilerplate code.

The worst-case scenario is where there are no state machine implementation guidelines or conventions, and the developer is responsible for hand crafting everything. This scenario opens up the possibility of the implementation not meeting formal state machine semantics. For example, the FSM definition states that a state machine can be in exactly one of a finite number of states at any given time. If the developer does not ensure, for example, run-to-completion semantics for event processing, then the "exactly one state" rule does not hold true. The run-to-completion semantics are easy to overlook or miss when you start your state machine implementation, especially where none of the state machine actions generate events (i.e., only external stimuli generate events).

However, if later you need to have a state action generate an event, but you did not implement run-to-completion semantics, you will not get the intended behavior of the state machine. And troubleshooting bugs that are the result of this violation of FSM semantics can be particularly challenging.

To summarize, then, code generation for finite state machines is good. Writing all the code from scratch is bad. Fortunately, there are several code generation options:

- Homegrown code templates, scripts, and code generators

- Third-party tools

  - Partial generation of just the execution code (e.g., Sinelabore)

  - Full generation of both execution and context code (e.g., IBM's Rhapsody tool)

When selecting a code generation tool, consider the following:

- Does the tool require an underlying runtime framework that the code generation is built on top of? In this situation, you will need to consider the footprint of the framework, that is, how much RAM and Flash is required.

- How does the tool manage memory? Some tools or frameworks require (or default to) a dynamic memory paradigm. For most embedded projects, dynamic memory allocation is undesirable.

- Can you immediately start drawing states and transitions? Or do you need to define and populate an underlying database with model and class structures? There are pros and cons to both ends of this spectrum; you just need to decide which paradigm best fits your team.

- Does the tool provide round-trip engineering? That is, if you edit auto-generated code, can those changes be discovered by the tool and incorporated into your state machine? Or, perhaps more fundamentally, is round-trip engineering even required or desirable? Generally, if a tool doesn't separate execution from context, then it could be desirable to have round-trip engineering.

I prefer using the low-cost drawing tool Cadifra and the code-generating tool Sinelabore. I then augment the output of these tools with my own homegrown scripts. Cadifra has no setup, configuration, or database; I can just start drawing states and transitions. Sinelabore consumes the output of various drawing tools (including Cadifra), which are UML state charts stored as XML documents, and generates the execution boilerplate code. The homegrown scripts are then used to massage the auto-generated output to provide header files that clearly define the context (i.e., to create an interface definition for all of the actions and guard methods). The scripts also provide the infrastructure for queuing state machine events so I can enforce the run-to-completion semantics for events. And because there is a separation between auto-generated execution code and the developer-supplied context, it means that there is never a need to edit the auto-generated files. Examples of what this approach looks like in real life are provided with the example thermostat source code. In the GitHub repository for PIM, look in the src/Storm/Equipment/Stage directory. The files of interest are

- genfsm.py—The script that invokes Sinelabore and then massages the output.

- Fsm.cdd—The Cadifra state diagram file.

- Fsm.pdf—A PDF illustration of the state diagram.

- Fsm_.cpp—The auto-generated "execution code" for the FSM. This is generated by Sinelabore and tweaked by the genfsm.py script.

- Fsm_ext_.h—Part of the output from the Sinelabore tool, which is in turn tweaked by the genfsm.py script.

- Fsm_trace_h—Part of the output from the Sinelabore tool, which is tweaked by the genfsm.py script.

- FsmContex_.h—The interface/class definition for the "context," that is, all of the actions and guards. This is generated by the genfsm.py script.

- FsmEventQueue_.h|.cpp—These files constitute the event queue for FSM events. This is generated by the genfsm.py script.

- BasicXYZ.h|.cpp—The remaining files provide the concrete "context" implementation. Note: There is more than one concrete context.

Tips, Hints, and Suggestions

Here are some tips, hints, and suggestions for designing and implementing finite state machines (in no particular order):

- Separate the context from the execution. In a perfect world, the context and execution code are in separate files. The benefits are

  - It is easier to understand the context. That is, you're not bogged down in the boilerplate code overhead of the diagram. For example, given the following hypothetical event and transition— `S1 -> ev1/actionA ->S2`—a developer needs to understand when and how `ev1` is generated and the contents of the `actionA` method. When the context is separated from the execution, this is straightforward and is not cluttered with the noise of the execution.

  - It allows for multiple instances of the same diagram with different contexts. For example, the PIM example's stage state machine (from Chapter 16) is used for both cooling and heating stages— that is, there are two different context implementations for the same execution diagram.

  - It simplifies auto-code generators because there is a clean separation of boilerplate code. That is, the execution and context definition are separated from the application-specific code, or the context implementation. Said another way, there is no need for your auto-code generator to support round-trip engineering.

- Events are required to have run-to-completion semantics. This means that if you start an action because an event was generated, and your action needs to generate new events, these new events cannot be processed until the current event completes. This oftentimes means implementing an event queue to capture pending events while processing the current event. Most of the time, this is only an issue when you are hand implementing state machines or you are creating your own code generator. As previously stated, violating the run-to-completion semantics is going to cause incorrect behavior that is usually intermittent and very hard to find and debug.

If there is any state where the state or a transition action can generate an event, you will need to create an event queue for that state machine. Even if you don't think you'll need it initially, you're probably still better off designing and implementing an event queue. Also, remember that when designing an event queue, you need to account for the queue overflow condition and define the application behavior when this happens.

- Guard methods should never have side effects. That is, if you are using C++, guard methods should be const methods. If you find yourself in a position where you need a guard method to have some overt action or side effect, this usually indicates that you should revisit your state machine design specifically to determine if you are missing actions or if the behavior has been modeled correctly.

- State chart semantics, for both UML and Harel, do not define or guarantee a processing order when you have multiple guards associated with a single-choice pseudo state. This means that the state machine author must define these guards such that one and only one of the guards will evaluate to true. In addition, the semantics of one and only one guard evaluating to true should be obvious when looking at the state chart (i.e., without having to review the implementation). The reason is because during the design phase, there is only the state chart—without an implementation—and the modeled behavior needs to be unambiguous.

- In addition to being very handy in modeling an event-driven behavior, the semantics of finite state machines also support both periodic behavior and a combination of event and periodic logic. The PIM example implementation of the stage FSM is event driven, but it is also executed at a periodic rate of once every two seconds to handle the processing logic related to calculating and expiring cycle times. Consequently, do not assume that only event or periodic logic is needed when developing your implementation patterns or code generators. You must support both. In my experience, it is common for the initial state machine design to be either exclusively event driven or exclusively periodic logic driven. But in many cases, over time, the design changes to require a combination of both event and periodic logic.

- All state machines can be described using a state chart or a state table. State charts are typically easier to read and understand. State tables are good for ensuring that modeled behavior has been fully captured because a state table requires that the behavior be considered for all states (or rows) for all defined events (or columns). In other words, it is easy to see if all the cells in the table have been filled in.

   When constructing state tables, it is often tempting to leave some cells blank when it seems obvious that "event X could never happen while in state Y." As a best practice in these situations, fill in each cell with a transition or explicit "ignore" or "can't-happen" markers. Even if you do not create a state table for every state machine as part of your design process, you still must consider what should happen in every state for all events.

- State chart semantics do not support events having arguments; they support events having guard methods, but not arguments. If the underlying application code passes "arguments" as part of the raw event generation, the context for the state machine is responsible for capturing the argument information and using that information either in action or the guard methods. In addition, you want to design your state chart such that the details of the underlying event argument information are not critical to reading and understanding the modeled behavior.

- Make all transitions in your state chart explicit. Avoid hiding transitional logic in the context code. For example, if an expired timer causes a transition from state A to state B, and a user event can also cause a transition from state A to state B, define both as discrete events. For example, Figure 10-6 shows how to handle multiple transitions.

Don't overload events

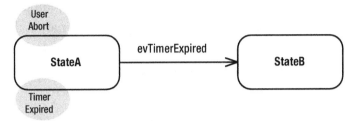

Define every event discretely

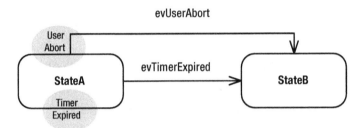

Figure 10-6. *Example of how not to overload events*

- By definition, a state machine diagram encapsulates history. For example, it may say that you can only get to State B if event Y occurred while in State A. Consequently, avoid having the context use internal variables or flags to remember previous conditions; these are essentially hidden states. It might be argued that exposing these hidden states can make the state chart unmanageable with respect to the number of states and transitions represented. If this scenario occurs, review your design to make sure you have a consistent level of abstraction in your state chart (i.e., you're not mixing high-, medium-, and low-level details into a single state chart). Only as a last resort should you go down the path of using internal variables to capture previous conditions.

- Name each state according to what is happening during the state or what is happening after the transition to the state has completed (e.g., "waiting for response"). If you have a lot of state names that end with -*ing*, you are on the right track. Do not name states as if they were actions. For example, `cycleEquipment` would be a poor state name choice; a better name would be `cyclingEquipment`.

- Guard names should be formed as questions that have yes or no answers (e.g., `isRetryAllowed`). Here are some names for the PIM example state FSM:

  - `isStartInOffCycle`

  - `isBeingSupplemented`

- Action names should be high level and describe what will happen. For example, it is better to name an action "`processResponse`" rather than a combination of "`parseResponseCommand`," "`lookUpResponseCommand`," and "`callResponseCallback`" actions.

CHAPTER 11

Documentation

PIM views documentation as a tool, not just a chore to be done to appease the process gods. Furthermore, documentation is more than just a record of what was designed and implemented; it is a development tool that adds value to any project by

- Providing a canonical reference

- Providing a higher level of abstraction for identifying, analyzing, and specifying solutions

- Providing a concrete medium for reviews

- Being easier and faster to rework than source code

- Bridging the gap between individuals and disciplines

- Providing training and onboarding materials

- Providing the basis for end user and support documentation

- Capturing the reasoning behind key decisions

By itself, a lack of documentation will not cause a project to fail. However, a lack of documentation compounded with other issues like people leaving the project, project leadership not providing technical oversight, insufficient test time, last-minute project staffing, volatile requirements, changing hardware, and such can cause a project to run significantly over budget and schedule. The reason is because without documentation, "the source code is the documentation," or rather "the source code is the *only* documentation." But source code is just too detailed, indirect, and difficult to derive ideas from—ideas like architecture, design, semantics, and requirements. Anyone looking for high-level information about the project is essentially forced to reverse engineer the code, which is often time consuming and painful for everyone involved. Not only is reverse engineering code a time sink, it is also prone to interpretation errors. Additionally, a lack of documentation is very much a technical debt, which jeopardizes the success of the next version of the project. (And there is always a next version of the project.)

© John T. Taylor, Wayne T. Taylor 2021
J. T. Taylor and W. T. Taylor, *Patterns in the Machine*,
https://doi.org/10.1007/978-1-4842-6440-9_11

By itself, an abundance of documentation will also not cause a project to fail. However, it can drive up the project's cost and extend the project's timeline with very little value add. As discussed in Chapter 2, there is a sweet spot, or Goldilocks amount, of documentation for a project. This sweet spot is different depending on the organization or industry, the templates that have been created, and the document control processes that are employed. And while formal documents are great, PIM encourages good content over formatting. That is, if you have a ten-page document with only two paragraphs of meaningful content, then something is wrong. Tools like a Wiki server, Microsoft's OneNote, and so on can be an effective way to capture content without getting bogged down in the formatting and the presentation details.

With PIM, the two cardinal rules for documentation are

- Document your header files
- Document first, then implement

Documenting Header Files

PIM considers header files to be "data sheets." In the header files, you want to summarize what the functions do, what the inputs and outputs are, and, most importantly, what the semantics of the functions are. The goal in PIM is to sufficiently document each header file to the point that developers do not have to search and reverse engineer the implementation to understand how to use the content of the header file. This is extremely important with highly decoupled designs because there may be more than one implementation for a given interface or class, and, because the implementations are decoupled, it is not always obvious where to find the actual implementations.

For example, in the PIM example code repository, there is an I/O abstraction for stream-based I/O (think Posix file descriptors). Part of the stream interface is an `isEos()` method that returns true if a stream being written or read has encountered an end-of-stream condition. There are over 20 different concrete implementations of this method depending on the platform, type of stream device (e.g., serial port, socket, file), and so on. So which of these implementations should a developer use as the "source of truth" for the semantics of the `isEos()` method? The answer is none of them. Out of sheer necessity, the canonical semantics needs to be documented in the `src/Cpl/Io/IsEos.h` header file.

The data sheet concept includes defining and capturing the semantics of the class or module. Unfortunately, on non-PIM inspired teams, developers rely on the implementation code to define the semantics; if anyone needs to know what the semantics are, they can reverse engineer the implementation. Sometimes the semantics are trivial or obvious, and other times even the original developer has trouble articulating the semantics.

The situation is further complicated when you need to sort out interface semantics from implementation semantics. For developers who want to follow the Liskov Substitution Principle—where consumers of a base class or interface can use objects of derived classes (i.e., an implementation of the class) without knowing it—how can those developers ensure their implementation faithfully implements the semantics of an interface if there is no natural language definition of the semantics? Furthermore, how can a developer correctly use an interface if the semantics have not been documented?

The code snippet in Figure 11-1 is from the `src/Cpl/System/Timer.h` header file and illustrates how semantics can be documented in header files.

```
/** This mostly concrete interface defines the operations that can be
    performed on a software timer. Software timers execute 'in-thread' in
    that all operations (start, timer expired callbacks, etc.) are
    performed in a single thread.

    Because the timer context (i.e. the timer owner), timer methods and
    callbacks all occur in the same thread, the timer context will never
    receive a timer expired callback AFTER the timer's stop() method has
    been called.

    NOTES:
        o The timer context must implement the following method:
          virtual void expired( void ) noexcept;

        o Because the timing source of an individual thread may NOT be a
          clean divider of the timer duration, the timer duration is taken
          as the minimum.  For example: if the timing source has a
          resolution of 20msec per count, and the timer duration on the
          start() timer call is 5 msec, then the timer will expire after
          the next full count, i.e. after 20msec, not 5msec.  IT IS THE
          APPLICATION'S RESPONSIBILITY TO MANAGE THE RESOLUTION OF THE
          TIMING SOURCES.
 */

class Timer:
{
public:
    /// Constructor
    Timer( TimerManager& timingSource );

    /**Constructor. Alternate constructor - that defers the assignment of
        the timing source
     */
    Timer();
```

Figure 11-1. *Example of documentation placed in header files*

```
public:
    /** Starts the timer with an initial count down count duration of
        'timerDurationInMilliseconds'.  If the timer is currently running,
        the timer is first stopped, and then restarted.
     */
    virtual void start( unsigned long timerDurationInMilliseconds );

    /** Stops the timer. It is okay to call stop() even after the timer has
        previously expired or explicitly stopped.
     */
    virtual void stop();

public:
    /** Callback notification of the timer's start time expiring. The
        Timer is placed in the stopped state when the start time expires.
        The Timer's 'Context' (aka a child class) is responsible for
        implementing this method.
     */
    virtual void expired( void ) = 0;

public:
    /** Sets the timing source.  This method CAN ONLY BE CALLED when the
        timer has never been started or it has been stopped
     */
    virtual void setTimingSource( TimerManager& timingSource );
};
```

Figure 11-1. (*continued*)

Do not duplicate comments between your header files and your .c|.cpp files. There should only be one true source, and that source needs to be your header files. This means comments describing a function belong in the header file, not in the .c|.cpp files. This does not mean, however, that the developer can leave all comments out of the .c|.cpp files; best practices for commenting inside of functions and methods should still be followed—just don't duplicate information. I have never encountered a situation where there were too many comments in a source code file. But I have encountered many, many source code files without any comments whatsoever.

If your development process includes the use of a documentation generator such as Doxygen, I recommend that you define the rules and coding standards related to the tool before any coding begins. In addition, the tool needs to be run frequently. If you implement the tool as part of your continuous integration, ensure that the tool runs without errors or warnings. This will help verify that the developers are following the documentation rules.

Document First, Then Implement

As a rule, software developers are documentation averse. Perhaps it's just human nature. But this tendency often leads to the anti-best practice of generating documentation after the coding has been completed. This anti-best practice is widespread across the entire development process from architecture and design to comments in the source code. While this approach may satisfy a project's deliverables and bring your work in line with the formal development process, it takes longer than if the documentation was done before the implementation. In fact, it negates much of the value add of creating documentation. Generating documentation is a tool for problem solving—that is, *it is a tool for figuring stuff out before writing code.* This applies to formal architecture and design documents as well as comments in the source code.

The reason creating documentation first is better and faster is because it is quicker and more efficient to iterate at the level of abstraction that human beings work best at—natural language and pictures. Consider that if you can't describe your design in natural language (with some supporting diagrams), how can you realistically expect to code it correctly? Or, if you can't describe it clearly, how can you expect someone else to understand your design? If you find yourself struggling to describe a feature in a design document, or struggling to write comments for a class, interface, or method, you probably need to go back to the drawing board because, at that point, any code you write almost certainly have to be redone or thrown out. To paraphrase Albert Einstein:

> *If you can't explain it simply, you don't understand it well enough ... [to code it].*

PIM recognizes that prototyping functionality is an important part of the development process. However, after you've got a particular bit of code working, don't keep going. Don't add enhancements or error handling. Rather, stop and create the documentation—especially the documentation that provides the context for where the newly working functionality exists, how it depends on operations that come before, or prepares for operations that are to come. In this way, PIM embraces just-in-time feature development, which includes the best practice of just-in-time documentation.

Finally, don't go overboard with a big bang approach where you document everything up front and then start coding. There are a few documents that I recommend you complete before jumping into implementation. However, when starting a new feature, story, or module, always do the problem-solving steps first which consist of items such as

- Creating the detailed design documentation

- Drawing the state chart, sequence diagram, timing diagram, and so on

- Fully defining and commenting the semantics of your header file content

After that, code away.

Documenting Your Development Process

PIM encourages generating a software development plan (SDP) at the start of a project before any design and implementation occurs. An SDP captures the details of the development process for the software team; in other words, it is the rules of engagement that the members of the development team will follow. For example, the SDP specifies what SCM and bug tracking systems will be used, what the SCM branching conventions are, how code reviews will be conducted, and so on. Creating the SDP is a vehicle for identifying and making decisions about how the software will be developed before you start development. In addition, all the developers on the team should have the opportunity to review the SDP and provide input before it is finalized.

The SDP is the kind of document that works well on a Wiki page because it is essentially just a glorified list of decisions, requirements, and constraints. Here are some examples of SDP content (in no particular order):

- SCM repository organization and locations

- SCM branching strategy

- Process models, for example, Agile, TDD, waterfall

- Coding standard requirements

- File organization

- Code review process

- Bug tracking and bug life cycle

- Build systems

- Unit test requirements

  - Manual

  - Automated

  - Code coverage

  - Unit test framework

- Continuous integration

- Build server

- CI builds

- Release builds

- Automated testing

- Release process and versioning

If you look at the preceding list, there is nothing in the list that requires "invention." It is simply capturing the stuff that the development team normally does on a daily basis. It is making the team's informal processes formal.

The value add of the SDP is that it eliminates many misunderstanding and miscommunication issues. It proactively addresses the "I didn't know I needed to …" problems that invariably occur when you have a bunch of people working together. This is especially true when a new team member is added to the project. A well-defined, and well-maintained, SDP is a great tool for transmitting key tribal knowledge to the new team member.

Document Your Software Architecture and Design

PIM recommends creating separate software architecture (SA) and software detailed design (SDD) documents. Chapter 5 describes what constitutes software architecture and what kinds of things need to be defined in that document. Along with the SDP, the software architecture document is the only other document that PIM prescribes be done at the start of the project.

The software detailed design document is a refinement of the SA document, bridging the gaps between the software requirements, the software architecture, and the source code. With the software architecture defined first, the SDD can be done just-in-time or on an agile story basis. Here are some examples of what is defined in an SDD (in no particular order):

- Design statements

- Class diagrams

- State charts

- Sequence diagrams

- Activity diagrams

- UI navigation

- Detailed algorithm definitions

- Memory and persistent storage layouts

- Communication protocols (commands, layers, framing, etc.)

- Error handling and reporting

- Logging (formats, media, priorities, severities, etc.)

- Alarm/alert management

- Driver model

- Scheduling (bare metal, RTOS, real-time performance, etc.)

Some additional things to consider when creating your SDD are

- Avoid including diagrams with no text explanations. Yes, a picture is worth a thousand words, but without supporting text, it might as well be a screensaver.

- Avoid duplicate information and details that are already captured in the SA document. This is a general best practice of making sure there is only one source for information.

- Avoid putting code fragments or header file details in the SDD because they will only be outdated once coding starts. For example, do not include class data members in your class diagram unless they are key to understanding the diagram. For code-level details (e.g., `typedefs`, `enums`, `structs`, etc.), use a documentation tool such as Doxygen that extracts comments from your code base as a companion document to the SDD.

Document Your Team's Best Practices

Whatever your organization's best practices are with respect to software development, they will need to be articulated and documented before you can expect the software team to follow them consistently. If your best practices are not documented, they do not exist. Well, technically, they do exist, but they exist as tribal knowledge. And the problems with tribal knowledge are that

- It can walk out the door.

- It is slow to propagate changes, refinements, and extensions of processes throughout the group, and it does so in an ad hoc manner.

- It is variable as it is open to individual interpretation and agendas.

- It is susceptible to misunderstandings that create confusion, rework, and delays.

As with the SDP, having your best practices formally documented sets clear expectations for developers, project managers, and management. Will your project fail if you don't document your best practices? No, but it will be a perpetual pain point throughout the project. Do you have to document best practices before you start a project? Ideally yes, but best practices are organic and evolve over time. While your project should initially allow time for the team to put best practices in writing, there should also be resources and time allocated in the middle and at the end of the project to keep them up to date.

CHAPTER 12

File Organization and Naming

Source code file organization is very often done organically. That is, developers start writing code and organizing their files based on their immediate needs, which at the beginning of a project usually do not include unit tests or code reuse. Consequently, later in the project when code reuse for unit tests and functional simulators becomes an issue, changing these now rigid source code directory structures can be very painful.

Project and company-wide file organization planning that is done early and deliberately is a strategic best practice. A well-thought-out, consistent file organization not only facilitates code reuse and the creation and maintenance of unit tests but it is also critical to your ability to build multiple images and executables from your code base.

Organizing Files by Namespace

Here is PIM's recommended approach to file organization:

- Organize your files by component dependencies, not by project. That is, do not create your directory structure to reflect a top-down project decomposition. Rather, organize your code by namespaces where nested namespaces are reflected as subdirectories in their parent namespace directory. By having the dependencies reflected in the directory structure, it is a quick and visual sanity check to avoid undesired and cyclical dependencies.

© John T. Taylor, Wayne T. Taylor 2021
J. T. Taylor and W. T. Taylor, *Patterns in the Machine*,
https://doi.org/10.1007/978-1-4842-6440-9_12

The C programming language standard does not support namespaces. However, the concept of namespace can still be implemented with C by applying the following convention: with functions, types, enums, variable names, preprocessor symbols, etc., that appear in header files, prefix the namespace on the names. For example, for a hypothetical function `hello_world()` in the `Foo::Bar` namespace, the function name would be `Foo_Bar_hello_world()`. The `hello_world()` function definition would be in a header file in the directory `Foo/Bar/`. The prefixing rule does not apply to symbols that are exclusive to a single `.c` file (e.g., file static functions and variables).

For example, a quick review of the `#include` statements of your project might show incorrect dependencies for the following use cases:

- An application-independent driver that is including application-specific header files.

- A file that is including a header file from a direct subdirectory. Parent namespaces should never depend on child or nested namespaces. By doing so, you create a circular dependency.

- Cyclical dependencies manifest themselves in header file `#include` race conditions. That is, the compile fails because of the order of the `#include` statements. There should never be a required or magic order for your `#include` statements.

- Place header files and their corresponding `.c|.cpp` files in the same directory. Do not create separate `source/` and `include/` directories.

- Create non-namespace directories for organizational purposes. However, for this use case, I recommend that non-namespace directories be easily recognized as such. That is, start with a leading underscore. For example, the PIM example code uses the convention of one `_0test/` directory per namespace to group together the unit test files for a namespace (e.g., `Storm\Component\_0test`, `Storm\Dm\_0test`, etc.)

- Reference header files with a full path relative to the root of your source. This means that your #include for header files will contain the namespace information for each header file.

  By doing this, file names (header and .c|.cpp files) do not have to be globally unique. The file names only need to be unique within a given directory and namespace. Directories and namespaces are your friends when it comes to naming because they provide a simple mechanism for avoiding future naming collisions. Having to refactor code to fix a naming conflict is a result of tactical thinking.

Note   Not requiring globally unique .c|.cpp file names can potentially have an impact on your build scripts. It is not uncommon for build scripts and makefiles to put all of the generated object files into a single directory. (The default QT[1] build scripts are an example of this.) Make sure you construct your build scripts in a way that path information about where a source code file is located is not lost when generating and referencing derived objects.

Here is an example of organizing by namespace from the PIM example code. The following namespaces are organized into the directory structure shown in Figure 12-1. Non-namespace directories are identifiable by names that start with a leading underscore ("_").

- Storm
- Storm::Component
- Storm::Component::Equipment
- Storm::Component::Equipment::Stage
- Storm::Dm
- Storm::Thermostat

---

[1]QT is a cross-platform open source framework for creating graphical user interfaces. https://en.wikipedia.org/wiki/Qt_(software)

- Storm::Thermostat::Main

- Storm::Thermostat::SimHouse

- Storm::TShell

- Storm::Type

- Storm::Utils

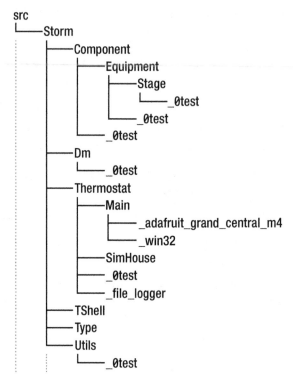

Figure 12-1. *Directory tree for namespaces*

Here is an example of the Storm/Component/AirFilterMonitor.h and Storm/Component/Equipment/Cooling.h header files with #include statements that contain the full namespace path:

File: Storm/Component/AirFilterMonitor.h
```
#include "Storm/Component/Base.h"
#include "Storm/Dm/MpSimpleAlarm.h"
#include "Storm/Dm/MpVirtualOutputs.h"
```

```
#include "Cpl/Dm/Mp/Uint32.h"
#include "Cpl/Dm/Mp/ElapsedPrecisionTime.h"
```

File: Storm/Component/Equipment/Cooling.h
```
#include "Storm/Component/Control.h"
#include "Storm/Component/Equipment/StageApi.h"
```

Organizing External Packages

While the previous section discussed best practices for organizing your source code, it did not mention how to manage the file organization for external source code. External source code (or packages) can be anything from purchased commercial software to open source projects to existing in-house code bases and libraries. Using external packages on your projects is a good thing; it is code reuse in action. However, it is also surprisingly difficult to do it right if you're not thinking strategically. If there is one and only one version of each external package over the entire life of your project (including maintenance and support), then it is easier. But if you have to manage different versions of external packages over time, or different versions concurrently, then things get messy, especially if you're trying to adhere to the OCP for both your source code and build scripts. (And PIM does consider build scripts to be "source code" when it comes to the OCP.)

Unfortunately, I don't have a best practice recommendation to solve this problem. I have a solution that I have used on many projects over the course of my career, but it is fundamentally flawed because it only works with projects that are infrequently released, which is typical for embedded projects. This infrequent release cadence can be attributed to the fact that releases of embedded software usually coincide with new hardware releases, which take longer to turn around than software releases.

Note   For a more in-depth discussion of how to manage external source code packages, see the "Outcast" section of Appendix E. This appendix also goes into a proposed, albeit work in progress, solution for package management that does not violate the OCP.

My solution is to include an xsrc/ directory that is a sibling to the src/ directory. Under the xsrc/ directory, there is a top-level subdirectory for each external package. The example source code on PIM's GitHub repository is organized this way. Figure 12-2 shows a simplified directory listing for the PIM repository.

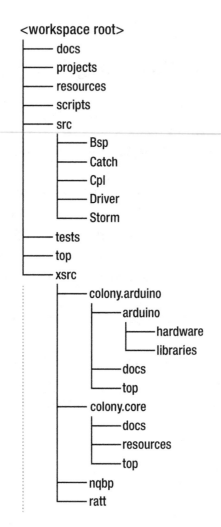

```
<workspace root>
├── docs
├── projects
├── resources
├── scripts
├── src
│       ├── Bsp
│       ├── Catch
│       ├── Cpl
│       ├── Driver
│       └── Storm
├── tests
├── top
└── xsrc
        ├── colony.arduino
        │       ├── arduino
        │       │       ├── hardware
        │       │       └── libraries
        │       ├── docs
        │       └── top
        ├── colony.core
        │       ├── docs
        │       ├── resources
        │       └── top
        ├── nqbp
        └── ratt
```

Figure 12-2. *xsrc tree listing from the PIM GitHub repository*

However, here's where things break down:

- How do you handle different or concurrent versions of packages?

- How are the different versions realized under the xsrc/ directory?

- What is the impact to the build scripts?

- What is the impact to #include statements in your in-house code?

- How do the #include statements in your in-house code reference files in an external package?

- Does one or more compiler search path options (-I) need to be added to the build script for each external package?

- Are your #include statements that reference external packages relative to the xsrc/ directory? If yes, what happens if you have multiple versions of the same package under the xsrc/ directory tree?

Naming

Just like file organization, naming conventions are a strategic best practice. PIM recommends that you define naming conventions that, at a minimum, provide protection against name collisions. This includes source code entities (class names, functions, preprocessor symbols, etc.) as well as file and directory naming conventions. The strategic goal for your naming conventions is to prevent future name collisions and to facilitate future source code reuse.

I worked on a telecom project that used a well-known RTOS for its operating system. Since our target hardware was not one of the prepackaged BSPs, we had to create our own BSP using the RTOS vendor's SDK. We kept having intermittent failures that were tracked down to our BSP, but we couldn't isolate the actual root cause. Finally, we discovered that the vendor's SDK contained a preprocessor macro called m_data, and we also had a variable in our custom BSP code named m_data. The net result was that while our BSP code compiled and linked, the runtime behavior was incorrect because of the macro expansion of the vendor's m_data macro. This is an example of a worst-case scenario of naming collisions. Typical naming collisions result in compile and link errors. However, fixing any naming collision requires modifying existing source code files, which PIM tries very hard to avoid.

Defining naming conventions will also draw you into a style conversation: uppercase vs. lowercase, camel case vs. snake case, and so on. This means that you will never get 100% agreement by the team members on a universal style for the project. Nevertheless, solicit input from the team when coming up with your naming conventions; then pick a single style and stick with it.

Naming Recommendations for C++

PIM's naming recommendations are slightly different depending on whether you are using C++ or C. Here are the naming recommendations for C++:

- Use namespaces and map your directory structure to your namespace structure (see "Organizing Files by Namespace" earlier).

- Namespaces and directories should have the same name and case. File names should have the same name and case as the primary class in the file. This simplifies finding source code files when you start with a symbol in the code. For example, using this convention, it would be simple to find the source code file that contains the method: Storm::Component::Equipment::IndoorHeating::reset().

- It would be in the file:

  src/Storm/Component/Equipment/IndoorHeating.h|.cpp.

- Typedefs and enums need to be encapsulated with namespaces or classes. Here is an example of how you can encapsulate an enum in a class:

```
class Foo
{
public:
    /// Magic values for balance status
    enum Balance_T { eLEFT=-1, eEVEN=0, eRIGHT=1 };
...
};
```

- All preprocessor symbols in a header file should be prefixed with associated namespace and file names, for example:

  File: src/Storm/Component/OperatingMode.h
```
#ifndef Storm_Component_OperatingMode_h
#define Storm_Component_OperatingMode_h
...
```

```
/** This constant defines the negative cooling offset (in degrees
    'F) for preferring cooling operating mode over heating mode
 */
#ifndef OPTION_STORM_COMPONENT_OPERATING_MODE_COOLING_OFFSET
#define OPTION_STORM_COMPONENT_OPERATING_MODE_COOLING_OFFSET 1.0F
#endif

...

#endif  // end header latch
```

File: src/Cpl/System/Trace.h

```
#define CPL_SYSTEM_TRACE_MSG(sect, var_args)   do { … } while(0)
```

Naming Recommendations for C

The C programming language standard does not support namespaces. However, the abstract concept of namespace can still be applied to C code. Conceptual namespaces are implemented as directories in your source code, and, in turn, this directory and file structure can be prefixed to all of the symbols in your header files. But this only applies to symbols in header files. For variables, functions, and macros that are exclusively scoped to a single file, you do not need to append any additional text.

Here is a hypothetical example of what a C implementation might look like. The Storm::Component::Equipment::IndoorHeating class would be defined as a set of data structures and functions in a file called src/Storm/Component/Equipment/IndoorHeating.h, which contains information that would look something like this:

```
#ifndef STORM_COMPONENT_EQUIPMENT_INDOORHEATING_H
#define STORM_COMPONENT_EQUIPMENT_INDOORHEATING_H

#include "Storm/Component/Control.h"
#include "Storm/Component/Equipment/StageApi.h"

/// Internal data for the Indoor Heating module
typedef
{
    StormComponentEquipement_StageApi_T* stage1;
    StormComponentEquipement_StageApi_T* stage2;
    StormComponentEquipement_StageApi_T* stage2;
} StormComponentEquipement_IndoorHeating_T;
```

```
/// Initialize the module
StormComponentEquipment_IndoorHeating_initialize
(
StormComponentEquipement_StageApi_T* instanceMemory,
...
);

/** This method will be called on a periodic basis (as determined by
    the calling Control Component instance) to perform active
    conditioning.
 */
bool StormComponentEquipment_IndoorHeating_executeActive
(
StormComponentEquipement_StageApi_T*    thisPtr,
StormComponentEquipment_Control_Args_T* args
);
...
#endif  // end header latch
```

Yes, the naming is very verbose in C. But, as I work on more C projects than C++, I can say from experience that you (and the team) will get used to it quickly. Additionally, with modern IDE's auto-completion features, there is not as much extra typing as you might think.

As in the preceding C++ example, all preprocessor symbols in a header file should be prefixed with their associated namespace and file names. This also includes enum values, because enum symbol values in C (defined in a header file) have a global scope.

For example, here is a problematic implementation that you will want to avoid:

```
/// Colors
typedef enum
{
eRED,           //!< eRED is a global symbol
eGREEN,
eBLUE
} Foo_Bar_Colors_T;
```

Instead, for the source file `src/Foo/Bar.h`, you should implement the enum as follows:

```
/// Colors
typedef enum
{
eFOO_BAR_COLORS_RED,    // eFOO_BAR_COLORS_RED is a global symbol,
                        // but has a unique name
eFOO_BAR_COLORS_GREEN,
eFOO_BAR_COLORS_BLUE
} Foo_Bar_Colors_T;
```

CHAPTER 13

More About Late Binding

As discussed earlier, one form of late binding is compile time binding. This is an abstraction technique that allows you to create different flavors of your project based on compile time settings. While it does add some additional complexity to the structure of your header files and build scripts, it also provides a reliable way to cleanly automate building multiple variants of your binary.

Two patterns that you can implement in your code to facilitate building different versions are LHeader and LConfig.

LHeader

With the Late Header, or LHeader, pattern, you defer which header files are actually included until compile time. In this way, the name bindings don't occur until compile time. This decoupling makes the module more independent and reusable, and it simplifies the construction of unit tests. The original motivation for creating the LHeader pattern was to create compiler- or platform-independent C code without using #ifdef/#else constructs in the source code files for each different platform that the source code is compiled for. The principle mechanism for this pattern is the C/C++ compiler's header search path options.

The LHeader pattern has four major components to it:

1. When creating a source code file, use a "naked" #include statement that references a header file that does not resolve to any header file in the baseline set of header search file paths. The file that is ultimately included at compile time is responsible for resolving the deferred name bindings in the source file, for example:

```
#include "colony_map.h" // Note: no path specified
```

© John T. Taylor, Wayne T. Taylor 2021
J. T. Taylor and W. T. Taylor, *Patterns in the Machine*,
https://doi.org/10.1007/978-1-4842-6440-9_13

2. Deferred name bindings are created by defining a preprocessor symbol that maps to another, yet to be resolved, symbol name, for example:

```
/** Defer the definition of the raw mutex type to the
    application's 'platform'
 */
#define Cpl_System_Mutex_T          Cpl_System_Mutex_T_MAP
```

3. Then on a per-project basis (or a per-unit test basis), a project-specific search path is added that allows the partial #include reference to be resolved to a project-specific instance of the header file name. For example, when building with the Visual Studio compiler, you can specify the compiler header search path using the -I command-line option. Here are the compiler header search paths that are used for building the PIM example thermostat application simulator. In this example, project\ Storm\Thermostat\simulation\windows\vc12 is the build directory.

```
-I\_workspaces\zoe\pim\src
```

```
-I\_workspaces\zoe\pim\projects\Storm\Thermostat\simulation\
windows\vc12
```

4. A per-project header file is created that resolves the deferred name bindings. Here is an example of the colony_map.h file located in the project\Storm\Thermostat\simulation\windows\vc12 directory. The file's content is

```
// strapi mapping
#include "Cpl/Text/_mappings/_vc12/strapi.h"

// Cpl::System mappings
#include "Cpl/System/Win32/mappings_.h"
```

The #include statements in the colony_map.h header file pull in specific mappings that resolve the Cpl::Text and Cpl::System interfaces. Here is an example of the Cpl/Text/strapi.h file:

```
/** Same as strcasecmp, but only compares up to 'n' bytes.  It has
    the same semantics as strncmp.

    Prototype:
        int strncasecmp(const char *s1, const char *s2, size_t n);
 */
#define strncasecmp             strncasecmp_MAP
```

And Cpl/Text/_mappings/_vc12/strapi.h resolves the mapping when building with the Visual Studio compiler.

```
#define strcasecmp_MAP          _stricmp
```

Implementation Example

The Colony.core C++ library implements the LHeader pattern for deferring the concrete mutex type. It relies on the PIM best practices for file organization and #include best practices.

1. The header file name colony_map.h is a reserved header file name. No other module, class, interface, and so on can use this file name.

2. Per PIM's recommended #include best practices, all #include statements are relative to the src/ directory. That is, path information is always part of #include statements. This means that there will not be an unintentional inclusion of the colony_map.h file.

3. The colony.* repositories use the NQBP build system. A feature of the NQBP build system is that all projects and unit test builds are performed in separate directory trees from the src/ directory tree. Each project and unit test build script is customized by adding its build directory—the directory where the executable image is

compiled and linked—to the compiler's header search path. This provides a unique per-project header search path. See Chapter 16 for additional details on NQBP.

4.   An instance of the colony_map.h header file is placed in each of the preceding build directories. The content of each colony_map.h header is a collection of #include statements (that reference files under the src/ tree) that resolve the deferred name binding.

The src/Cpl/System/Mutex.h header file defines a concrete mutex that has deferred binding.

```
#ifndef Cpl_System_Mutex_h_
#define Cpl_System_Mutex_h_

#include "colony_map.h"

/** Defer the definition of the a raw mutex type to the application's
    'platform'
 */
#define Cpl_System_Mutex_T              Cpl_System_Mutex_T_MAP
...
#endif // end Header latch
```

Figure 13-1 illustrates how the deferred name binding is resolved. The project build script has the following common header search paths.

```
-I\_workspaces\zoe\pim\projects\Storm\Thermostat\simulation\windows\vc12
-I\_workspaces\zoe\pim\src


pim/projects
└─Storm
   └─Thermostat
      ├─adafruit-grand-central-m4      // Target build
      │  └─windows
      │     └─gcc
      │        colony_map.h            // #include "Cpl/System/FreeRTOS/mappings_.h"
      └─simulation
         ├─linux                       // Linux simulator
         │  └─gcc
         │     colony_map.h            // #include "Cpl/System/Posix/mappings_.h"
         └─windows                     // Windows simulator
            └─vc12
               colony_map.h            // #include "Cp l/System/Win32/mappings_.h"
pim/src
├─Bsp
├─Cpl
│  ├─Checksum
│  ├─Container
│  ├─Dm
│  ├─Io
│  ├─Itc
│  ├─Json
│  ├─Math
│  ├─Memory
│  ├─Persistent
│  ├─System
│  │     Mutex.h                       // #include "colony_map.h"
│  │  ├─BareMetal
│  │  │  mappings_.h                   // #define Cpl_System_Mutex_T_MAP  int
│  │  ├─Cpp11
│  │  │  mappings_.h                   // #define Cpl_System_Mutex_T_MAP
│  │  │                                // std::recursive_mutex
│  │  ├─FreeRTOS
│  │  │  mappings_.h                   // #define Cpl_System_Mutex_T_MAP
│  │  │                                // SemaphoreHandle_t
│  │  ├─Posix
│  │  │  mappings_.h                   // #define Cpl_System_Mutex_T_MAP
│  │  │                                // pthread_mutex_t
│  │  └─Win32
│  │     mappings_.h                   // #define Cpl_System_Mutex_T_MAP
│  │                                   // CRITICAL_SECTION
│  ├─Text
│  ├─TShell
│  └─Type
└─Driver
```

Figure 13-1. *PIM project/ and src/ directory listing*

Caveat Implementor

The preceding implementation works well most of the time. Where it breaks down is when interface A defers a type definition using the LHeader pattern and interface B also defers a type definition using the LHeader pattern and interface B has a dependency on interface A. This use case results in a cyclic header include scenario, and the compile will fail. If you are using C++, this use case typically does not occur. However, when using PIM with C code, you will run into it—though it is not a frequent occurrence. When this use case is encountered in either C++ or C, the following constraints are imposed:

1. The project-specific reserved header file (e.g., `colony_map.h`) shall only contain #include statements to other header files. Furthermore, this reserved header file (e.g., `colony_map.h`) shall *not* have a header latch (i.e., no `#ifndef MY_HEADER_FILE` construct at the top or bottom of the header file).

2. The header files, which are included by the project-specific `colony_map.h` header file and which resolve the name bindings, shall have an additional symbol check in their header latch. The additional symbol check is for the header latch symbol of the module file that originally declared the name whose binding is being deferred. For example, the extra symbol check for the `pim/src/Cpl/System/Win32/mappings.h` file would be

```
// Header latch symbol from the Mutex interface
#ifdef  Cpl_System_Mutex_h_

// Traditional header latch for my file
#ifndef Cpl_System_Win32_mappings_h_
#define Cpl_System_Win32_mappings_h_
...
#endif // end header latch
#endif // end interface latch
```

The conventions described earlier are only required when there are nested deferred typedefs. In the example code, the actual `Cpl/System/Win32/mappings.h` header file does not use the extra interface latch because none of the `Cpl::System` interfaces have nested deferred typedefs. Nevertheless, it is recommended that you always follow the "no header latch in the reserved header file" rule. It has a minimal downside, and if you do find yourself with nested deferred typedefs, you won't get frustrated with failed compiles because you forgot to remove the header latch in the reserved header file. Diagnosing compile time failures due to cyclic header `#include` statements is usually very frustrating; it is something you want to avoid.

LConfig

The Late Config, or LConfig, pattern is a specialized case of the LHeader pattern that is used exclusively for configuration. The LConfig pattern provides for project-specific header files that contain preprocessor directives or symbol definitions that customize the default behavior of the source code.

The LConfig pattern uses a globally unique header file name, and it relies on a per-project unique header search path to select a project-specific configuration. That is, it uses the same basic mechanisms as the LHeader pattern; however, LConfig is not used for resolving deferred function and type name bindings. Configuration settings are settings that override defaults or magic constants and are used to enable or disable conditionally compiled code. The Colony.core C++ library uses the reserved file name `colony_config.h` for the LConfig pattern. The following are examples of the LConfig pattern:

Symbol definition in the src/ tree

```
#include "colony_config.h"     // LConfig pattern reserved header file

// Actual size value be overridden at compile using LConfig
#ifndef OPTION_FOO_BAR_MAX_BUFFER_SIZE
#define OPTION_FOO_BAR_MAX_BUFFER_SIZE     128
#endif
...
uint8_t my_buffer[OPTION_FOO_BAR_MAX_BUFFER_SIZE];
...
```

Configuration in the src/ tree

```
#include "colony_config.h"      // LConfig pattern reserved header file
...
// Defined in colony_config.h to enable tracing
#ifdef USE_CPL_SYSTEM_TRACE
...
#define CPL_SYSTEM_TRACE_MSG(sect, var_args)        do { ... } while(0)
...
#else
...
#define CPL_SYSTEM_TRACE_MSG(sect, var_args)
...
#endif // end USE_CPL_SYSTEM_TRACE
```

Example colony_config.h (in a project directory)

```
#ifndef COLONY_CONFIG_H
#define COLONY_CONFIG_H

// Make the buffer small to simply testing
#define OPTION_FOO_BAR_MAX_BUFFER_SIZE   5

// Enable tracing (for debugging my unit test)
#define USE_CPL_SYSTEM_TRACE

#endif
```

Because the LConfig pattern is only used to define magic constants and preprocessor directives for conditionally compiled code, it does not suffer from the potential circular header includes found in LHeader.

CHAPTER 14

Initialization and the Main Pattern

When your application runs, the initialization phase may be simple or very complex. Simple is where all of your code can start at any time regardless of what else may or may not have started. Complex is where the initialization of a module may depend on another module already being started.

Here is a hypothetical example. If you were working with three modules—power-on self-tests, a nonvolatile RAM driver, and a logging sub-system—the desired start-up sequence would be

1) Power on the self-tests (POST).

2) Start the nonvolatile RAM driver.

3) Start the logging module.

Figure 14-1 is an illustration of how this would look.

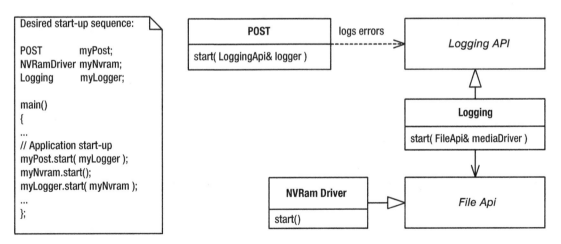

Figure 14-1. *Example of a start-up order*

© John T. Taylor, Wayne T. Taylor 2021
J. T. Taylor and W. T. Taylor, *Patterns in the Machine*,
https://doi.org/10.1007/978-1-4842-6440-9_14

The challenge here is that the power-on self-test will want to report errors and warnings using the logging sub-system. This is a "chicken or egg" situation because the power-on self-test module executes before the logging module has been started, and the logging module cannot be started until the nonvolatile RAM driver has been started.

One solution would be to initialize each of the three modules "just enough" so they can be referenced or used by the other modules without crashing. This would be followed by a second start-up phase that fully initializes each module. For example, in this scenario, the first initialization step of the logger module would be to initialize its internal buffers so that it can cache and accept log entries, but it would not attempt to write the log entries to the nonvolatile media. The second start-up phase of the logger module would then finish the initialization and begin writing log entries to the nonvolatile media. This would include any log entries buffered between the first and second initialization steps. This is illustrated in Figure 14-2.

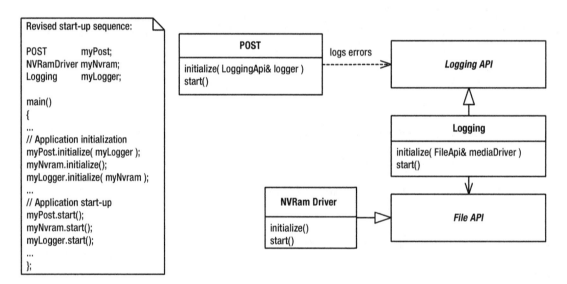

Figure 14-2. *Two-phase start-up example*

While this example is somewhat contrived, it is meant to illustrate the start-up dependencies your application modules can have on your sub-systems. For real-world projects, the start-up sequence gets even more complicated if the application is a multi-threaded application. The issues you might encounter with multi-threaded applications are

- You need to initialize a module or sub-system before the thread scheduler is enabled. This would be the initialization that occurs when the application is running as a single thread and interrupts have been disabled.

- You need to initialize a module or sub-system after the thread scheduler is enabled and interrupts are enabled. And the initialization needs to occur in the thread that the module or sub-system executes in.

Things can also get complicated if you are using C++, and you need to statically allocate one or more objects. Issues you might encounter with C++ statically allocated objects are

- Statically allocated C++ objects have their constructors execute as part of the C++/C start-up runtime code. This means the constructors execute before main() is called. In addition, the destructors for these objects execute after main() exits. Since PIM strongly discourages dynamic memory, a PIM application will have many statically allocated C++ objects.

- The C++ standard does not guarantee these statically allocated objects will be created in any specific order. The C++ standard also does not guarantee the destructors will execute in any particular order.

- The underlying operating system and other system services may not be available till after main() begins executing. For example, the BSP code for the PIM thermostat application example, running on the Arduino hardware, initializes the Arduino framework and starts FreeRTOS in main(). All this happens after the constructors for the statically allocated objects have executed.

Staged Initialization

To address these various start-up issues, PIM recommends the following:

- For C++ code, constructor methods should not call or use methods of other objects and should not make any OSAL or system service calls. The role of the constructor should be restricted to initializing member variables, which includes storing references and pointers to other classes that are passed as constructor arguments. In the following example, if the instances of both the Foo and Bar classes are statically allocated, it would yield an error. The problem is that while it may appear to run fine using one compiler, it may crash with a different compiler. Or, it might run fine the first couple of times you compile, but as more statically allocated objects are created (i.e., there is a change in the order that the compiler creates static objects), then it will crash.

```cpp
class Foo
{
public:
    /// Constructor
    Foo() { ... }

    /// Reset the instance to its initial state
    void reset() { ... }
};

class Bar
{
public:
    /// Constructor
    Bar( Foo& helper ) :m_helper( helper )  // Save the reference
    {
        m_helper.reset();   // POTENTIAL ERROR;
    }
```

```
protected:
    /// Reference to my helper object
    Foo& m_helper;
};
```

To ensure that the Bar object always runs correctly when statically allocated, Bar needs an additional method that would be called after main() begins to execute in order to complete all of the initialization required by Bar. This extra method is shown here in bold:

```
class Bar
{
public:
    /// Constructor
    Bar( Foo& helper ) :m_helper( helper )  // Save the reference
    {
    }

    /// Reset the instance to its initial state
    void reset() { m_helper.reset(); ... } // Safe to reset my
                                           // helper object

protected:
    /// Reference to my helper object
    Foo& m_helper;
};
```

The exception to this recommendation is when an object self-registers itself with a container or another entity in its constructor. For example, in the Colony.core C++ library, model points self-register themselves into a model point database. The registration mechanism works whether the object was statically allocated or allocated from heap after `main()` began executing. The details of how to make this C++ magic work with statically allocated objects have to do with how the compiler initializes the BSS segment (which the C++ standard guarantees).[1] You can find several example objects self-registering with containers in the `Colony.core` C++ library.

- For multi-threaded applications, break up the initialization of modules and sub-systems into at least two phases. The first phase should run before multiple threads are running and interrupts are enabled. The second phase should run later in the context of the module or sub-system's thread. Each initialization phase should also have corresponding stop or shutdown methods. PIM recommends that you define a naming convention for these various initialization methods to make it obvious to developers the context of when these methods should be used. For example:

  - Use `initialize()` for initialization that is performed before the thread scheduler and interrupts are enabled.

---

[1] The BSS segment, which contains all uninitialized static data, including the memory for statically allocated C++ objects, is guaranteed by the compiler to be initialized to all zeros. This initialization happens before the C++ constructors for the statically allocated objects execute. This means that if the logic for a C++ constructor were to initialize all of its data to all zeros, then that object would already be in the "proper state" before the constructor is executed. The implementation of the container classes in the Colony.core C++ library sets all of their member data to zero when they are constructed. In addition, each container class has a constructor with a unique argument signature that does not initialize any of its data. That is, it relies on the BSS initialization for proper initialization. This constructor is used specifically for creating statically allocated container instances. In turn, this allows other statically created object instances to successfully add themselves to a statically allocated container because constructor execution order is no longer an issue.

- Use the open() and close() for *triggering* the in-thread initialization and in-thread shutdown, respectively. These methods are actually synchronous inter-thread communication calls. This means the open() and close() methods are thread aware and are responsible for implementing the semantics of the inter-thread communication calls. (More on this later.)

- Use start() and stop() for *performing* in-thread initialization and in-thread shutdown, respectively. Unlike open() and close(), these methods have no thread awareness; that is, they assume that the caller is responsible for the correct thread context. For example, a sub-system has a single pair of open() and close() methods, and the sub-system's implementation of the open() and close() methods calls start() and stop() on its set of private modules that will execute in the same thread.

ALWAYS PAIR YOUR INITIALIZATION METHODS

An open() method should always have a corresponding close() method, even if there are no actions for the close() method to perform. As the application development continues, especially when following an agile or just-in-time development process, there is a good chance you will eventually have actions to perform with the close() method. Similarly, if you have a start() method, always have a stop() method.

If a module does not need one or more of the staged initialization steps, then don't implement it. However, consider the practice of "limiting operations in C++ constructors to ensure proper operation when an object is statically allocated" to be a must-follow best practice. But even then, if all objects are allocated from the heap during start-up, this practice can be skipped as well.

About Open/Close with Inter-thread Communication

For a multi-threaded device, there is always a certain amount of start-up and initialization that needs to occur in specific threads. For example, the PIM thermostat example application has the persistent storage sub-system run in its own thread. (This is the NVRAM thread. See the `Cpl::Persistent::RecordServer` class.) Part of the start-up of this sub-system requires registering for change notifications of the model points that are being persistently stored. The subscription mechanism for model points requires that subscriptions occur in the same thread where the "callbacks" will occur (i.e., the thread that the change notification executes in). What this means is the persistent storage sub-system has start-up code that has to execute in the NVRAM thread.

The aforementioned open/close methods are synchronous ITC calls where messages are sent from the main thread—the thread that is managing the overall start-up of the system—to the NVRAM thread. When the main thread calls the open() method, an ITC message is placed into the NVRAM thread's ITC message queue, and the NVRAM thread is signaled to wake up. The NVRAM thread then wakes up and dispatches the "open" message (that calls the persistent storage sub-system) to process the message while executing in the NVRAM thread. After the persistent storage sub-system completes its initialization, it returns the ITC message back to the main thread. Because the open ITC message is synchronous, the main thread blocks until the ITC message has been returned (from the NVRAM thread). The synchronous semantics are important here for start-up because they allow the main thread to sequentially complete the initialization of a module or sub-system before moving on to the next one. This means that once the open() call to Module A completes (i.e., the main thread unblocks and resumes execution), the system can assume Module A is fully started and is ready for use.

The close() call is the inverse of the open() call. That is, it allows for a graceful shutdown of a module or sub-system. In the case of the PIM thermostat example, with the persistent storage sub-system, the close() method is used to unsubscribe from the model point change notifications. The close() ITC calls also have synchronous ITC semantics, which means when the close() call to Module A completes, the system can assume that Module A is fully shut down.

Figure 14-3 illustrates a generalized example using open/close ITC calls to perform an in-thread start-up and shutdown of a module.

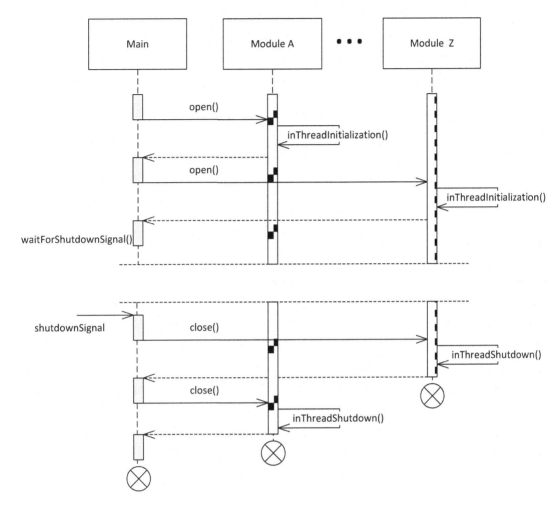

Figure 14-3. *ITC start-up/shutdown sequence*

Main Pattern

The Main pattern states that an application is built by wiring together independent components and modules. The Main pattern consists of

- The resolution of interface references with concrete implementations.

- The initialization and shutdown sequencing.

- The optional sequencing (or runtime execution) of a set of components and modules. The "set of components and modules" can be the entire application, a sub-system, a feature, or any combination thereof.

Typically, the Main pattern is also responsible for the creation of the components and modules that are being wired together. There are two variants of the Main pattern: Main minor and Main major. Main minor is when the Main pattern is applied to a feature or sub-system. Main major is when the Main pattern is applied to creating an application.

Main Minor

To start, consider the Main pattern when it is applied to a feature or a sub-system. I call this Main minor. Figure 14-4 is a high-level class diagram for the `Storm::Thermostat::Algorithm` class, and the `Algorithm` class is the implementation of the Main minor pattern for the HVAC control algorithm feature.

So do you need to use the term "Main" in your classes or namespace when using the Main patterns? No, there is no requirement to use the name "main" anywhere. That said, for the Main minor variant, I recommend using the name of the feature or sub-system for the namespace that contains the implementation classes and files. For the Main major variant, I recommend creating a namespace of "Main" to contain the implementation classes and files.

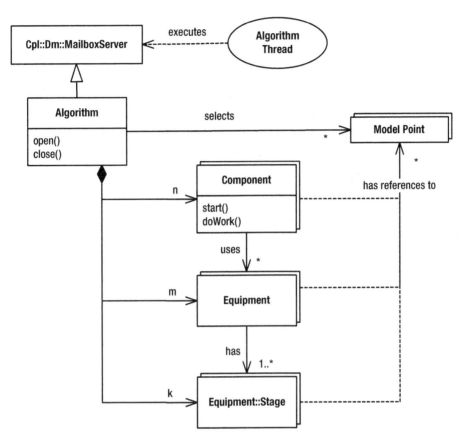

Figure 14-4. *Example of a control algorithm*

The algorithm class in Figure 14-4 does the following:

- It creates a collection of control objects, that is, the Component, Equipment, and Equipment::Stage instances.

- It wires together the control objects by providing model point and control object references.

- It performs the initialization sequence for the control objects.

- It manages and defines the runtime execution order for the control objects. The control objects are executed periodically (every two seconds) in a specific order.

The algorithm class is extremely specific in that it supports the following HVAC configurations:

- Single-stage air conditioner with a furnace (up to three stages of heat)

- Stand-alone furnace (up to three stages of heat)

If you wanted to support other HVAC configurations, a different algorithm class would need to be created that supports additional/different HVAC configurations.

All of the `Component`, the `Equipment`, and the `Equipment::Stage` classes take references to model points in their constructors. Since the algorithm class creates these objects, it contains the knowledge of which model points need to be passed to which control object. Figure 14-5 shows the model point references for each control object.

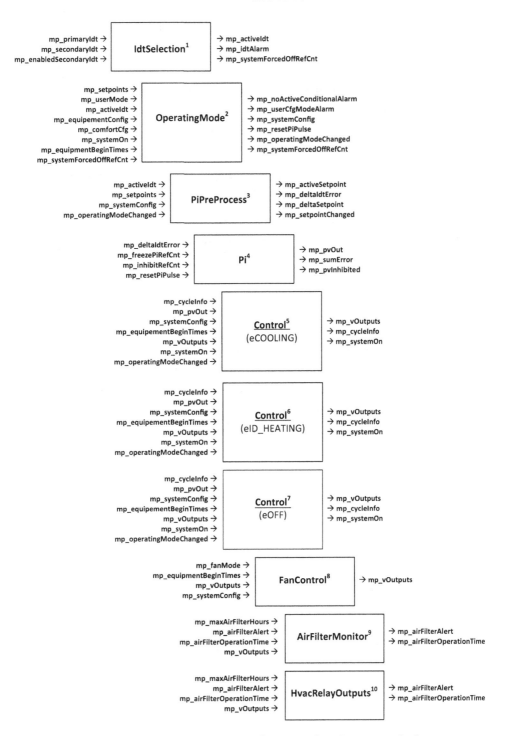

Figure 14-5. *Input/output model point references for the control objects*

In Figure 14-5, the order of execution is indicated by a superscript number in each class. If there are changes to the algorithm design, then the number of control objects, or the ordering of execution, or model point references may change. For example, you may need to add a new control class or instance that supports using a heat pump. What does not change, however, are the existing individual control classes.

The algorithm class is dependent on all of the individual control classes and specific model point instances, but it does not have any platform dependencies. When implementing a Main minor pattern, it is desirable to not have platform dependencies. However, if it makes sense to have platform dependencies in your Main minor pattern, then do so. The downside is that the feature or sub-system is now restricted to a certain platform, which may be incompatible with automated unit tests and a functional simulator.

Main Major

In Chapter 7, I introduced the concept of using the Main pattern to reuse application code to create something like a functional simulator. This is a use case for Main major, the pattern that is intended to bind all of the application's platform-independent code to a specific platform. Figure 14-6 shows the relationships between platform-independent code (and who creates them) for a specific platform.

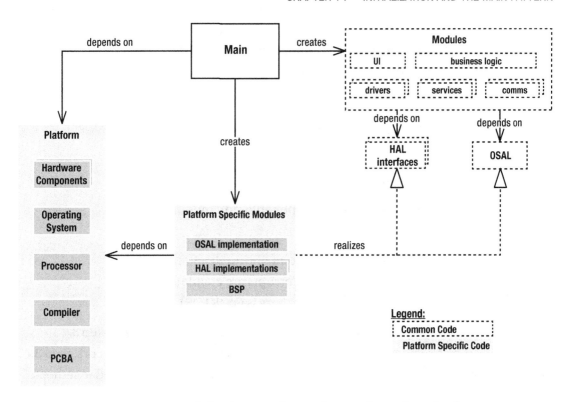

Figure 14-6. *Integration of platform-independent code with a platform*

So this is great in theory. But how do you go from the diagram to implementation? In practice, some of the platform-specific bindings will be done at compile or link time. These bindings are not explicitly part of the Main major pattern. The Main major pattern only addresses runtime creation and initialization.

It might be helpful at this point to briefly review how an embedded application gets executed. The following sequence assumes the application is running on a microcontroller:

1. The interrupt service routine for the reset vector is executed.

2. The compiler included C/C++ runtime code executes. This includes items such as initialization of static variables, execution of constructors for statically allocated C++ objects, and potentially some minimal board initialization.

3. The main() function is called. When and what happens in the main() function is obviously application specific. However, in general terms, the following actions occur:

   a. All remaining board, or BSP, initialization is completed.

   b. The OS/RTOS is initialized. The thread scheduler may or may not be started at this time.

   c. Control is turned over to the application.

   d. The various sub-systems, components, and modules are initialized and started.

   e. The application runs. At this point, the application is fully constructed and initialized, interrupts are enabled, and the thread scheduler is running (if there is OS/RTOS).

In the preceding sequence, the Main major pattern comes into play in step 3. Steps 3.a and 3.b are where all of the platform creation and initialization occurs. Step 3.c is where the application's sub-systems, components, and modules are wired together. What this means is that all of the code required for steps 3.a and 3.b should be separated from step 3.c because 3.a and 3.b are highly platform dependent, and there is a minimal value in trying to reuse this start-up code.

However, for step 3.c, there is value in having a common application start-up across different platforms, especially as the amount and complexity of the application start-up code increases. The tricky part is that even for step 3.c, there are still platform-specific dependencies. The easiest approach to solving these platform dependencies is to use link time bindings. Figure 14-7 shows high-level pseudocode for how the Main major pattern is implemented for the PIM thermostat application running on the target hardware and as a functional simulator under a PC.

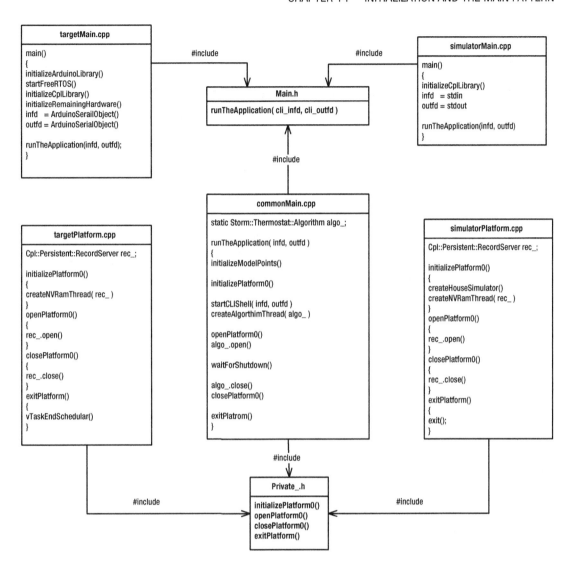

Figure 14-7. *Pseudocode for a Main major pattern implementation*

Because the thermostat example is relatively simple (i.e., not a complete application), Figure 14-7 does not show how application-level components are wired together. The reason is because all of the wiring happens in the Storm::Thermostat::Algorithm class (i.e., a Main minor instance). You can add the necessary wiring logic to your commonMain.cpp file or defer the wiring to a "Main minor" such as the algorithm class or any combination thereof.

Table 14-1 shows where the files represented in Figure 14-7 exist in the PIM source code tree.

Table 14-1. *File locations in the PIM repository*

Diagram File	Actual File
targetMain.cpp	projects/Storm/Thermostat/adafruit-grand-central-m4/windows/gcc/main.cpp
simulatorMain.cpp	projects/Storm/Thermostat/simulation/windows|linux/main.cpp
commonMain.cpp	src/Storm/Thermostat/Main/Main.cpp
targetPlatform.cpp	src/Storm/Thermostat/Main/_adafruit-grand-central-m4/platform.cpp
simulatorPlatform.cpp	src/Storm/Thermostat/Main/_simulation/platform.cpp

## CHAPTER 15

More Best Practices

PIM is all about the benefits that come from incorporating best practices into your development process. Generally, the more best practices you follow, the easier your life is, and the better your chance of delivering your project on schedule. To that end, this chapter describes some best practices that will make your software development life easier and reduce the headaches along the way. I realize that there will be situations and technical considerations that may not allow you to follow these best practices, but do not ignore them.

What follows is something of a hodgepodge of topics that address some of the critical aspects of any embedded project.

Avoid Dynamic Memory Allocation

With embedded projects, using dynamic memory, or allocating memory from the heap, has the associated problems:

- Memory eventually is exhausted. This is potentially a problem with any software in any environment, but in the embedded projects, the memory heap is not only finite but extremely limited. If you're using dynamic memory, you need to ensure that your application can continue to run if an allocation function fails or is delayed indefinitely.

- Heap memory gets fragmented from repeated allocate and free operations. Even if there is enough total memory available for an allocation request, if there is not a contiguous block of free memory large enough for the allocate request, the call will fail.

- "Heap allocate" and "heap free" operations are nondeterministic. That is, the amount of time it takes to complete an allocate or free operation is not bounded in time, and the allocate operations have the possibility of failing.

© John T. Taylor, Wayne T. Taylor 2021
J. T. Taylor and W. T. Taylor, *Patterns in the Machine*,
https://doi.org/10.1007/978-1-4842-6440-9_15

Typically, most embedded devices are required to run days, months, years without a reset or a power cycle. Running your device for a couple of hours is unlikely to cause an allocate request to fail. However, running an application that uses dynamic memory for three months dramatically increases the probability of an allocate request failing due to fragmentation. For an embedded device that has real-time constraints, the nondeterminism of the dynamic heap operations is usually a nonstarter from the get-go.

All this leads to best practice of not using dynamic memory allocation. Well, technically, the best practice is do not use dynamic memory allocation after start-up of the application. It is okay to allocate memory from the heap at start-up, but not after the system is up and running. This practice guarantees the system will not fail over time due to lack of memory, and it avoids any issues with respect to real-time processing and the nondeterministic nature of the heap.

Not using dynamic memory allocation, however, does not mean you can't use dynamic objects. If the application needs dynamic objects, then the application should provide private pools of memory that are specific to the set of dynamic objects in question. By having private memory pools for a given set of objects, the application can ensure that these private pools do not fragment and that the amount of time the allocate and free operations take is well bounded. Many third-party frameworks and C++ libraries provide such functionality (including the Colony.core C++ library). However, since the private memory pools will have a fixed size (i.e., up to N objects can be allocated), there is still an issue of potentially running out of memory. Ensuring that the out-of-memory use case does not occur becomes a burden of the software architecture and the developers.

Another misconception about not using dynamic memory is that containers (linked lists, sorted lists, dictionaries, etc.) cannot be used or that the containers have to be fixed sizes. This is not true. Containers can be built using intrusive listing. Intrusive listing means that the individual elements that are put into the container contain all the overhead and metadata required by a container's linkage mechanism. In C++, this can be done via simple inheritance for the element types. In C, however, the burden of properly creating data structures that represent list items is placed on the developer (i.e., enforced only by convention).

The result of employing intrusive listing is containers that can hold an infinite number of elements (assuming infinite RAM). It also means that if an element exists, it can be inserted into the container without needing to allocate additional memory. A downside of the intrusive listing approach is that at any given time an individual element can be in, at most, one container. Fortunately, this use case does not come up often, and there are ways to resolve it (e.g., with the Proxy pattern[1]) without resorting to traditional containers that rely on dynamic memory allocation. The Colony.core C++ library makes extensive use of intrusive containers.

Documenting Header Files

PIM's best practice is that header files are "data sheets." Ideally, this means that a given header file documents the syntax, semantics, usage, and the dos and don'ts of the module or class in sufficient detail that the consumer of the header file can understand how to use it without reverse engineering the .c|.cpp files. (See Chapter 11 for an in-depth discussion on why this is a good thing.)

PIM recommends that you

- Fully document your header files. The following code snippet is from the src/Cpl/System/Timer.h header file and illustrates how to document the semantics, usage, constraints, thread behavior, and so on:

```
/** This mostly concrete interface defines the operations that can be
    performed on a software timer.  Software timers execute 'in-thread'
    in that all operations (start, timer expired callbacks, etc.) are
    performed in a single thread.

    Because the timer context (i.e. the timer owner),
    timer methods and callbacks all occur in the same thread, the
    timer context will never receive a timer expired callback AFTER
    the timer's stop() method has been called.
```

---

[1]The Proxy pattern is a structural design pattern that provides a surrogate or placeholder for another object to control access to it. [*Design Patterns: Elements of Reusable Object-Oriented Software* (1994), Erich Gamma, Richard Helm, Ralph Johnson, John Vlissides.]

```
    NOTES:
        o The timer context must implement the following method:
                virtual void expired( void ) noexcept;

        o Because the timing source of an individual thread may
        NOT be a clean divider of the timer duration, the timer
        duration is taken as the minimum.  For example: if the
        timing source has a resolution of 20msec per count, and the
        timer duration on the start() timer call is 5 msec, then the
        timer will expire after the next full count, i.e. after
        20msec, not 5msec. IT IS THE APPLICATION'S RESPONSIBILITY TO
        MANAGE THE RESOLUTION OF THE TIMING SOURCES.
 */
class Timer:
{
public:
    /// Constructor
    Timer( TimerManager& timingSource );

    /** Constructor. Alternate constructor - that defers the
        assignment of the timing source
     */
    Timer();

public:
    /** Starts the timer with an initial count down count duration of
        'timerDurationInMilliseconds'.  If the timer is currently
        running, the timer is first stopped, and then restarted.
     */
    virtual void start( unsigned long timerDurationInMilliseconds
);

    /** Stops the timer. It is okay to call stop() even after the
        timer has previously expired or explicitly stopped.
     */
```

```
    virtual void stop();

public:
    /** Callback notification of the timer's start time expiring.  The
        Timer is placed in the stopped state when the start time
        expires. The Timer's 'Context' (aka a child class) is
        responsible for implementing this method.
     */
    virtual void expired( void ) = 0;

public:
    /** Sets the timing source.  This method CAN ONLY BE CALLED
        when the timer has never been started or it has been
        stopped
     */
    virtual void setTimingSource( TimerManager& timingSource );
};
```

- Do not duplicate comments from your header files into your .c|.cpp files. When in doubt on where a particular comment belongs, put it in the header file.

- Comment each namespace. The easiest way to accomplish this is to have a README.txt file in each namespace directory. This is especially important when there is a collection of modules or classes in the namespace. The README.txt provides a logical place that is easily locatable for documenting semantics and usage that span all the modules in the namespace.

- Use Doxygen or an equivalent tool to extract information from your header files and from your namespace-specific README.txt files. Doxygen renders this information in a searchable, hyperlinked format which makes a great companion to your formal detailed design documentation because it lets you include code-level details that are always up to date.

Include Doxygen as part of the CI process. Require that Doxygen run successfully without errors as part of "passing a build." It is also recommended that you "fail a build" if there are Doxygen warnings. Just like compiler warnings, most Doxygen warnings are benign, but not all. And just like compiler warnings, trying to resolve or correct the warnings after you have written thousands of lines of code is painful.

Interfaces and More Interfaces

In Chapter 3, I made the claim that the use of abstract interfaces is the golden hammer for pounding out decoupled modules. This is part of the Dependency Inversion Principle.

As stated earlier, an abstract interface does not have to be a collection of either pure virtual or virtual methods in C++. In the context of PIM, an abstract interface is any interface that defines a behavior that has a deferred binding for its implementation. That is, it is not a source time binding. While pure virtual or virtual methods in C++ are one mechanism for a deferred binding, there are also other deferred binding times.

Compile Time Binding

An example of compile time bindings is the Late Header pattern (LHeader) that uses the preprocessor to defer a binding to compile time. In the LHeader section of Chapter 3, there is an example of deferring the concrete type definition for a mutex. However, the LHeader can be used with functions. The following example listing shows how to define the HAL interface for accessing a UART's registers using the LHeader pattern. While the LHeader is not the most user-friendly pattern, it is very efficient in that the "abstract function calls" are the "implementation function calls." That is, you do not have the "function calling a function" scenario. Here are some partial snippets of code that illustrate how this works:

src/Driver/Uart/Hal.h

```
/** @file

    This file defines a hardware abstraction layer (HAL) for accessing a
    hardware register based UART.
```

NOTE: NO 'Initialization' method is provided/defined in this interface, this is intentional! The initialization of the baud rate, number of start/stop bits, etc. is VERY platform specific - which translate to very cumbersome/inefficiencies in trying to make a generic one size-fits-all init() method.

What does this mean? Well first the application is RESPONSIBLE for making sure that the platform specific initialization happens BEFORE any of the Cpl drivers are started. Second, this interface ASSUMES that the required 'Uart Handle' is returned/created (at least conceptually) from this platform specific init() routine.
```
    */

#include <stdint.h>
#include "colony_map.h"

/*-------------- PUBLIC API ---------------------------------------------*/
/** This data type defines the platform specific 'handle' of a UART.   The
    'handle' is used to unique identify a specific UART instance.
 */
#define Driver_Uart_Hal_T                    Driver_Uart_Hal_T_MAP

/*-------------- PUBLIC API ---------------------------------------------*/
/** This method places the specified byte in to the transmit data register
    and initiates a transmit sequence.

    Prototype:
        void Driver_Uart_Hal_transmitByte( Driver_Uart_Hal_T hdl,
                                            uint8_t byteToTransmit );
 */
#define  Driver_Uart_Hal_transmitByte    Driver_Uart_Hal_transmitByte_MAP

/** This method enables the UART transmitter


    Prototype:
        void Driver_Uart_Hal_enableTx( Driver_Uart_Hal_T hdl );
 */
#define  Driver_Uart_Hal_enableTx        Driver_Uart_Hal_enableTx_MAP
```

```
/** This method returns the last received byte, independent of any Rx
    errors

    Prototype:
        uint8_t Driver_Uart_Hal_getRxByte( Driver_Uart_Hal_T hdl );
 */
#define  Driver_Uart_Hal_getRxByte      Driver_Uart_Hal_getRxByte_MAP

/** This method enables the UART receiver
    Prototype:
        void Driver_Uart_Hal_enableRx( Driver_Uart_Hal_T hdl );
 */
#define  Driver_Uart_Hal_enableRx       Driver_Uart_Hal_enableRx_MAP
```

The following header files, which are specific to the BSP for the Renesas RX62n MCU, provide the implementation of the HAL interface. The first header file, uarts.h, defines the actual concrete implementation. The second header file, hal_mappings.h, is where the compile binding magic happens; this is where the abstract HAL interface symbols get mapped to concrete functions.

src/Bsp/Renesas/Rx/u62n/Yrdkr62n/uarts.h

```
/** This method requests that the specified byte be transmitted (i.e.
    it loads the TX data register and starts the TX process)
 */
#define Bsp_uartTransmitByte(p,b)   \
    BSP_SCI_INDEX_TO_INSTANCE(p).TDR=(b)

/** This method enables RX & TX at the same time. NOTE: The 62N
    effectively does not allow enabling RX & TX at different times.
 */
#define Bsp_uartEnableRX_TX(p)        \
    BSP_SCI_INDEX_TO_INSTANCE(p).SCR.BYTE |= 0x30

/** This method returns the last byte received
 */
#define Bsp_uartGetReceivedByte(p)  \
    BSP_SCI_INDEX_TO_INSTANCE(p).RDR
```

src/Bsp/Renesas/Rx/u62n/Yrdkr62n/hal_mappings_.h

```
// Driver::Uart
#include "Bsp/Renesas/Rx/u62n/Yrdkr62n/uarts.h"

///
#define Driver_Uart_Hal_T_MAP                    uint8_t

///
#define Driver_Uart_Hal_transmitByte_MAP         Bsp_uartTransmitByte

/// Enable BOTH RX & TX because that is the way the chip works
#define Driver_Uart_Hal_enableTx_MAP             Bsp_uartEnableRX_TX

///
#define Driver_Uart_Hal_getRxByte_MAP            Bsp_uartGetReceivedByte

/// Enable BOTH (see above)
#define Driver_Uart_Hal_enableRx_MAP             Bsp_uartEnableRX_TX
```

Link Time Binding

Link time binding is the easiest abstract interface to create. Simply define a set of functions or classes, and then have a separate implementation for the interface. You do this by setting up your build scripts to build and link whichever implementation you need for your application. The following is the fatal error interface from the Colony.core C++ library. Yes, this is a C++ example, but all of the methods in the FatalError class are static class functions (i.e., functionally equivalent to a C function wrapped inside a class).

src/Cpl/System/FatalError.h

```
/** This class defines methods for handling fatal errors encountered by
    an application.  The implementation of the methods is platform
    dependent.
 */
class FatalError
{
```

```
public:
    /** This function is used to process/log a FATAL error.  The supplied
        error message will be logged to a "storage media" along with other
        useful info such as the current task, stack dump, etc. In addition,
        THE APPLICATION AND/OR SYSTEM WILL BE "STOPPED".  Stopped can mean
        the application/system is exited, restarted, paused forever, etc.

        The type of "storage media", additional info, stopped behavior,
        etc. is defined by the selected/linked implementation.

        NOTE: Applications, in general should NOT call this method - the
        application should be DESIGNED to handle and recover from errors
        that it encounters/detects.
     */
    static void log( const char* message );

    /** Same as above, but "value" is also logged.  This method allows
        additional information to be logged without resulting to a string
        formatting call (which may not work since something really bad just
        happen).
     */
    static void log( const char* message, size_t value );

    /// Printf style formatted message
    static void logf( const char* format, ... );

public:
    /** Same as log(..) method, except NO "...other useful info
        such as current task,..." is logged, AND the "storage media" is
        restricted to 'media' that is ALWAYS available.

        This allows routines that are supplying the extra info OR routines
        that write to media to be able to log fatal errors WITHOUT creating
        a recursive death loop.
     */
    static void logRaw( const char* message );

    /// Same as log(..) method, except NO 'extra info' and restricted media
    static void logRaw( const char* message, size_t value );
};
```

There are several implementations of this class—based on the target platform. For example:

src/Cpl/System/Win32/_fatalerror/FatalError.cpp
```cpp
void FatalError::log( const char* message )
{
    fprintf( stderr, "\n%s%s\n", EXTRA_INFO, message );
    Shutdown::failure( OPTION_CPL_SYSTEM_FATAL_ERROR_EXIT_CODE );
}

void FatalError::log( const char* message, size_t value )
{
    fprintf( stderr, "\n%s%s [%p]\n", EXTRA_INFO, message, (void*) value );
    Shutdown::failure( OPTION_CPL_SYSTEM_FATAL_ERROR_EXIT_CODE );
}

void FatalError::logf( const char* format, ... )
{
    va_list ap;
    va_start( ap, format );

    fprintf( stderr, "\n%s", EXTRA_INFO );
    vfprintf( stderr, format, ap );
    fprintf( stderr, "\n" );
    Shutdown::failure( OPTION_CPL_SYSTEM_FATAL_ERROR_EXIT_CODE );
}

void FatalError::logRaw( const char* message )
{
    log( message );
}

void FatalError::logRaw( const char* message, size_t value )
{
    log( message, value );
}
```

src/Cpl/System/FreeRTOS/_fatalerror/FatalError.cpp

```cpp
void FatalError::log( const char* message )
{
    if ( xTaskGetSchedulerState() == taskSCHEDULER_RUNNING )
    {
        Cpl::Io::Output* ptr =
            Cpl::System::Trace::getDefaultOutputStream_();

        ptr->write( EXTRA_INFO );
        ptr->write( message );
        ptr->write( "\n" );

        // Allow time for the error message to be outputted
        Cpl::System::Api::sleep( 250 );
    }

    Shutdown::failure( OPTION_CPL_SYSTEM_FATAL_ERROR_EXIT_CODE );
}
void FatalError::log( const char* message, size_t value )
{
    if ( xTaskGetSchedulerState() == taskSCHEDULER_RUNNING )
    {
        int             dummy = 0;
        Cpl::Io::Output* ptr   =
            Cpl::System::Trace::getDefaultOutputStream_();

        ptr->write( EXTRA_INFO );
        ptr->write( message );
        ptr->write( ". v:= " );
        ptr->write( Cpl::Text::sizetToStr( value,
                                        buffer_.getBuffer( dummy ),
                                        SIZET_SIZE, 16 ) );
        ptr->write( "\n" );

        // Allow time for the error message to be outputted
        Cpl::System::Api::sleep( 150 );
    }
```

```
    Shutdown::failure( OPTION_CPL_SYSTEM_FATAL_ERROR_EXIT_CODE );
}

void FatalError::logf( const char* format, ... )
{
    va_list ap;
    va_start( ap, format );

    if ( xTaskGetSchedulerState() == taskSCHEDULER_RUNNING )
    {
        buffer_ = EXTRA_INFO;
        buffer_.vformatAppend( format, ap );
        Cpl::System::Trace::getDefaultOutputStream_()->write( buffer_ );
    }

    Shutdown::failure( OPTION_CPL_SYSTEM_FATAL_ERROR_EXIT_CODE );
}

void FatalError::logRaw( const char* message )
{
    log( message );
}

void FatalError::logRaw( const char* message, size_t value )
{
    log( message, value );
}
```

C++ Pure Virtual and Virtual Constructs

If C++ is an option for your project, take full advantage of the language's ability to create
abstract interfaces and virtual methods that have runtime bindings.

Data Model

While the data model is not an abstract interface in a traditional sense, it does provide a similar decoupling effect as an abstract interface. While you can refer to Chapter 9 for an in-depth discussion of the data model pattern, here is a summary, in no particular order, of the different data model pattern semantics and best practices discussed there:

- Model points contain data, not objects. In addition, model points do not contain business rules or enforce policies other than potential basic value range checking rules.

- Model points should be uniquely typed by their contained data values and their usage semantics. For example, it provides the definition of what constitutes a change for change notifications.

- There is no synchronization between model points. Operations on a single model point instance are atomic. When synchronization across model points is required, it must be provided by the application.

- Never cache a model point value across function calls. It is okay to read a model point value in a method and then use a local value (i.e., model point value stored in an automatic variable[2] of the method) for the rest of the method call. But never read a model point value and then store it in a class member or global variable for later use.

- Always check the valid state of a model point before operating on the read value. The application cannot assume that a model point always has valid value, and any module interacting with the model point needs to include logic for dealing with the invalid data.

- A model point's change notification semantics guarantee that a client will get a notification when there is a change to the model point's value or state. However, it does not guarantee notifications for all changes, just the last one.

---

[2]In C/C++, an automatic variable is a local variable within a set of scope braces { }.
 https://en.wikipedia.org/wiki/Automatic_variable

- PIM recommends that all model points be statically instantiated. By statically creating the model points, it avoids the whole dynamic memory issue. Additionally, this ensures that all model point instances are always in scope.

- Use a naming convention, or a C++ namespace, that will protect you from polluting the global namespace with all of your model point instance names.

- PIM recommends that the application instantiate all model points in their invalid state. This ensures that there are no false valid-to-invalid transitions for model points that have their true initial values set from external interfaces. It also reinforces the behavior of first checking the model's state.

- With non-application-specific or nondomain-specific classes and modules (i.e., generic middleware, drivers, etc.), always provide references or pointers to model point instances. That is, for nonspecific classes and modules, avoid hard-coded model point instance names.

- With application-specific and domain-specific classes (i.e., classes that are not generic, as opposed to say a driver that can be reused across many applications), it is okay to use hard-coded model point instance names. This reduces the constructor and initialization overhead of passing around references and pointers to model point instances.

- PIM recommends that your data model framework support text-based serialization of model points and that all model point types have this feature. This allows for inspecting and updating model points from a CLI or debug console interface in a general manner instead of constructing case-by-case CLI commands to access model points.

- PIM recommends that your data model framework support symbolically named model point instances. This feature is required if you are supporting serialization.

- PIM recommends that your data model framework support the concept of locking model point values. Locking is where an entity can freeze or lock a model point's value, and all subsequent write operations to the model point's value will silently fail. This feature is especially helpful for testing and debug scenarios.

Build System

The PIM repository is set up to use the NQBP build system. However, PIM itself is build system agnostic. Nevertheless, PIM does impose the following requirements and best practices for a build system and build scripts:

- Builds need to be command line based to support automation. This requirement is not an absolute, but it is a rare use case where building from a developer's IDE and building from a fully integrated CI tool set yield the same results.

- The continuous integration build machine and the developers use the same build scripts. (This is an absolute requirement.)

- The build should create the application (including all variants) and support an unlimited number of unit tests. The build scripts must scale because the number of unit tests or application variants increases over time.

- Adding a new file to the build scripts should require low to no effort for the developer. Adding new directory should also be low effort. Remember PIM is all about the OCP and extending code without modifying existing source files. This means that you will be adding new files and directories all the time.

- For any build script file that is located in the same directory as the source code, the script should not have any "unique to the final output" details (e.g., compiler flags, linker directives, -D symbols, etc.). The reason is because any given directory may be built for different output images. For example, it could be built as part of the application and additionally as part of a unit test image.

- The build scripts should have the ability to selectively build directories. That is, the build scripts should never assume that it is okay to recursively build everything in a directory including all of its subdirectories. Once again, the reason is because whether the build is creating the application, the functional simulator, or a unit test, the subdirectories which need to be used can differ.

- Build scripts must be constructed such that path information about where a source code file is located is not lost when generating and referencing derived objects. The reason is because PIM does not guarantee globally unique file names.

- Build scripts must be constructed such that the generated object files are not placed in the same directory as the source code. The reason is because PIM encourages the use of compile time bindings, which means that the generated object file from a file can or will be different depending on what is being built (e.g., application, functional simulator, unit test). Furthermore, PIM encourages the use of multiple compilers because the compiler used for automated unit tests is typically not the compiler used when building for the target hardware.

- The build engine should be host, compiler, and target independent. Because PIM encourages automated unit tests and functional simulator builds, you will be building with multiple compilers for multiple target platforms and, additionally, possibly dealing with multiple host environments.

CHAPTER 16

PIM Thermostat Example

Throughout this book, I've attempted to explain best practices and patterns that can make embedded software development more successful and efficient. However, in some cases, nothing is quite as helpful as looking at some source code from a good working example. To that end, I created a sample application that illustrates most, if not all, of the principles covered in this book. The source code is available to be freely downloaded from my GitHub site (`https://github.com/johnttaylor/pim`), and this chapter serves as the documentation for that code.

The thermostat example is a working application that illustrates PIM in action; however, it is not a complete application. For example, there is no real end user interface in the example code (except for a command-line interface). But, again, the purpose of the thermostat application is not to be a finished or polished application, but rather a nontrivial, working, real-world example of PIM.

Features and Requirements

Here is a quick summary of the functionality of the thermostat application:

- It can control a single-stage air conditioner with a furnace (up to three stages of heat).

- It can control a stand-alone furnace (up to three stages of heat).

- There is PID control for regulating temperature.

- There is an "auto mode" for determining heating or cooling operation.

- There are basic alarms for configuration errors.

- There are air filter monitoring and alarms for changing the air filter.

© John T. Taylor, Wayne T. Taylor 2021
J. T. Taylor and W. T. Taylor, *Patterns in the Machine*,
https://doi.org/10.1007/978-1-4842-6440-9_16

- There is persistent storage of the thermostat configuration and user settings.

- It has a functional simulator that runs under Windows and Linux.

- It has a primitive house simulator to provide temperature feedback to the PID control.

- It uses an Adafruit Grand Central M4 Arduino board (featuring an Atmel SAMD51 microcontroller) as its target hardware.

- It has a command-line interface (for both target and PC platforms).

Table 16-1 lists the formal requirements for the thermostat application. The requirements are intentionally terse because the goal was not to build a fully functional thermostat, but rather to build just enough of an application to be a meaningful example. However, the design and implementation were done with consideration of future requirements (e.g., support for a heat pump, multistage compressors, etc.).

Table 16-1. *Requirements for the example thermostat application*

Requirement	Description
E001	Shall be able to control a one-stage cooling unit.
E002	Shall be able to control up to a three-stage furnace.
E003	Shall be able to provide variable indoor fan speed signal when an indoor unit is equipped with a variable speed motor.
E004	Shall be able to control a fixed speed indoor fan motor.
E005	Shall be able to connect a remote indoor temperature sensor that shall be used for temperature control (instead of the onboard temperature sensor). If the remote sensor is detected as bad, temperature control shall revert to the onboard sensor.

(continued)

Table 16-1. (*continued*)

Requirement	Description
C001	Shall be able to control indoor temperature to zero error (i.e., a simple error control is not acceptable). However, without variable capacity HVAC equipment, zero error control will not be realizable. However, the control algorithm should be sufficiently capable of zero error if variable capacity equipment were available.
C002	Shall provide an "auto mode" that will intelligently determine which mode—heating or cooling—the thermostat should be operating in.
C003	Shall provide the customer the ability to run the HVAC system in either "fan auto" or "fan continuous" mode.
C004	Shall track the number of hours that the indoor fan is operating, and after a configurable number of hours, alert the homeowner that the indoor air filter needs to be replaced.
A001	Shall provide an alarm if there is a failure of the outdoor unit. This requirement only applies when the physical HVAC equipment is capable of reporting such failures to the thermostat (e.g., a communicating HVAC system).
A002	Shall provide an alarm if there is a failure of the indoor unit. This requirement only applies when the physical HVAC equipment is capable of reporting such alarm/failures to the thermostat (e.g., a communicating HVAC system).
A003	Shall provide an alarm if there is temperature sensor failure.

Target Hardware

The thermostat example runs on an ARM Cortex-M4 microcontroller. It also has a supporting functional simulator that executes on Windows and Linux as console applications. Figure 16-1 describes the hardware platform.

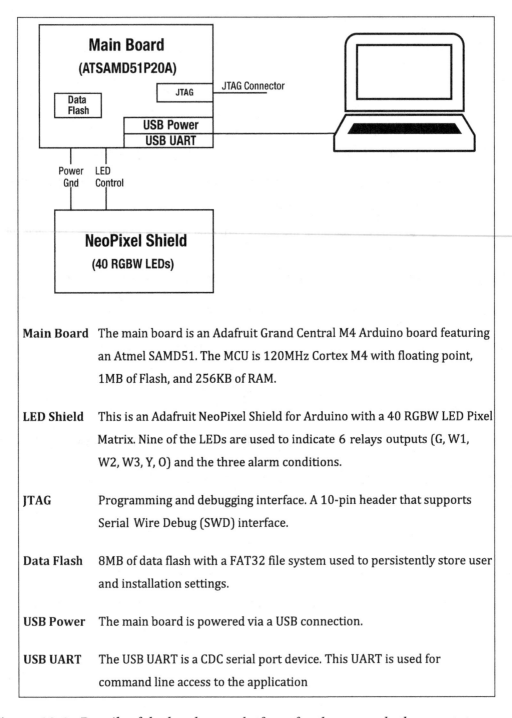

Main Board The main board is an Adafruit Grand Central M4 Arduino board featuring an Atmel SAMD51. The MCU is 120MHz Cortex M4 with floating point, 1MB of Flash, and 256KB of RAM.

LED Shield This is an Adafruit NeoPixel Shield for Arduino with a 40 RGBW LED Pixel Matrix. Nine of the LEDs are used to indicate 6 relays outputs (G, W1, W2, W3, Y, O) and the three alarm conditions.

JTAG Programming and debugging interface. A 10-pin header that supports Serial Wire Debug (SWD) interface.

Data Flash 8MB of data flash with a FAT32 file system used to persistently store user and installation settings.

USB Power The main board is powered via a USB connection.

USB UART The USB UART is a CDC serial port device. This UART is used for command line access to the application

Figure 16-1. *Details of the hardware platform for the example thermostat*

Installation and Setup

The source code for the thermostat example can be found on GitHub in the following repository: https://github.com/johnttaylor/pim. The example code is functional on both a Windows and a Linux PC.

There are, however, some limitations when using Linux as your host environment:

- Building for the target hardware is not supported. But building the simulator for Linux is supported.

- The code coverage scripts are not guaranteed to work.

- The ratt scripts are not guaranteed to work. ratt is a test tool built on top of the Python pexpect library that is used for performing some of the automated testing of the algorithm code.

- Doxygen is not supported.

Here are the minimum prerequisites for both Windows and Linux:

- Python 3.6 or newer.

- At least one compiler installed.

- Git client installed. This is optional if, instead of cloning the repository, you want to work with a downloaded zip file from GitHub.

Note   Detailed instructions on how to install compilers, Python, git, and other third-party tools are outside the scope of this book.

Additional items you will need to run on the target platform include

- An Adafruit Grand Central M4 Arduino board.

- A compatible JTAG programmer with a 10-pin header and connector. I use a Segger JLINK.

- A GCC-ARM Cortex M/R cross compiler for ATSAM51/Arduino. I recommend using the Arduino IDE to install this compiler. Remember that only the Windows host environment is supported when building for the target hardware.

- A serial terminal application (e.g., PuTTY for Windows or minicom for Linux).

Linux Setup

On Linux, you will need to perform the following setup:

- Install the GCC compiler on your Linux PC. Install the entire GCC toolchain and tools. After installation, it is assumed that the GCC compiler is in the command path.

- Clone the PIM repository to your PC. The repo can be installed anywhere on your PC; however, the root path to the repo location cannot contain any spaces.

- Run the env.sh script using the source shell command. This script is at the root of the cloned repository. Here is an example:

    ~/work/pim $ **source env.sh**

The env.sh shell script only needs to be run once per terminal window.

At this point, you are ready to build any of the linux/gcc projects or unit tests.

Windows Setup

On Windows, you will need to perform the following setup:

- Install at least one compiler. The following is the list of compilers for Windows that are used for building the thermostat example and majority of the unit tests. (There are some unit tests from the Colony.core C++ library that require additional compilers; however, these compilers are not needed for the thermostat example.)

    - Microsoft Visual Studio—The community edition is free and works very well. You need a version of Visual Studio that supports the C++11 language standard. If you only want to use and install one compiler, this is the one I recommend.

- GCC for Windows—This is also known as the mingw-w64 compiler (`http://mingw-w64.org/doku.php`). Install the 64-bit version. Additionally, you will want to install a version of the compiler toolchain that supports generating both 32-bit and 64-bit applications because the `mingw_w64` build scripts default to 32-bit builds.

- GCC-ARM Cortex M/R cross compiler for ATSAM51/Arduino— This compiler is used when building for the target hardware. The compiler can be installed using the Arduino IDE.

- Clone the PIM repository to your PC. The repo can be installed anywhere on your box; however, the root path to the repo location cannot contain any spaces. Also, be careful not to put the repo too deep in your file system. That is, you don't want the path to the root of the repo to be too long as, once the build process starts putting paths on everything, you might bump up against the Windows path length limitation.

- Set up supporting scripts so that, when building on Windows, the PIM environment can find your installed compilers. You must edit these scripts for each installed compiler. These scripts are located in the `top/compilers/` directory. There needs to be a Windows batch file for each installed compiler. The individual scripts are responsible for updating the environment for that compiler, for example, adding the compiler to the Windows command path, setting environment variables needed by the compiler or debug tools, and so on.

  Also, each script provides a "friendly name" that is used to identify the compiler when running the `env.bat` script. The actual batch file script names are not important; that is, it does not matter what the file names are as long as you have a unique file name for each script. Here is an example of the `top/compilers/vcvars32-vc16.bat` file:

```
01|@echo off
02|IF "/%1"=="/name" ECHO:Visual Studio VC16 (32bit) compiler
  |for |Windows & exit /b 0
03|
04|call "C:\Program Files (x86)\Microsoft Visual
  |Studio\2019\Community\VC\Auxiliary\Build\vcvars32.bat"
```

Line 2 is where the "friendly name" is set. And line 4 simply calls the batch file supplied by Visual Studio. You will need to edit this line to match your local installation.

Here is an example of the top/compilers/atsamd51-arduino-v7.bat batch file:

```
01|@echo off
02|IF "/%1"=="/name" ECHO:GCC-ARM Cortex M/R cross compiler for
  |ATSAM51/Arduino & exit /b 0
03|
04|:: Core Arduino tools
05|set ARDUINO_TOOLS=C:\Users\User\AppData\Local\Arduino15\
  |packages\adafruit
06|set ARDUINO_COMPILER_VER=7-2017q4
07|set ARDUINO_BSP_VER=1.5.7
08|
09|:: Additional/extras
10|set SEGGER_TOOLS_JLINK="e:\Program Files (x86)\SEGGER\JLink"
11|set SEGGER_TOOLS_OZONE="e:\Program Files\SEGGER\Ozone V3.10a"
12|
13|echo:GCC ARM-Cortex M4 (%ARDUINO_COMPILER_VER%), Adafruit's
  |Grand Central BSP (v%ARDUINO_BSP_VER%) setup
```

Line 2 is where the "friendly name" is set. Lines 5–7 define where you installed the Arduino compiler. You will need to edit these lines to match your local installation. The Arduino compiler is not added to the Windows command path, because the PIM build scripts directly use ARDUINO_xxxx environment variables. Lines 9–11 set up the environment for using the Segger JLINK JTAG debugger. If you are not planning to use a JLINK, these lines can be deleted. In addition, if you need to add additional lines to support your JTAG tools, this is the place to add them.

- Run the env.bat file. From a command window (i.e., a DOS box), change to the root of the cloned repository and from there run the env.bat script. It might look something like this:

```
c:\work\pim> env.bat
```

Running the script without any arguments will display the list of available compilers. To select a compiler toolchain, run the script again with the number of the compiler toolchain you want to use, for example:

```
c:\work\pim> env.bat 1
```

The env.bat shell script only needs to be run once per command window per compiler. To select a different compiler, simply rerun the env.bat script again and specify a different number. (Depending on how the compiler environment is set up, you may not always be able to run the env.bat an unlimited number of times for a given compiler because the environment space gets used up. If this happens, simply close your terminal window and open a new command window.)

At this point, you are ready to build any of the windows/<compiler> projects or tests, where <compiler> matches your compiler toolchain. The possible values for <compiler> are

- windows/vc12—Any Visual Studio compiler that support C++11

- windows/mingw_w64—Any MinGW_64 compiler that supports C++11

- adafruit-grand-central-m4/windows/gcc—The ARM Cortex M/R cross compiler for the ATSAM51 Arduino

Building

The PIM repository directory structure separates the source code directories from the directories where the builds are performed. In the following top-level directory structure, application builds and unit tests are built in the projects/ and tests/ directory trees, respectively. The source code resides under the src/ or xsrc/ directory trees.

```
<workspace root>
├──────docs
├──────projects        ; Build applications/released images
├──────resources
├──────scripts
├──────src
├──────tests           ; Build unit tests
├──────top
└──────xsrc
```

To build an application or unit test, simply navigate to a leaf directory inside the projects/ or tests/ directories and run the nqbp.py script. All projects and unit tests are built by running the nqbp.py script.

Building on Linux with the GCC Compiler

The following example is the script that builds the functional simulator. The example starts with running the env.sh script. However, the env.sh script only needs to be run once per compiler per terminal window.

```
~/work/pim $ . ./env.sh
Environment set (using native GCC compiler)
~/work/pim $ cd projects/Storm/Thermostat/simulation/linux/gcc
~/work/pim/projects/Storm/Thermostat/simulation/linux/gcc $ nqbp.py


===========================================================================
= START of build for:  thermostat-simulation.out
= Project Directory:   pim/projects/Storm/Thermostat/simulation/linux/gcc
= Toolchain:           GCC
= Build Configuration: posix64
= Begin (UTC):         Sun, 26 Jul 2020 17:10:17
= Build Time:          1595783417 (5f1db8f9)
===========================================================================
= Cleaning Built artifacts...
= Cleaning Project and local Package derived objects...
= Cleaning External Package derived objects...
= Cleaning Absolute Path derived objects...
====================
= Building Directory: src/Storm/Thermostat/Main
= Compiling: Main.cpp
=
= Archiving: library.a
====================
= Building Directory: src/Storm/Thermostat
= Compiling: Algorithm.cpp
= Compiling: ModelPoints.cpp
```

```
=
= Archiving: library.a
...

=====================
= Building Project Directory:
main.cpp
=====================
= Linking...
================================================================================
= END of build for:     thermostat-simulation.out
= Project Directory     pim/projects/Storm/Thermostat/simulation/linux/gcc
= Toolchain:            GCC
= Build Configuration: posix64
= Elapsed Time (hh mm:ss): 00 00:38
================================================================================
~/work/pim/projects/Storm/Thermostat/simulation/linux/gcc $
```

Building on Windows with the Visual Studio Compiler

The following example is the script that builds the functional simulator. The example starts with running the env.bat script. However, the env.bat script only needs to be run once per compiler per terminal window.

```
c:\work\pim>env.bat
NO TOOLCHAIN SET

1 - GCC-ARM Cortex M/R cross compiler for ATSAM51/Arduino
2 - GCC-AVR cross compiler for Atmel AVR/arduino
3 - GCC-RX cross compiler for Renesas RX
4 - MINGW64 v5.1.0 compiler for Windows
5 - GCC-ARM Cortex M/R cross compiler for NRF52/Arduino
6 - Visual Studio VC14 (32bit) compiler for Windows
7 - Visual Studio VC16 (32bit) compiler for Windows
8 - Visual Studio VC16 (64bit) compiler for Windows

c:\work\pim>env.bat 7
```

```
******************************************************************
** Visual Studio 2019 Developer Command Prompt v16.3.10
** Copyright (c) 2019 Microsoft Corporation
******************************************************************
[vcvarsall.bat] Environment initialized for: 'x86'

c:\work\pim>cd projects\Storm\Thermostat\simulation\windows\vc12
c:\work\pim\projects\Storm\Thermostat\simulation\windows\vc12>nqbp.py

===========================================================================
= START of build for: thermostat-simulation.exe
= Project Directory    pim\projects\Storm\Thermostat\simulation\windows\vc12
= Toolchain:           VC++ 12, 32bit (Visual Studio 2013)
= Build Configuration: win32
= Begin (UTC):         Sun, 26 Jul 2020 17:04:01
= Build Time:          1595783041 (5f1db781)
===========================================================================
= Cleaning Built artifacts...
= Cleaning Project and local Package derived objects...
= Cleaning External Package derived objects...
= Cleaning Absolute Path derived objects...
====================
= Building Directory: src\Storm\Thermostat\Main
Main.cpp
=
= Archiving: library.lib
====================
= Building Directory: src\Storm\Thermostat
Algorithm.cpp
ModelPoints.cpp
=
= Archiving: library.lib

...

====================
= Building Project Directory:
```

```
main.cpp

====================

= Linking...

===========================================================================

= END of build for:    thermostat-simulation.exe
= Project Directory    pim\projects\Storm\Thermostat\simulation\windows\vc12
= Toolchain:           VC++ 12, 32bit (Visual Studio 2013)
= Build Configuration: win32
= Elapsed Time (hh mm:ss): 00 01:11

===========================================================================

c:\work\pim\projects\Storm\Thermostat\simulation\windows\vc12>
```

Build Directory Naming Conventions

PIM encourages building functional simulators and a large number of unit tests. This translates to using multiple compilers and multiple target platforms (e.g., target hardware, PC console applications, etc.). To prevent name collisions, PIM recommends that you think strategically about what your directory structure will look like for your build directories. That is, start out from day one with conventions that include managing different compilers and different target platforms.

The PIM repository separates released entities from unit tests using the projects/ and tests/ directories, respectively. The separation is an attempt to remove the noise of the unit test builds from the builds that create images and applications that are formally tracked. The concrete definition of what should be built in which directory is

- The projects/ tree contains any application or entity that is not an automated or manual unit test.

- The tests/ tree only contains build directories for automated and manual unit tests.

For projects, the PIM repository uses the following naming convention:

projects/<project-name>/<hostplatform>/<compiler>

where

<project-name>—Is one or more subdirectories that identify what the project is. Things to consider are application variants (e.g., different products within a product family), target hardware vs. a simulated platform, and so on.

<hostplatform>—Is the host platform required for executing the build. Typically, this is Windows or Linux.

<compiler>—Is the compiler being used. There is no formal naming structure for a compiler name; just be consistent with naming across all of your projects and test builds.

For unit tests, the PIM repository uses the following naming convention:

```
tests/<component-path>
      /_0test/[<qualifier>/][<targetplatform>/]<hostplatform>/<compiler>
```

where

<component-path>—Is one or more subdirectories that is the namespace directory path of the component being tested. For example, the `<component-path>` for the `src/Cpl/Container` component is `tests/Cpl/Container`.

<qualifier>—Is an optional parameter that can specify one or more subdirectories. The typical use case for this parameter is where there is more than one unit test executable for a single component or namespace. For example, for the `src/Cpl/System` component, there are unit tests verifying the operation of the component running in real time as well as unit tests using simulated time. Here is an example:

```
tests/Cpl/System/_0test/realtime, tests/Cpl/
System/_0test/simtime
```

<targetplatform>—Is an optional parameter that can be one or more subdirectories. The use case for this parameter is when you have a common unit test code that executes across different platforms. For example, the `src/Cpl/File` component can be targeted to use any of the following as the underlying implementation:

- The C standard library FILE* functions

- POSIX file descriptors

- Native Win32 file functions

When testing the Cpl::File component using the FILE* functions, the unit test still needs to be built under Linux and Windows. Consequently, using ansi as the <targetplatform> qualifier, you end up with these two directory trees:

```
tests/Cpl/Io/File/_0test/ansi/linux
tests/Cpl/Io/File/_0test/ansi/windows
```

> **<hostplatform>**—Is the host platform required for executing the build. Typically, this is Windows or Linux.
>
> **<compiler>**—Is the compiler being used. There is no formal naming structure for a compiler name; just be consistent with naming across all of your projects and test builds.

PIM recommends that you have a naming convention for your unit test executable names. Having a consistent naming convention for your test images can greatly simplify your CI build scripts when it comes to building and executing unit tests. For instance, the NQBP build engine has two support scripts—bob.py and chuck.py—that will recursively build and execute unit tests. This translates to single statements in your CI scripts that can be used to build and execute all unit tests under a specified directory tree. For example, here is the command-line usage for the bob.py and chuck.py scripts that would build using the Visual Studio compiler and execute the built unit tests (four at a time in parallel) under the tests/ directory.

```
c:\work\pim\tests>bob.py vc12
...
c:\work\pim\tests>chuck.py -4 --match a.exe -dir vc12
```

Table 16-2 is an example of a naming convention.

Table 16-2. *Unit test naming convention*

Unit Test Image Name	Description
a.exe | a.out	Name for all automated unit tests that can be executed directly and that can be run in parallel with other unit tests.
aa.exe | aa.out	Name for automated unit tests that can be executed directly and cannot be run in parallel with other unit tests. For example, this could be a unit test that uses a hard-coded TCP/IP socket port number.
b.exe | b.out	Name for all automated unit tests that are invoked via a script that can be run in parallel with other unit tests.
bb.exe | bb.out	Name for unit tests that are invoked via a script that cannot be run in parallel with other unit tests.
a.py	Name for all scripts that can be run in parallel with other unit tests that are responsible for invoking a test image. For example, the unit test for the `Cpl::Io::Stdio` component verifies input/output from STDIO. The `a.py` scripts pipe the test text to the `a.exe` unit test image.
aa.py	Name for all scripts that cannot be run in parallel with other unit tests that are responsible for invoking a test image.

PIM Thermostat Application Usage

This section provides some basic getting started instructions for executing the PIM thermostat application. Once you are up and running on the hardware, or the simulator, you can experiment with the various CLI commands and poke under the covers by directly reading and writing model points.

Running on the Target Hardware

The build scripts are set up to build a stand-alone firmware image (no bootloader) for the Atmel SAMD51 microcontroller. In addition, you will need a compatible JTAG programmer to program the image onto the board. There are supporting scripts (in the build directory) that will program the board and launch Segger's Ozone debugger tool. These scripts are specific to the Segger tools.

The target board is powered via USB, and the same USB connection provides a serial UART interface for communicating with the board from your PC. This UART connection is used for the application's command-line interface (CLI). For more details, see the "Command-Line Interface (CLI)" section.

Functional Simulator

To run the functional simulators, simply build the simulator and then execute the output image. The command-line interface for the application runs over STDIO.

Command-Line Interface (CLI)

Running the CLI is mostly the same for the thermostat example running on the target hardware or as a simulator. The only differences are there are some target platform-specific CLI commands. For example, the threads command behaves differently depending on the target platform. The following sections provide snippets from a sample session using the Windows simulator. There are no meaningful differences when running on the Linux simulator or on the actual target hardware.

CLI—Basic Help

The CLI has a *help* command. Issuing help with no arguments displays a terse list of supported commands. Typing help * or help <cmd> provides verbose help. You can get to the CLI by running the thermostat-simulation.exe program.

```
c:\work\pim\projects\Storm\Thermostat\simulation\windows\vc12>_win32\
thermostat-simulation.exe

--- Your friendly neighborhood TShell. ---

$$$ help
bye [app [<exitcode>]]
dm ls [<filter>]
dm write {<mp-json>}
dm read <mpname>
filter
filter clear|ack
filter set <numhours>
```

```
help [* | <cmd>]
house [<odt>]
house enable <odt>
house disable <idt>
log
log enable <fname>
log disable
state [usarlct]
threads
tprint [<text>]
trace [on|off]
trace section (on|off) <sect1> [<sect2>]...
trace threadfilters [<threadname1> [<threadname2>]]...
trace level (none|brief|info|verbose|max)
trace here|revert
user mode eOFF|eCOOLING|eHEATING|eAUTO|eID_HEATING
user fan eAUTO|eCONTINUOUS
user setpt <cool> <heat>
wb
wb enot enable|disable
wb acc true|false
```

CLI—Running Cooling

The command sequence found in Table 16-3 can be used to exercise the thermostat's cooling operation.

Table 16-3. *Commands for running the example thermostat in cooling mode*

Step	Command	Description
1	state	Displays the current state of the thermostat.
2	house enable 95	Enables the house simulator with a simulated outdoor temperature of 95°F. Range is -20°F to 120°F.
3	user setpt 70 60	Configures the thermostat's cooling and heating setpoints to 70°F and 60°F, respectively. The cooling setpoint range is 55°F to 95°F. The heating setpoint range is 5°F to 90°F. In addition, the heating setpoint must always be less than the cooling setpoint.
4	user mode eAUTO	Sets the thermostat's heating or cooling mode to automatic.
5	user fan eAUTO	Sets the thermostat's fan operation mode to automatic.
6	state	Displays the updated state of the thermostat.
7		Wait for 30 seconds to allow the PID algorithm to determine whether active cooling is required.
8	wb enot disable	For white-box testing, temporarily disable the minimum off time so that the equipment will turn on immediately.
9	state	Displays the updated state of the thermostat. The system is actively cooling at this point.

Here is an example of the preceding sequence:

```
--- Your friendly neighborhood TShell. ---

$$$ state
ThermostatMode=eAUTO, FanMode=eAUTO, CoolSetpt=70.00, HeatSetpt=60.00,
idt=75.00, odt=<n/a>
SystemOn=off, OpMode=eCOOLING, Idu=eFURNACE, Odu=eAC, IduStages=0,
OduStages=1, force=0
g=off, bk=0,  w1=off, w2=off, w3=off,  y1=off, y2=off,  o=COOL
pv=90.00, error=5.00, sum=150.00, pvInhibit=no, freezeCnt=0, inhibitCnt=0
IdtSensorAlarm:              pri=no, sec=no, priAck=no, secAck=no, critical=no
NoActiveConditioningAlarm: active=no, ack=no, critical=no
UserCfgModeAlarm:            active=no, ack=no, critical=no
```

```
AirFilterAlert:                 active=no, ack=no, critical=no
Cycle=eOFF, BeginOn=00:00:00.000, TimeOn=0, BeginOff=00:00:00.000, TimeOff=0
Outdoor: BeginOn=00:00:00.000, BeginOff=00:00:00.008
Indoor:  BeginOn=00:00:00.000, BeginOff=00:00:00.008
System:  BeginOn=00:00:00.000, BeginOff=00:00:00.008
00 00:01:00.028
```

$$$ **house enable 95**
```
Cmd simulator ENABLED.
```

$$$ **user setpt 70 60**
```
CoolSetpt=70.00, HeatSetpt=60.00
```

$$$ **user mode eAUTO**
```
New thermostat mode = eAUTO
```

$$$ **user fan eAUTO**
```
New fan mode = eAUTO
```

$$$ **state**
```
ThermostatMode=eAUTO, FanMode=eAUTO, CoolSetpt=70.00, HeatSetpt=60.00,
idt=75.00, odt=95.00
SystemOn=off, OpMode=eCOOLING, Idu=eFURNACE, Odu=eAC, IduStages=0, OduStages=1,
force=0
g=off, bk=0,  w1=off, w2=off, w3=off,  y1=off, y2=off,  o=COOL
pv=90.50, error=5.00, sum=155.00, pvInhibit=no, freezeCnt=0, inhibitCnt=0
IdtSensorAlarm:             pri=no, sec=no, priAck=no, secAck=no, critical=no
NoActiveConditioningAlarm: active=no, ack=no, critical=no
UserCfgModeAlarm:           active=no, ack=no, critical=no
AirFilterAlert:             active=no, ack=no, critical=no
Cycle=eOFF, BeginOn=00:00:00.000, TimeOn=0, BeginOff=00:00:00.000, TimeOff=0
Outdoor: BeginOn=00:00:00.000, BeginOff=00:00:00.008
Indoor:  BeginOn=00:00:00.000, BeginOff=00:00:00.008
System:  BeginOn=00:00:00.000, BeginOff=00:00:00.008
00 00:01:00.095
```

$$$ **wb enot disable**
```
enot = DISABLED (Equip Min Off Time)
```

```
$$$ state
ThermostatMode=eAUTO, FanMode=eAUTO, CoolSetpt=70.00, HeatSetpt=60.00,
idt=70.10, odt=95.00
SystemOn=ON, OpMode=eCOOLING, Idu=eFURNACE, Odu=eAC, IduStages=0, OduStages=1,
force=0
g=ON, bk=100,  w1=off, w2=off, w3=off,  y1=ON, y2=off,  o=COOL
pv=17.16, error=0.10, sum=156.30, pvInhibit=no, freezeCnt=0, inhibitCnt=0
IdtSensorAlarm:              pri=no, sec=no, priAck=no, secAck=no, critical=no
NoActiveConditioningAlarm: active=no, ack=no, critical=no
UserCfgModeAlarm:          active=no, ack=no, critical=no
AirFilterAlert:            active=no, ack=no, critical=no
Cycle=eON_CYCLE, BeginOn=00:01:22.008, TimeOn=362, BeginOff=00:00:00.000,
TimeOff=0
Outdoor: BeginOn=00:01:22.008, BeginOff=00:00:00.008
Indoor:  BeginOn=00:00:00.000, BeginOff=00:00:00.008
System:  BeginOn=00:01:22.008, BeginOff=00:00:00.008
00 00:01:28.813
```

Documentation

The starting point for additional documentation is the file top/start_here.html in the PIM repository. The start_here.html file is a TiddlyWiki file. Essentially, it is a Wiki page contained in a single HTML file with no Wiki server required. The file contains various details such as requirements, software architecture, software development plan, and so on.

Another item in the top/ directory is the run_doxygen.py script. This script, which must be run from the top/ directory, runs Doxygen on all of the source code in the src/ tree. The Doxygen output will be placed under the top-level docs/ directory.

The prerequisites for running the Doxygen script are

- Python 3.6+.

- Doxygen, version 1.8.15 or higher—The location of the Doxygen executable needs to be included in the Windows command path. See www.doxygen.nl/index.html.

- Graphviz, version 2.38.0 or higher—The location of the Graphviz executable must be included in the Windows command path. See `https://graphviz.org/`

- Microsoft help compiler—The location of the help compiler needs to be included in the Windows command path. The `run_doxygen.py` script generates a single Microsoft help file from the set of web pages. The advantage of the help file, aside from being a single file, is that it supports searching for text inside comments in the source code. To download the help compiler, `htmlhelp.exe`, see `www.microsoft.com/en-us/download/details.aspx?id=21138`

About NQBP

NQBP is a Python-based build engine that I have used in some form or another over many years building projects. NQBP stands for *Not Quite Benv–Python*. The primary features of NQBP that I have come to rely on are

- Adding a new file in an existing directory requires zero effort.

- Adding a new source directory to a build is done simply by adding the new directory's name and path as a single-line entry to a single file.

- Supporting both Windows and Linux host platforms.

- Not having to deal with makefiles.

Here is a more detailed list of NQBP features:

- Multihost build engine for C, C++, and assembler builds.

- Targeted specifically for embedded development.

- Speed.

- Command line based.

- Supports many compiler toolchains.

- Source code reusability. That is, NQBP assumes that code will be shared across many projects.

- Reusability of compiler toolchains. That is, after a particular compiler toolchain has been created or defined, it can be reused across an unlimited number of projects.

- Highly effective on small- to medium-sized projects.

What NQBP is not:

- It is not a make-based build engine. In fact, NQBP does no dependency checking at all; it never checks to see if anything has changed.

- It is not an optimal choice for large projects (that are over 100,000 lines of code).

Installing NQBP

NQBP is largely preinstalled in the PIM repository. The underlying Python scripts for NQBP are located in the xsrc/nqbp directory tree. NQBP relies on specific environment variables being set with the env.bat and env.sh scripts. These variables are described in Table 16-4.

Table 16-4. *NQBP environment variables*

Variable	Description
NQBP_BIN	The full path to the root directory where the NQBP package is located.
NQBP_PKG_ROOT	The full path to the package that is actively being worked on. For the thermostat example, this is the root directory of the PIM repository on your PC.
NQBP_WORK_ROOT	The full path of the directory containing one or more packages being developed. For the PIM repository, this is the parent directory of the NQBP_PKG_ROOT.
NQBP_XPKGS_ROOT	The full path of the root directory containing external or third-party source code. For the PIM repository, this is the NQBP_PKG_ROOT/xsrc directory.
NQBP_XPKG_MODEL	The mode in which external or third-party source code is referenced by the build scripts. For the PIM repository, the value of this variable is mixed. If you reuse NQBP for your projects, typically you would not set this variable or set it to legacy. This variable is used to enable support for building under the Outcast development model. See Appendix E.

NQBP Usage

NQBP separates the build directories from the source code directories. It further separates the build directories into two buckets: unit tests (the `tests/` directory) and applications (the `projects/` directory). The NQBP build scripts will only work if they are executed under one of these two directories. Whether you have both or only one of these directories is strictly your choice. The following diagram illustrates the directory structure when using `legacy` or `mixed` external package models. See Appendix E.

```
<NQBP_WORK_ROOT>
  └──────<NQBP_PKG_ROOT>        ; Typically this is the root of your SCM repo
          ├──────<abc>
          ├──────projects        ; Build applications/released images
          ├──────<xyz>
          ├──────src             ; Source code directory
          ├──────tests           ; Build unit tests
          └──────<NQBP_XPKGS_ROOT> ; recommended name for this directory is 'xsrc'
```

NQBP Build Model

The default build behavior for NQBP is to always perform a clean build. It deletes all previously built files and then builds all of the source code. The build-all paradigm is actually faster for building small projects than having a makefile check all of the header file dependencies and then only build what has changed. However, as projects increase in size, this will no longer hold true. That said, NQBP provides numerous command-line options to perform selective builds (i.e., to build only a single file, to build only a single directory, to only build a set of directories, etc.). The recommendation is that if you only changed a .c|.cpp|.s|.asm file or files, perform a selective build. That is, just build the files you edited. If you change a header file, then it is easier to just build everything rather than attempt to identify the #include dependencies impacted by your change.

NQBP Object Files vs. Libraries

When NQBP compiles directories, it places all the object files into a library file for each directory built. The exception is NQBP does *not* create a library file for the objects in the build directory (i.e., the directory where you run the nqbp.py script). During the link phase, it links your executable image against the object files in the build directory and the individual libraries it created during the compile phase. This has the positive effect of only including the code your application uses from a specific directory instead of including all of the object files for an entire directory into your application. Once again, the exception to this rule is all object files in the build directory are always linked into the application.

For example, if your application uses the `Cpl::Container::Dictionary` class, but does not use any of the other classes from the `Cpl::Container` namespace, at compile time the NQBP build scripts will compile the entire `Cpl/Container` directory. However, at link time, your application will only link in the `Cpl::Container::Dictionary` object code from the library. This is the C/C++ language–defined behavior for linking against libraries.

There is one downside to this approach: if there are no references in your application code to a variable or function in an object file that is placed in a library, then it will not be linked. Oddly enough, there can be required variables and functions that need to be linked that are not explicitly referenced. Here are some example cases:

- C/C++ runtime code—This includes things like the code that executes when the reset interrupt occurs, that is, the microcontroller's vector table. Your application does not have an explicit function call to any of the entries in the vector table. The vector table is typically placed into RAM at a very specific location by the linker script.

- Self-registered (with a container) C++ modules—For this scenario, there is no calling module that references the self-registered instances directly by their names, only indirectly using a reference from the container. The Catch2 unit tests are an example of this. Each Catch2 test case self-registers with the test runner. At runtime, the test runner walks through its list of tests to execute the individual tests.

NQBP provides a mechanism—`.firstobjs` and `.lastobjs` parameters—to explicitly force linking against an arbitrary set of object files in addition to linking against directory libraries. When linking directly against object files, the object files are unconditionally included in the final image. See the `tests/Storm/Component/_0test/linux/gcc/mytoolchain.py` file for an example of this.

NQBP Build Variants

NQBP supports the concepts of build variants. A build variant is where the same basic set of code is compiled and linked against different targets. For example, the automated unit test for the Cpl::Dm namespace using the MinGW compiler has three build variants: win32, win64, and cpp11. Here is a description of these variants:

- win32 is a 32-bit application build using the native Win32 API for threading.

- win64 is a 64-bit application build using the native Win32 API for threading.

- cpp11 is a 64-bit application build using the C++11 threading interfaces.

Each build variant can be built independently from the others. That is, if you build variant A, it does not delete the final output files of variant B, but it will delete the intermediate object and library files. NQBP does not consider a debug build a build variant. This means building with debug or without debug enabled will overwrite the previous build variant's final output files.

NQBP Build Scripts

Some of the Python scripts that NQBP uses are common across projects, and others are unique to individual projects. Table 16-5 describes the primary components that make up a complete build script.

Table 16-5. *Components of a complete build script with NQBP*

Component	Description
`<compilerToolchain>.py`	This script contains the compiler and linker script commands, options, configurations, etc. that are needed to use a specific compiler to build a specific set of outputs. After a compiler toolchain has been created, it can be reused on an unlimited number of projects. These scripts are located under the `nqbp/nqbplib/toolchains` directory. If you are using a compiler that NQBP does not currently support, you will need to create a compiler toolchain script. See the `nqbp/top/start_here.html` file for details on how to do this.
`nqbp.py`	This script is used to perform the builds. A copy of this script must be placed in each build directory. The content of this script is minimal; it basically calls scripts inside the `nqbp/nqbplib` directory to perform the actual builds.
`mytoolchain.py`	This script is used to specify which compiler toolchain to use and to provide project-specific customization of the referenced compiler toolchain. Each build directory is required to have a `mytoolchain.py` file.
`libdirs.b`	This file is used to specify which directories to build. Each build directory is required to have a `libdirs.b` file.
`sources.b`	This file is optional. When used, this file specifies which .cl.cppl. asml.s files in a given directory to build. By default, NQBP builds all .cl.cppl.asml.s files found in directories specified by the `libdirs.b` file or in the build directory itself.

Selecting What to Build with NQBP

The principal mechanism for selecting which files to build is the `libdirs.b` file in the build directory and the optional `sources.b` files in source directories. The `sources.b` file simply contains file names which are listed singly on separate lines of the file. The `libdirs.b` file contains the directory names which are listed singly on separate lines of the file and specify which directories to compile and link. However, there is additional syntax and semantics for the `libdirs.b` file.

- Directories are referenced relative to the NQBP_PKG_ROOT directory.

- Entries in the file can reference another libdirs.b file within the projects/ or tests/ directory trees. The syntax for this is to use a relative directory path qualifier to the reference included in your libdirs.b file.

- Blank lines or lines starting with # are ignored.

- Environment reference variables can be referenced using leading and trailing $ characters to identify directories or partial directory paths.

- An entry that starts with <build-variant> enclosed within square brackets ([ ]) will only be compiled when <build-variant> matches the build variant specified when NQBP is invoked.

- An optional pipe symbol (|) can be used to include multiple variants inside the square brackets. For example, you could specify [arm7|arm9].

- Entries with no variant prefix specified are compiled for all variants.

- Entries can specify an optional trailing list of source files (in the specified directory) to either be omitted from the build or to only be included in the build. The less than character (<) is used to specify a build-only list of files. The greater than character (>) is used to specify an excluded list of files.

- Here are some examples of lines that can be included in a libdirs.b file:

```
# Build the src/foo directory in my package
src/foo
```

```
# Build the src/foo directory but do NOT build the hello.c
# and world.cpp files
src/foo > hello.c world.cpp
```

```
# Build the src/foo directory but ONLY build the hello.c
# and world.cpp files
src/foobar < hello.c world.cpp
```

```
# Build the third-party module Uncle under the xsrc/ directory
xsrc/Uncle/src
```

```
# Build using an absolute path that the base path is specified
# by an environment variable
# where ARDUINO_TOOLS=c:\Progra~2\Ardunio
$ARDUINO_TOOLS$/hardware/arduino/cores/arduino

# Directory specific to the 'cpp1' variant
[cpp11] src/Cpl/System/_cpp11

# Build all directories specified in the following file
# (relative to my build directory)
../../../libdirs.b
```

There are additional options when building with the Outcast model that are not present here.

NQBP Extras

NQBP also provides some additional scripts and features that are not directly used for building but are used to leverage or support the NQBP engine. Table 16-6 lists a few of these supported scripts.

Table 16-6. *NQBP scripts that are used to leverage the NQBP engine*

Script	Description
bob.py	The bob script is a tool that recursively builds multiple projects or tests. Bob can only be run under the projects/ and tests/ directory trees. In addition, bob provides several options for filtering and specifying which projects or tests actually get built. For example, the following statement will build only tests that use the Visual Studio compiler. It also passes the -gt options to the nqbp.py build scripts. c:\work\pim\tests>**bob.py vc12 -gt**
chuck.py	The chuck script is a tool that recursively runs executables or scripts. chuck can only be run under the projects/ and tests/ directories. Like bob, chuck provides several options for filtering and specifying which executables or scripts are run. For example, the following statement will execute all of the a.exe unit tests built using the Visual Studio compiler ten times: c:\work\pim\tests>**chuck.py --match a.exe --dir vc12 --loop 10**
tca.py	The tca script is a wrapper script that is used to invoke the gcovr tool that generates code coverage reports and metrics. For example, the following statement generates coverage metrics for just the Cpl::Container module or namespace: tca.py rpt --filter .*Cpl/Container.* The tca script is run after the unit test executable has been run at least once. Note: In the PIM repository, only the mingw_w64 32-bit builds are configured to be instrumented to generate code coverage metrics.

In the PIM repository, the env.bat and env.sh scripts create macros (or aliases) for the bob.py and chuck.py scripts that allow these scripts to be invoked without having to specify their path or add their path to the system's command path.

Colony.core

Colony.core is a C++ class library that provides basic system services and the operating system abstraction layer (OSAL) that the thermostat example is built on. Colony.core is its own repository in GitHub (`https://github.com/johnttaylor/colony.core`) that has been directly integrated into the PIM repository. Table 16-7 describes the features, services, and functionality provided by Colony.core.

Table 16-7. *Features, services, and functionality of Colony.core*

Service	Description
Cpl:: Checksum	A collection of checksum, CRCs, and Hash classes.
Cpl:: Container	Classes for various types of containers. All of the containers use intrusive listing mechanisms. That is, every item that is put into a container contains the memory and fields that are required to be in the container. No memory is allocated when an item is inserted into a container, and all of the containers can contain an infinite number of items (RAM permitting). There are two major side effects of intrusive containers: • All items or classes that are put into containers must inherit from the base class Cpl::Container::Item. • A given item can be in at most one and only one container.

(*continued*)

Table 16-7. (*continued*)

Service	Description
Cpl::Dm	A data model framework. The framework provides a multi-threaded framework for the data model architecture pattern. The implementation has the following features:

- Type safety (for the model point's value type).
- Atomic operations (e.g., all read/write operations are thread safe).
- Change notifications.
- Separate valid/invalid states for the model point's value.
- Invalid status is an integer that supports application-specific invalid codes.
- The data in the model is always in RAM with the ability to have persistent storage on a nonvolatile media.
- Serialization. The framework supports both binary and text-based serialization of model point's value as well as any supporting metadata. The text serialization uses JSON formatting.
- Command-line debug shell support for reading and writing all model point instances are included.
- Locking. This is where an entity can lock a model point's value, and all subsequent write operations to the model point's value will fail silently.
- Association of static data. The application can define and bind nonmutable information specific to each model point instance such as valid data ranges, units of measure, symbolic names, etc.
- Type information. The frameworks support each model point type having a unique, text-based type identifier.

Note that the framework can also be used with bare-metal application (i.e., without threads).

Service	Description
Cpl::Io	Common interfaces for reading and writing data to and from streams and files. Essentially, the Cpl::Io* namespaces provide platform-independent interfaces for operations that would typically be done using POSIX file descriptors or Windows file handles.

(*continued*)

Table 16-7. (*continued*)

Service	Description
`Cpl::Itc`	Classes for message-based inter-thread communications (ITC) as well as event flags. The ITC message mechanism has the following characteristics:

- The ITC model is a client-server model, where clients send messages to servers. Messages can be sent asynchronously or synchronously.
- Data flow between clients and servers can be unidirectional or bidirectional as determined by the application. Because this is an inter-thread communication, data can be shared via pointers since clients and servers share the same address space.
- Data is shared between clients and servers using the concept of a payload. In addition, a convention of ownership is used to provide thread-safe access to the payload.
  - A client initially owns the payload. That is, the client can access the data in the payload without the use of critical sections.
  - When a client sends or posts a message, there is an implicit transfer of ownership of the payload. After sending the message, the client is obligated to not access the payload contents.
  - When a server receives a message, the server now owns the payload and can access the data in the payload without the use of critical sections.
  - When a server returns a message, there is an implicit return of ownership of the payload back to the client. After returning the message, the server is obligated to not access the payload contents.
- No dynamic memory is used. Clients are responsible for providing all required memory for the individual messages. This translates to no hard limits to the number of messages a server can receive. It also means that the application does not have to worry about overflowing message queues or mailboxes. Another side effect of the memory paradigm is that there are no broadcast messages.
- Messages and payloads are type safe. That is, they are handled and dispatched with no type casting required.

The ITC event flag mechanism has the following characteristics:

- Each thread supports up to N unique event flags. Event flags are not unique across threads. That is, the semantics associated with event flag1 for Thread A are independent or the semantics associated with event flag1 for Thread B.
- An individual event flag can be viewed as a binary semaphore. Waiting, however, is done on the thread's entire set of event flags.
- A thread can wait for at least one event to be signaled. When the thread is waiting on events, and it is then signaled, all of the events that were in the "signaled" state when the thread was unblocked are cleared.

(*continued*)

Table 16-7. (*continued*)

Service	Description
Cpl:: Json	A parser and formatter for JSON. This is actually a third-party file for serializing and deserializing JSON strings. The module is targeted for the Arduino platform but works on any platform. The advantage of its Arduino roots is that it has a no `malloc` option. (Copyright Benoit Blanchon 2014-2019. MIT License. `https://github.com/bblanchon/ArduinoJson`)
Cpl:: Math	Classes and utilities related to numeric operations.
Cpl:: Memory	Interfaces that allow an application to manually manage dynamic memory independent of the actual heap.
Cpl:: Persistent	A basic persistent storage mechanism for nonvolatile data. The persistent sub-system has the following features: • The sub-system organizes persistent data into records. The application is responsible for defining what the data content of a record is. It is the responsibility of the concrete record instances to initiate updates to the persistent media. A record is the unit of atomic read/write operations when using persistent storage. • On start-up, the records are read, and the concrete record instances process the incoming data. • All persistently stored data is checksummed to detect data corruption. Be aware, however, that the CRCs are only validated on start-up. • Record instances are responsible for defaulting their data (and subsequently initiating an update to the persistent media) when the stored data has been detected as corrupt. • The sub-system is independent of the physical persistent storage media. • The record server can process an unlimited number of records. It is also okay to have more than one record server instance.
Cpl:: System	A platform-independent foundation of abstractions and classes related to program execution. These are basic operating system abstraction layer (OSAL) interfaces. The interfaces and abstractions are designed to support multi-threaded applications. Additionally, a bare-metal, no threads required, implementation is also provided for these OSAL interfaces.

(*continued*)

Table 16-7. (*continued*)

Service	Description
Cpl:: Text	Utilities that provide yet another string class and additional text processing. What makes the Cpl::Text::String class different from other string classes is that it supports a "zero dynamic memory allocation" interface and implementation. There is also a dynamic memory implementation of the string interface for times when strict memory management is not required.
Cpl:: TShell	A text-based command shell framework that can be used to interact with an application. One example is a debug shell (or maintenance port) that provides you with white-box access to running the application. Note, however, that TShell is only a framework; the application is responsible for connecting it to the application and providing application-specific commands.

Colony.Apps

Colony.Apps is the native GitHub repository for the thermostat example (https:// github.com/johnttaylor/colony.apps). It has been integrated into the PIM repository to simplify using the example code. Originally, the Colony.Apps repository was intended to include multiple example applications built on top of the other Colony.* repositories. Currently, the only example application is the thermostat example.

Colony.Arduino

Colony.Arduino is another Colony.* repository in GitHub that has been integrated into the PIM repository (https://github.com/johnttaylor/colony.arduino). It provides the Colony.* ecosystem with support for several Arduino boards and libraries. In the context of the PIM, it provides the BSP for the Grand Central M4 board and the NeoPixel library for the LED shield used with the Grand Central M4 board.

RATT

RATT is a Python-based automated test tool built on top of the Python pexpect package. The RATT tool is also a GitHub repository (https://github.com/johnttaylor/ratt). The PIM repository uses the RATT tool for running automated integration tests that exercise the control algorithm in simulated time.

RATT was specifically created to perform automated testing of Units Under Test (UUTs) that support a command-line interface, but it can also be used with any application that supports interactive behavior (e.g., stdio) with the parent process that launched the application. The following is a summary of RATT's features:

- It is a pure Python module and runs on Windows and Linux.

- It has an interactive mode in addition to running scripts.

- It can list all available scripts and provides help for each script.

- Test scripts are written in Python.

- Test scripts can be located anywhere and in multiple locations.

- Works with UUTs connected via

  - A serial port

  - stdio (i.e., console applications)

  - Telnet/SSH (a telnet client application is required)

## CHAPTER 17

The Tao of Development

This book is about patterns. And, up to this point, the patterns discussed have been focused on improving software design and coding. But beyond software, there are other patterns in the development process that bear consideration—patterns outside the machine, as it were.

Over the course of many years working as a software engineer, I've seen the same things over and over again. At different companies, I've seen the same ideas about design, the same approaches to project management, the same group dynamics, the same mistakes, and, sometimes, the same successes. Consequently, I thought it might be worthwhile to share some of these observations. While I've codified these observations into a set of rules, they are really just things you would hear me say if you were around me at work. And I say these things a lot. Maybe because sometimes it just helps to say them out loud.

John's Rules of Development

Some of these rules are original, and others have been shamelessly paraphrased or borrowed from coworkers. As with all generalized rules, there are always exceptions, except for rule #1.

1. Never trust the software guys.

    This rule covers a multitude of sins such as

    - Software developers always have bugs in their code.

    - Software developers are terrible at estimating effort.

    - Software developers' priorities do not always align with program managers' priorities.

    - Software developers are either too conscientious (e.g., this must be a 100% solution) or not conscientious enough (e.g., "we don't need no stinking testing").

© John T. Taylor, Wayne T. Taylor 2021
J. T. Taylor and W. T. Taylor, *Patterns in the Machine*,
https://doi.org/10.1007/978-1-4842-6440-9_17

In all seriousness, I use rule #1 with managers, project managers, program managers, peers, and my spouse, to remind everyone that software guys are human, and, as such, our work has imperfections.

2. Software is not soft, it's hard.

    Software is complex, challenging, and time consuming and requires skilled professionals—no matter how much management, marketing people, and customers would like it to be otherwise. Unfortunately, in the embedded space, software development is a tertiary activity. Many stakeholders simply do not *grok* the software development process. So, in addition to developing software, you also get to spend time and energy educating folks about why things are taking longer than their emotional expectations.

3. "Similar but different" is still different.

    Early on, software developers are introduced to the magic of subroutines. Then they learn about generic libraries, classes, and frameworks whose miraculous functionality reduces a lot of the grunt work and heavy lifting of coding. However, once we have a hammer, it tends to become a golden hammer. This leads to a tendency to hit similar things with the same hammer, even though they are different. The classic example of this would be treating squares and rectangles the same since a square is a rectangle. However, a rectangle is not a square, and you will encounter errors if you create a single interface for handling rectangles and squares. In short, *do not force things to be the same*. And always follow the Liskov Substitution Principle (LSP).

4. The hardware is always late.

    Hardware is hard, lead times are a bitch, and PCBAs cost money. Enough said.

5. There are always new requirements.

    The only constant in life is change. This is especially true with
    software requirements. You can rage against change, or you can
    embrace it. I discovered in my career that embracing change and
    finding ways to construct designs to be "change tolerant" was
    much easier on my blood pressure. In addition, while change is
    constant, you can never fully anticipate what will change. This
    leads to the corollary principle: 80% of your code never changes,
    but the 20% that changes can come as a surprise. The simplest
    way, then, to address not knowing what code will need to be
    changed in the future is to start with the assumption that all of the
    code will change.

6. Don't ask open-ended questions.

    One of my first software projects as an intern was to automate a
    test station for testing a protection circuit inside a compressor
    to prevent motor damage. There were no formal, documented
    requirements, and I was told to work with one of the mechanical
    engineers on what the test station needed to do. I naively asked
    the mechanical engineer, "what does the test station need to
    do?" His response was a verbal list of requirements, which I went
    off and implemented. After I was finished, I demonstrated the
    test station. The response was, "that's great, but how about we
    add A, and do X instead of Y?" This cycle of getting new verbal
    requirements, reimplementation, demonstration, followed by a
    change of verbal requirements continued over the course of the
    entire summer.

    The lesson I took from this is that customers often don't know
    what they want, and it is futile to expect that at some point they
    will. Consequently, if you ever want to be done with a project,
    only ask if they want option A or option B. Never present an
    option C.

7. Testers are your friends.

   There is always some tension between the test team and the development team. This is understandable because it's a tester's job to find and report all of the mistakes the developer has made. That said, a friendly tester will make your life better, if for no other reason than they can give you a "heads up" on problems and give you a chance to fix or identify a root cause before the bug becomes "public." And having to explain a bug to a stakeholder when the root cause is unknown is an uncomfortable experience. To put it another way, an alienated tester will cause you heartache and pain.

8. Just move the cursor to the right.

   Most software developers struggle when it comes to writing documentation. (I include myself in this group; it's why I have a coauthor for this book.) Documentation tasks can seem overwhelming. Sometimes, the best way to start is to just start typing, not worrying about format, good grammar, logical progression, and so on—just to set down ideas in some form. After some content is "on paper," as it were, it is a much simpler task to then organize, format, and wordsmith it into a finished document. To say it another way, writing and editing are two separate mental processes; don't try to do them both at the same time. Just start by moving the cursor to the right ... and keep it moving ...

9. They only remember the number, never the preconditions.

   My first introduction to this management principle was when I gave a PowerPoint presentation to the directors and VP of engineering about the development for a new controller. On the first slide, in big bold red lettering was the caveat that the proposed timeline of six months did not start until tasks A, B, and C were completed. However, somehow the directors and VP left the meeting with the idea that the new controller project would be done in six months from today. I tried later to remind them that six months was dependent on A, B, C being completed first, but their response was "yes, but you said six months." Know that even if your manager asks you for a nonbinding swag for when a piece of work will be finished, your answer will be binding.

10.   Money is always an issue.

I have been involved in too many planning sessions where the solution to saving a project schedule was to throw money at the problem. That is, we could hire new developers, invest in hardware and tools, and colocate everyone to a common site. As stakeholders were leaving the meeting, we were filled with a sense of accomplishment. However, after the reality of spending the money—or, more precisely, not spending the money—set in, the schedule was doomed. Unfortunately, the stakeholders' expectations for the schedule did not change even though the money was not spent (see rule 9). Consequently, never base your plans on the assumption that additional money beyond the current budget allocation will be available.

11.   Never believe never.

Never is a trap. It's similar to having a pet cat roll over on its back and present its nice soft fluffy stomach to be petted. Inviting as it is, as soon as you touch the cat's fur, claws and fangs will dig into your hand. The same thing happens when a stakeholder, marketing genius, customer, system engineer, and so on state that "the product will *never* have to do X, and you shouldn't spend any time or effort accommodating it in your design." Over and over, I've been told "never," and then all of sudden, X becomes a must-have feature that I get to spend my nights and weekends working on. Here are some examples:

- "This is just a prototype and doesn't need to be production quality code." But after the demo, management now needs it to ship tomorrow.

- "The contract manufacturer will develop the end-of-line testing software." This usually lasts until someone actually gets the quote from the CM for the work.

- "There will only be one version of the hardware and one version of software that has to be supported at any given time." This usually goes away as soon as you release a version of hardware to customers and start on the next board spin.

12. All developers are not created equal.

    This is about setting expectations. Whether you are an individual contributor, technical lead, frontline manager, or director, be prepared for the human element. It is also a bit of a personal rant against the corporate culture—the actual culture, not the pretty posters on the wall—that treats developers as commodities that are all interchangeable. Developers are individuals. As individuals, they all differ in their experiences, interests, abilities, and skills (both technical and personal). Don't assume that your coworkers are just like you.

13. If you can't write it down, you can't code it.

    This is a paraphrase from the Albert Einstein quote, "If you can't explain it simply, you don't understand it well enough." If you can't describe your design in natural language, with some supporting diagrams, how can you realistically expect that you can code it correctly? And how can you expect someone else to understand your design or implementation?

    Here is a very simple sanity check you can make when designing a feature. If you are struggling to create the design document, or struggling to write comments for a class or interface, you probably need to think through the problem more thoroughly. Do not spend time writing code that will almost certainly have to be reworked or thrown away. My personal habit is to write the comments first, before starting on the implementation. Incorrect assumptions and bad design choices quickly show up when you write out the comments for a piece of software. Another good way to catch bad design choices is simply by talking out loud with another developer about it.

    A corollary to this rule is, if it doesn't make sense when you say it out loud, start over.

Wayne's Rules of Development

Some of these rules are overstated for effect. That is, while there may be exceptions and contexts where a rule might not entirely apply, adding the extra language made them seem less pithy.

1. People are messy.

   Code works or it doesn't. Compilers and linkers work the same way every time you use them, and when something unexpected happens, it's usually because the internal logic or semantics of the tools weren't understood well enough. Unfortunately, software gets developed by people who use these tools, and people are messy. They get married, they get divorced, they get their appendix out, they get stuck in the Florida Keys, they don't like to wear socks but do like to take their shoes off in a shared office space. All the unexpected and frustrating things people do will, to one degree or another, affect the project. And there's really nothing you can do about it except recognize that it will happen. When messy things happen and interfere with my schedule or my responsibilities, I find it oddly calming to shrug and say "people are messy."

2. Projects have a beginning, middle, and end.

   This sounds really obvious, but it is fascinating to see that software projects are nearly always managed the same way from start to finish, even though people are doing very different work at the beginning than they are at the end. I have always advocated that the beginning of a project would be best managed with a waterfall methodology, and then, somewhere in the middle of a project, it should be managed with Agile. Expectations about what is getting done, how it is getting done, and how long it should be taking should always be considered in the context of whether you're at the beginning, middle, or end of a project.

3. All software resists shipment.

    No matter what your release date, there are always last-minute
    features that become critical and last-minute bugs that are
    uncovered. All of these things will reset your release timeline.
    Additionally, there can be noncode, nontechnical activities
    that slow things down like licensing reviews and export control
    paperwork. And the bigger the project is, the more people there
    are that can come up with reasons and roadblocks that force a
    reset of the release timeline. Don't be fooled into thinking, then,
    that after the last line of code has been written, the hard part is
    done. You have to beat software out the door with a stick.

    I always advocate that, toward the end of the project, you practice
    pulling together formal releases. This will expose a lot of hiccups
    and reveal the additional work that needs to be done that you
    haven't been seeing. If you can, make sure there is time in the
    development schedule to cut at least three practice releases to get
    the release process smoothed out.

4. Levels of indirection decay over time.

    Levels of indirection are what make it possible to reuse code
    and build lots of different things with minimal additional work.
    However, the cost of this sort of architecture is an additional
    complexity. In cognitive terms, more mental energy is required
    to keep the levels of indirection in mind when you're working
    with the software. And like energy in the real world, entropy will
    eventually catch up with higher energy levels.

    I worked on a project years ago that I thought was really ingenious.
    From the same source, I could build three different variants of
    the product in multiple languages (including branding for an
    OEM product). When I eventually left the company, I trained
    my replacement on the organization and build process, and that
    person hated all the levels of indirection. That person insisted
    that the only way forward was to break up the system into three

different source trees that would be kept in sync manually. I was flabbergasted. But all my boss could say was "that's the person I've got to take over the job. You want to stick around and keep it running?"

Pursuing a PIM strategy is always a good idea because it will make your life easier and make you nimbler and more efficient. But be aware that it will require constant care and feeding on a people level. That is, it requires continual training and ongoing communication with your team about what you're doing and how it supports the team's goals in order to keep things humming along smoothly. As mentioned in the introduction, good software engineering practices require discipline by the developers and stakeholders.

5. A working prototype is everything and nothing.

    A working prototype is the greatest thing in the world. It is a proof that the idea you have can be turned into a reality. Unfortunately, when management sees a prototype, they often think that 80% of the work is done and that a product release is just around the corner. But a prototype is functionally closer to 0% of the work. As difficult as it may be, after you've got your prototype working, you should set it aside and create all your design documents. This will be easier because the prototype has shown you the work that needs to be done. And, after you've completed your design documents, don't go back and extend your prototype; rather, start at zero implementing your design.

6. Design reviews are better than code reviews.

    In my experience, the perennial problem with code reviews is that they miss the forest for trees. That is, code reviews tend to focus on the syntax of the code and don't really look at the semantics or the overall design of the software. In my experience, code reviews can catch implementation errors, but they don't often expose design flaws. And design flaws are much harder and more expensive to fix than implementation errors.

In a perfect world, you would want to perform both code reviews and design reviews. But if you're pressed for time, you're better off reviewing code by asking "What are the semantics of this class or module? Where does your code implement those semantics?" Or, alternatively, "What is the algorithm for this function? How does your code implement it?"

APPENDIX A

Terminology

This appendix provides definitions for the terms used throughout this book. These definitions, provided in Table A-1, are how I use the terms, and they are not necessarily authoritative nor canonical definitions you might find in Wikipedia or in IEEE standards.

Table A-1. *Terminology used in this book*

Term	Definition
Abstract interface	In the context of PIM, this is any interface that defines a behavior that has a deferred binding for its implementation. That is, it is not a source time binding.
Component	This is equivalent to a C++ namespace. It contains zero or more modules or subcomponents. In the context of file systems, a component is represented as a directory.
Component scope	This is analogous to package scope in Java. It is not analogous to protected scope or private scope qualifiers in C++. When an interface/file/method/class is designated as component scope, it is only accessible by other modules in the same component or its subcomponents.
Declaration	A declaration introduces one or more names into a program. When you declare a variable, function, class, etc., you are saying that in the project there is something with this name, and it has this type.
Definition	A definition is a unique specification of an object, variable, function, class, etc. Creating a definition means specifying all the information necessary to create the thing in its entirety.

(*continued*)

© John T. Taylor, Wayne T. Taylor 2021
J. T. Taylor and W. T. Taylor, *Patterns in the Machine*,
https://doi.org/10.1007/978-1-4842-6440-9

Table A-1. (*continued*)

Term	Definition
DIP	Dependency Inversion Principle
DMA	Direct Memory Access
EEPROM	Electrically Erasable Programmable Read-Only Memory
ISP	Interface Segregation Principle
Loose coupling	This is where an individual module—with little or no knowledge—makes use of other modules. Another definition would be that loosely coupled components adhere to the Dependency Inversion Principle (DIP) and only depend on entities that are unlikely to change (e.g., abstract interfaces).
LSP	Liskov Substitution Principle
Module	This is the definition or implementation of a set of functionality; it is analogous to a class in C++. A typical module consists of a single .h file and a single .cl. cpp file. Just as C++ allows you to have pure virtual classes, parent classes, child classes, etc., PIM's definition of modules allows you to define a module with many source files that can reside in different components (or directories).
OCP	Open-Closed Principle
Package	This is a formally versioned and released collection of components. With respect to a file system, a package is the parent directory of all its components.
PIM	This is an acronym for this book: *Patterns in the Machine*.
Platform	This is the combination of operating system (if any), physical hardware (MCU/CPU), and compiler toolchain.
Public scope	This is analogous to the C++ public scope qualifier. When an interface/file/method/class/etc. is designated as public scope, it is accessible by any other module.
SA	This is an acronym for software architecture.

(*continued*)

Table A-1. (*continued*)

Term	Definition
SCM	This is an acronym for software configuration management. SCM is the process or tools used to store, track, and control changes to the source code. For example, git is an SCM tool.
SDD	Software detailed design
SDP	Software development plan
SPI	Serial Peripheral Interface. This is a synchronous serial communication interface used for short distance communications.
SRP	Single Responsibility Principle
Target hardware	This is the embedded hardware that an application runs on. For example, the target hardware for a product might be an ARM Cortex-M microcontroller.
Target platform	This is the embedded platform that an application runs on. For example, the target platform for an application might be an ARM Cortex-M microcontroller running FreeRTOS, built with the gcc-arm-none-eabi cross compiler on a Windows machine.
Technical debt	This reflects the implied cost of additional future work that is incurred by choosing a partial, limited, or easy solution instead of a final, complete, robust solution.
UUT	Unit Under Test

APPENDIX B

State Machine Notation

I have worked in a lot of shops where each developer had his or her own concept of what a state machine is. Besides the obvious confusion and relearning that is required when someone new joins the team, many times these individualized concepts of state machines were such that they could not be realized in a state chart diagram. The situation was analogous to the developer saying, "I can code it, but I can't explain it." Similarly, in the case where developers used customized state chart notation, the results were often internally inconsistent. This was problematic because there was no way to verify that the implementation met the intent of the state chart.

PIM encourages the use of UML state charts. But there are several types of state machines: Mealy machines, Moore machines, Harel state charts, UML state charts, and so on. If you opt to not use UML state charts, at least select a formally defined machine type or notation (e.g., Moore, Mealy-Moore, etc.)

Table B-1 summarizes the features and differences between the various state machine types. In addition to using UML state charts, PIM recommends that you define "state machine standards" for your team. These are analogous to coding standards that you called out in your software development plan (SDP). By doing this, you provide consistency within the development team as well as simplify the learning curve for cross-functional team members (i.e., system engineers, testers, etc.). Additionally, by adhering to formal state machine semantics, you can use your diagrams and charts with standardized implementation patterns and code generators.

© John T. Taylor, Wayne T. Taylor 2021
J. T. Taylor and W. T. Taylor, *Patterns in the Machine*,
https://doi.org/10.1007/978-1-4842-6440-9

Table B-1. *State machine standards compared*

	Mealy	Moore	Mealy-Moore	Harel	UML
States and transitions	Y	Y	Y	Y	Y
Transitions have actions	Y		Y	Y	Y
States have actions		Y	Y	Y	Y
Hierarchical, composite states				Y	Y
Orthogonal regions/concurrent states				Y	Y

Figure B-1 contains some basic UML state chart notation, and Figure B-2 gives an example of how that notation is used.

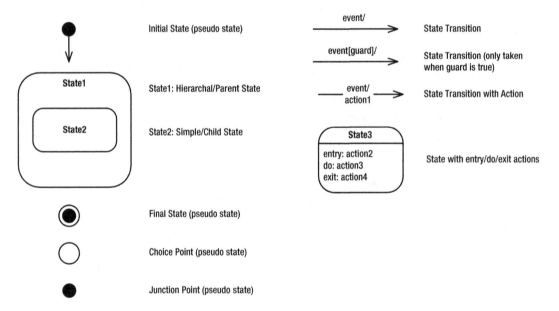

Figure B-1. *State machine notation*

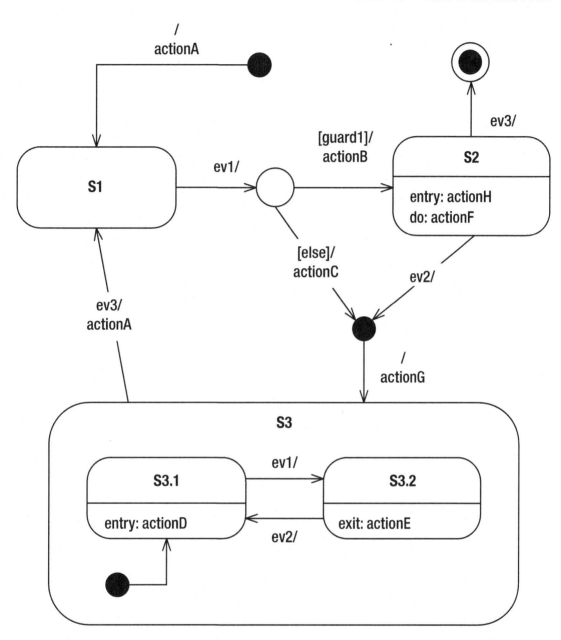

Figure B-2. *Example of a state machine notation*

APPENDIX C

A UML Cheat Sheet

In some cases, I try to illustrate relationships in diagrams that use UML conventions. Sometimes, the labeling and arrow types I use have specific meanings, so here is a cheat sheet of my most commonly used conventions.

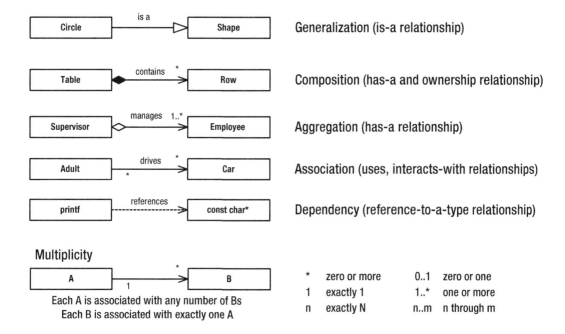

Arrows represent the direction of the relationship
(e.g. the file A.h would contain the statement: #include "B.h")

© John T. Taylor, Wayne T. Taylor 2021
J. T. Taylor and W. T. Taylor, *Patterns in the Machine*,
https://doi.org/10.1007/978-1-4842-6440-9

APPENDIX D

Why C++

PIM applies equally to C and C++. And yet most of the examples in the book are C++. The reason for this is because much of the PIM example code comes from, or is based on, open source projects that I have been developing over the course of many years. Since these were my personal projects, I used my language of choice which is C++. Nevertheless, the majority of my professional projects have used C. For example, the first two professional projects where I implemented the data model pattern were C projects.

So why C++? To put it simply, it provides more and has manageable downsides. All those claims you may have heard that C++ is too heavy and has too much overhead for small microcontrollers are mostly nonsense. Consider that the Arduino platform, which started with small microcontrollers, is actually C++ under the covers. I would argue that the same application written in C++ would have the same runtime performance as if it were written in C. To clarify what I mean by the "same application," I mean the same architecture, the same design, and an equivalent implementation. For example, if the C implementation did not use function tables for polymorphism, then the C++ code would not use virtual functions in its implementation.

Table D-1 enumerates some of the advantages of using C++. This is not an in-depth discussion of any particular C++ features; rather, it summarizes the benefits of the features in C++.

© John T. Taylor, Wayne T. Taylor 2021
J. T. Taylor and W. T. Taylor, *Patterns in the Machine*,
https://doi.org/10.1007/978-1-4842-6440-9

Table D-1. *Benefits of C++ on embedded projects*

Feature	Benefit
Type checking	C++ provides more compile time type checking than C. Consider how templates work and that out-of-the-box C++ does not support implicit types. Also, in my experience, the need to use explicit casting (e.g., to cast a void* to MyType_T*) is greatly reduced because of class inheritance in C++. Anything that enables the compiler to detect errors is a good thing. Those of us that had the opportunity to write C code using a pre-ANSI C compiler understand how big of a win it is to have strict type checking.
Namespaces	C only provides global namespace (and file scoped namespaces). In theory, if your application is small, then the potential for name collision in the global namespace is low. However, if you bring third-party code into a small application, the chances of a name collision significantly increase. PIM is all about preemptively avoiding name collisions because resolving name collisions means you have to edit existing, proven source code. With name collisions, it is true that "an ounce of prevention is worth a pound of cure."
References	When interviewing potential new hires, I like to ask "what are the advantages of C++ references?" Invariably, I get the answer of being able to use the dot notation instead of the pointer notation inside a method. Well, yes, references do provide a cleaner syntax. But the big bang for the buck for references is that a reference is guaranteed to point to something, whereas a pointer is not. This means that the developer does not have to check for a null pointer reference before using the reference. (If every C programmer always checked that all pointers were not NULL before attempting to dereference them, C would be a better place.)
Encapsulation	The class structure in C++ that binds data with a set of functions is much cleaner—and compiler enforced—than in C where data structures can be passed to an arbitrary collection of functions. In addition, the class constructor/destructor mechanism provides for guaranteed initialization and cleanup of classes instead of relying on the developer to do this.

(*continued*)

Table D-1. (*continued*)

Feature	Benefit
Runtime bindings	Runtime bindings, or dynamic polymorphism, in C++ are "virtual" and "pure virtual" methods. As stated in Chapter 3, deferred bindings are a good thing when it comes to decoupling dependencies. While polymorphism is not needed for every class—and for an embedded project perhaps not needed for most classes—it is a clean and compile-safe way to create and use runtime bindings. Yes, I can implement the equivalent of virtual functions in C, but it is not pretty and requires type casting, which means you lose compiler-enforced type safety.
String handling	The ability to have a String class instead of raw `char*` pointers and a set of string functions (e.g., `strcpy`, `strcmp`, etc.) is a huge win. I am still amazed today at how many experienced developers do not understand the semantics of `strncpy()`. For example, `strncpy()` does not guarantee that the result is null terminated nor that the max number of bytes to be copied will leave space for the null terminator. By itself, the encapsulation of 98% of the C string handling into a String class makes it worthwhile to use C++. A good String class is not just a convenience, it's self-preservation.[1]

[1]So why does the PIM example code not use C++'s `std::string` class? The issue with the `std::string` class and the standard template library (STL) in general is its extensive use of the dynamic memory allocation. And in most embedded systems, dynamic allocation is frowned upon. Yes, I know that string class and the STL provide the ability to have custom allocators for the memory handling, but this gets messy with providing an allocator instance every time a string class is instantiated. Having a String class that does not rely on or assume dynamic memory is a much cleaner approach.

Unfortunately, no programming language is perfect. There are some downsides to using C++ on embedded projects. Some of those downsides are

- Little or no compiler support for older microcontrollers or specialized hardware architectures.

- Potential for longer compile and link times. However, with modern compilers and multicore PCs, this may be a minor consideration.

- A general lack of C++ experience on development teams.

There can also be a tendency to overdo things with C++. That is, in my experience, I have seen three categories of C++ projects:

- C with classes—There is nothing inherently wrong with this type of implementation. It just incurs a lost opportunity cost for not taking advantage of a cleaner and quicker implementation using C++.

- Objects gone wild—This is the worst kind of C++ project. It is easy to get caught up in the wonder and power of objects and design patterns. But if this results in complex class hierarchies and excessive levels of indirection, it will get in the way of runtime performance and maintainability. You end up with code that only the original author can understand. I confess to having fallen into this trap more than once, and I have paid a high price in refactoring time and programming effort to dig myself out. (If you're interested in researching the details of a sad tale of design hubris, you can look at my first C++ implementation of the data model pattern in the Colony.core repository. Hint: It was under the Rte namespace.)

- Goldilocks—Obviously, this is a project that falls somewhere between the preceding two categories. It is also very subjective. That is, one developer's Goldilocks project is another developer's objects gone wild. Only hindsight, and perhaps code longevity, can measure whether your C++ project is a Goldilocks project with respect to good usage of the C++ language.

APPENDIX E

About Package Management with Outcast

Outcast is a paradigm and an open source project that attempts to integrate package management (think logistics of true code reuse) with the day-to-day development process. It is still in the proof of concept stage. I'm discussing it here because the native development environment for the PIM thermostat example actually consists of several packages that are managed by the Outcast tools. To simplify the usage of the example code for PIM readers, all of the separate packages have been consolidated into a single package (or Git repository). The PIM repository is essentially a read-only repository in that the canonical source for its content comes from the Colony.* repository packages. This consolidation is mostly transparent, but you will see traces of Outcast in the NQBP build scripts.

Before going into more details about Outcast, I should define what I mean by package and package management. A package is a formally versioned and released collection of components in *source code form*. In the context of PIM, these are not binary packages. Packages also include metadata such as their version identifier, dependencies on other packages, descriptions, and so on. Package management involves the creation of the package containers, distributing the packages, and consuming the packages.

Why does all this matter? The reason is because after you have created a code base, you have to be able to leverage it. Typically, what I have observed is there is a single code base that supports a single product, or there is a code base that supports a family of products. The plan is usually to have everything released at the same time. This approach works when the releases are infrequent (which is very common in the firmware world) and the exception cases are kept to a minimum.

© John T. Taylor, Wayne T. Taylor 2021
J. T. Taylor and W. T. Taylor, *Patterns in the Machine*,
https://doi.org/10.1007/978-1-4842-6440-9

But occasionally there are times when you need an individual product release within the product family. Typically, this is treated as a "one-off scenario." Packages, then, are an attempt at reuse that can avoid case-by-case builds. Packages become the unit of reuse. That is, entire packages are available for reuse, not individual source code files. Because packages are formally released and have a concept of dependencies on other packages, they provide a source code reuse strategy that can scale to a large number of packages as well as a large number of versions. However, "can scale" and "this is how you scale" are not the same thing. Outcast attempts to provide the "this is how you scale" solution.

Outcast

The Outcast open source project (https://github.com/johnttaylor/Outcast) was created to explore how to incorporate package management at the start of the development process rather than tacking it on after the fact. Currently, the Outcast project is still a work in progress. However, the key takeaways from this project are

- The release process is not a lightweight process, even when automated.

- Having larger, fewer packages is more manageable than having many smaller packages. This goes back to the overhead associated with releasing a package.

- Infrequent releases are better than releasing "all of the time." With infrequent releases, you can reduce the overhead of performing the actual releases as well as the overhead of consumers evaluating and incorporating the new releases.

- A mechanism needs to be provided where a developer does not have to wait for a formal release before having access to new or fixed functionality in a package.

- The contents of a reusable package need to be available to potential clients.

- There should be an automated way to inform the client of the new package contents or provide search capabilities to those who might want the functionality.

- There should be best practices defined that require searching available packages before reinventing the wheel.

Outcast Model

The Outcast model supposes that all source code is contained in a package and that packages may or may not have dependencies on other packages. From a development perspective, there is a workspace that contains an active package and all of the packages that the active package depends on. As the name implies, the active package is what a developer is currently working on.

The contents of the active package are managed directly through an SCM (e.g., the active package is a local Git repository). The dependent packages are then accessed through a level of indirection. This extra layer of indirection allows for seamless switching between different releases of the dependent packages including accessing a dependent package directly from its SCM repository.

Outcast uses the two top-level directories in the workspace named xpkgs/ and xinc/ for the indirection. Both directories use symbolic links to reference a specific package release. Two directories are used as follows: the xpkgs/ directory is used to simplify how the NQBP build scripts are constructed, and the xinc/ directory is used to collapse all of the non-active packages' header files into a single directory tree. This allows a single header search option like -I to work for all dependent packages, as opposed to needing separate -I options for each dependent package which does not scale as the number of dependent packages goes up.[1] The Outcast project provides tools for mounting (and unmounting) dependent packages into the xpkgs/ and xinc/ directories. Here is the workspace file organization:

---

[1]Remember dependencies are transitive. So even if a package has only one explicit dependency, the realized dependencies can be much greater. For example, A depends on B and B depends on X and Y. This means that the realized dependencies for A is {B, X, Y}—not just B.

```
└─<WorkspaceRoot>
   ├─xpkgs ; Root directory for 'mounted' packages
   │  ├─<symlink_ext_pkg#1> ; Symbolic link to an external or local Packages
   │  │                      ; directory
   │  ├─<symlink_ext_pkg#2> ; Symbolic link to an external or local Packages
   │  │                      ; directory
   │  └─...
   ├─xinc  ; Root directory for symbolically linked headers files for each
   │    ; mounted package.
   │  ├─<namespace1> ; Include directory retains the namespace organization
   │  │              ; of the individual packages
   │  └─...
   └─<namespace2>
      └─...
   ├─<local_pkg #1> ; Local package, i.e. contents are pulled/pushed
   │                ; directly to your SCM
   └─<local_pkg #2> ; Local package, i.e. contents are pulled/pushed
                    ; directly to your SCM
```

This directory listing is the workspace for the Colony.Apps repository in the native
Outcast environment.

```
└─<WorkspaceRoot>
   ├─xpkgs              ; Root directory for 'mounted' packages.  All subdirs
   │                    ; are symbolic links
   │  ├─catch           ; Unit test framework
   │  ├─colony.arduino  ; Arduino support for the Colony.core framework
   │  ├─colony.core     ; C++ Library for OSAL and system services.
   │  ├─ratt            ; Python based automated test tool
   │  └─nqbp            ; Build engine
   ├─xinc               ; Root directory for symbolically linked headers
   │                    ; files for each mounted package.
   │  ├─Bsp
   │  ├─Catch
   │  ├─Cpl
   │  ├─Bsp
   │  └─Driver
```

```
├─colony.apps        ; Active Package
│   ├─docs
│   ├─projects
│   ├─resources
│   ├─src
│   ├─tests
│   └─top
└─colony.core        ; Dependent package - but using the latest,
                     ; non-released snapshot
```

The Outcast paradigm of using a level of indirection to access dependent packages essentially creates a logical view of where all of the packages—both native and mounted—are effectively under the same top-level physical directory tree (i.e., under the src/ directory). This is what makes it possible to collapse all of the mounted packages' header files in the xinc/ directory. It is also what makes creating the single PIM repository from many separate repositories possible without having to modify or edit any of the packages' source code files. However, the creation of the PIM repository did require some modification to the build scripts due to how the Arduino libraries were copied into the Colony.Arduino repository. The copying of the Arduino tools was only done as simplification for consumers of the PIM project. If the PIM repository required the reader to install the Arduino libraries via the Arduino IDE, then there would be no modification to the build scripts when creating the PIM repository.

APPENDIX F

Requirements vs. Design Statements

I have never worked on a project that did not have software requirements. I have, however, worked on many projects—dare I say, most—that have had

- Ambiguous requirements

- Incomplete requirements

- Conflicting requirements

- Excessively onerous requirements

Since by definition requirements define what it is you are constructing, they are a big deal. And in theory, it should be simple: a requirement is a "what," and a design is the "how" that meets the requirement. The problem is that one stakeholder's what is another's how, and vice versa. There will be gaps between where requirements end and detailed design can start, but it is better to acknowledge the gaps, and fill them in with "design statements," rather than to thrash around trying to get the "right level" of requirements from the stakeholders.

Here is a real-world example from one project I worked on. The project included a thermostat for commercial HVAC equipment. The software team received one requirement from marketing for the thermostat that said, "control indoor space temperature to +/- 1 degree Fahrenheit under steady state conditions." Disregarding the missing requirements for what should happen during the nonsteady-state conditions (e.g., setpoint changes, operating constraints imposed by the HVAC equipment, etc.),

285

© John T. Taylor, Wayne T. Taylor 2021
J. T. Taylor and W. T. Taylor, *Patterns in the Machine*,
https://doi.org/10.1007/978-1-4842-6440-9

the first obstacle was to figure out what type of control logic should be used. Should it be simple delta error control, proportional-integral-derivative control (PID), or something else? The software team had enough experience with HVAC controls to know that thermostat algorithms are nontrivial, but we were not process control engineers. Said another way, the software team needed detailed control algorithms: a high-level "what" was insufficient to design and implement. The problem was not that it was rocket science to define the control algorithms; rather, it was getting the right resource assigned to the project to define them. The problem was compounded by the fact that the marketing group kept insisting that the project requirements were defined (i.e., "everything is done") and that it was solely a software team issue. In this particular case, the "whats" the software developers needed were the control algorithm definitions, which were the "hows" to the marketing group.

I don't have a "one-size-fits-all" solution to the requirement paradox. The reason is because the way requirements are managed, formalized, and so on is specific to industries, domains, and companies. The problem is that at the end of the day, your software gets tested against the requirements. So, if the requirements are too high level, how do you identify what constitutes comprehensive test coverage? If the requirements are too detailed, you will have a large test burden of black-box and white-box testing approaches. For example, the level of formality for requirements for a medical device will almost always be orders of magnitude more detailed than the requirements for a start-up company's IoT device.

What I do have is a recommendation for how to bridge the gap from a high-level "what" to a high-level "how" that can then be used to drive a detailed software design. If you have a high-level requirement, then develop *design statements* that provide the missing details. In the preceding example, the thermostat control algorithm definitions could be considered design statements. With this approach, when system test time rolls around, the test group verifies the formal software requirements *and* the design statements. By verifying both, you will get a good baseline for the depth and breadth of your test coverage.

As a final thought, the actual name—design statements—is not important; you can use whatever terminology or label best fits your organization. For example, at one company I worked at, the design statements were captured in an "Engineering Response" document that filled in the next level of detail for marketing's high-level requirements. The target audience for the document was not just the marketing team, but the development and test teams since the Engineering Response effectively became the software requirements for development and test. What you should not do is use the term *requirements* for your design statements. There is too much baggage, perspectives, and religion associated with the term requirements. By using a different name, you can save yourself a lot of frustration.

Index

A

Abstract interface, 28, 29, 32, 38, 39, 42
Adafruit Grand Central M4, 220, 223
Agile, 4, 10, 23, 161, 189, 261
Ansi, 233
Arduino, 33, 36, 37, 43, 45, 46, 48, 54, 67,
    88, 93, 220, 225, 226, 252, 283
ArduinoJson, 252
ARM, 221, 227, 267
Atmel SAMD51, 220, 234
Automated unit testing, 6, 10–14, 28, 91, 115

B

Batch files
    env.bat, 225
Binding time
    dynamic, 38
    polymorphic, 38, 39
    static
        compile time, 39–41
        link time, 39, 41
        source time, 39, 40
Board support package, 48, 67, 77
Branching, 14, 113, 114
BSP, see Board support package
Build identifier, 114, 115
Build machine, 13–15, 81, 96, 108,
    110–112, 116, 117

Build system, 13, 14, 65, 78, 80, 81, 92, 113,
    116–118, 160, 165, 167, 169, 175,
    209, 216, 217, 225, 233, 234,
    240–246, 281, 283

C

C#, 103, 104
Cadifra, 21, 147
Catch2, 92, 243
CI, see Continuous integration
Closed to extension, 26
CMake, 80, 81, 92, 117
Code coverage, 10, 86, 89–91, 95,
    223, 248
Colony.Apps, 253, 282
Colony.Arduino, 253, 283
Colony.core, 32, 33, 35, 51, 67, 124, 177, 181,
    188, 202, 209, 224, 249–253, 278
Command-line build script, 116
Command-line interface (CLI), 32, 33,
    199, 215, 234–236
Component-Based
    vsDevelopment (CBD), 19, 120
Continuous integration, 3, 10, 13–15, 79,
    81, 92, 95, 107–118, 158, 160, 216
Cortex, 221, 223, 225, 227, 267
cpp11, 244
CruiseControl, 108

V

Vector table, 243

W

Watchdog, 8, 9, 69
Waterfall, 4, 10, 159, 261
Wiki, 20, 24, 154, 159, 239

win32, 87, 106, 244
win64, 244
Windows, 12, 38, 41, 67, 77, 85, 103, 106, 118, 221, 223–227, 233, 235, 239, 240, 250, 254, 267

X, Y, Z

XML, 147

Printed in the United States
By Bookmasters